The Dark Lord

The Dark Lord

Cult Images and the Hare Krishnas in America

Larry D. Shinn

The Westminster Press
Philadelphia

Book design by Gene Harris

First edition

Published by The Westminster Press®
Philadelphia, Pennsylvania

PRINTED IN THE UNITED STATES OF AMERICA

9   8   7   6   5   4   3   2   1

Library of Congress Cataloging-in-Publication Data

Shinn, Larry D., 1942–
    The dark lord.

    Bibliography: p.
    1. International Society for Krishna Consciousness—
United States. 2. Hare Krishnas—United States.
I. Title.
BL1285.835.U6S55 1987   294.5′51   86-32480
ISBN 0-664-24170-0 (pbk.)

For my father, Dwight Shinn
who by his living taught me
the meaning of tolerance

and for my mother, Doris Shinn
who has always encouraged her children
to seek the truth and to speak it plainly

Contents

Preface

It is truly a delight when a scholar stumbles onto an area of research off the prescribed path he or she had previously charted. It is even more exciting when that detour produces surprising new experiences that challenge the pathfinder's assumptions and views about what the new terrain is and how it should be described. Both of these experiences happened to this author while on the circuitous route that led to this book.

What I bring to this investigation of the cults and the Hare Krishnas is twenty years of study of the religious traditions of the world. From the dusty streets of Palestine in the early 1960s through several lengthy sojourns in India in the 1970s, I have been stimulated to learn about the religious lives of persons whose orientation is different from my own. Such experiences led me to Princeton University to study the religions of India and, in particular, the devotional *(bhakti)* Hindu traditions that focus on the cowherd deity named Krishna. I was intrigued to learn from my study of Krishna theology how similar it was to my own Protestant heritage. Little did I know, however, that such cross-cultural religious interests would lead me, ten years into a teaching and scholarly career, throughout America and India to study the American Hare Krishnas.

As I headed to California in the summer of 1980, I viewed my excursion as a three-week field trip to collect interview data from Hare Krishna devotees that I could use as illustrative material for a book on religious conversion. I was just beginning a fifteen-month leave to study the psychological literature on conversion at the Institute for the Advanced Study of Religion at the University of Chicago. Even though I thought the American Hare Krishnas were not apt to be authentically Indian, I assumed that to listen to the stories of young persons attracted to a faith so different from their family traditions would provide valuable insights into the religious conversion process. I was only half right.

What I found in my three weeks of interviewing and observation in the Krishna communities in Los Angeles, San Francisco, and Berkeley was an American Krishna tradition that was authentically Indian and self-consciously so. To step into the Krishna temple in Berkeley or Dallas is to enter a world of images, cuisine, and activities that can be found throughout northern India in homes and communities devoted to Krishna. Consequently, the first surprise for this investigator was the authenticity of the Krishna tradition I had thought was little more than just another quasi-Indian import. As we will see in chapter 2, the founding guru of the Hare Krishnas is best described as a Hindu missionary who brought to America an Indian form of ecstatic devotion to God that rivals in its intensity of feeling the evangelical Christianity preached in his Indian homeland.

The second surprise in store for me on my stay in California was to learn how dangerous the stereotypes associated with the "cults" can be. As I sat through two days of the trial described in chapter 1, the outline for this book began to emerge out of the ashes of the scholarly study of conversion I had intended to pursue. As I listened to the testimony of the young Krishna devotee named Rebecca Foster, I was struck by the sincerity of the religious quest that had led her to the Krishnas. As I heard the description by Rebecca's family of her "brainwashing by a cult," I slowly began to realize how powerful and pervasive the cult images and stereotypes in America really are.

The following years have been an exhilarating if sometimes frustrating and circuitous tour through a mansion of many rooms entered through the back door of that California trip. One room of this mansion is filled with the history and development of the Krishna tradition in India and America that provides a natural link to my previous training and interests. Another room of this mansion is overflowing with more than two thousand pages of transcripts and dozens of tapes from the over 110 interviews I have conducted with Krishna devotees. These interviews lasted an average of three hours each and included people ranging from new gurus and temple presidents to farm laborers and kitchen workers. Still another room is decorated with the sights, sounds, and impressions from my participant observation in fourteen Krishna temples in the United States and two in India. On four trips totaling nearly three months, I followed the daily temple life and routine of Krishna devotees in these sixteen communities.

Finally, I made my way through two rooms that seem to have an impenetrable barrier between them. One is a room filled with anticult studies done by persons who study the cults from afar through ex-devotees and then make generalized proclamations about all the cults. The reading public knows this room and its books well. The adjacent room is one filled with a wide array of social-scientific studies of particular marginal religious and nonreligious groups that are mostly unknown to the lay audience. On the one hand, I have attended nearly a dozen cult conferences run by anticult groups and authors. I have interviewed leaders of the American Family Foundation and other such anticult groups as well as psychologists and sociologists who support such organizations. On the other hand, I have participated in several social science conferences that focused upon the new religions in America or upon marginal social groups. I have also interviewed Moonies and members of similar groups to have some basis of comparison for my more concentrated study of the Hare Krishnas in America.

It is upon my completed tour of the whole mansion described above that this book is based. Additionally, the 1980–81 year I spent at the Divinity School of the University of Chicago has been influential on this current study.

Therefore I extend my gratitude to Martin Marty, then director of the Institute for the Advanced Study of Religion at Chicago, for his cordial welcome and for his institute's quiet setting for a year-long study. Special thanks also go to Peter Homans and Robert Moore, who took time out to discuss Freud and Jung with me and to point me in the direction of current studies in the interstice between psychology and religion. The onerous task of typing transcripts from the hundreds of hours of taped interviews was borne cheerfully by Lyn Boone and Nancy Shinn.

My former colleagues in the Department of Religion at Oberlin College, Grover Zinn, Gordon Michalson, Gilbert Meilaender, James Dobbins, Michael White, and Elliot Ginsburg, all endured my excited discoveries and offered their own thoughtful perspectives and encouragement. Paul Dawson of Oberlin's Government Department steered me toward the work of Milton Rokeach that marked one important detour in my research and eventually led to the interpretive structure that undergirds my discussion of "submission" in chapter 4. Paul stimulated me to rethink the proper role of the interview material now central in each chapter of this book.

Gordon (Mike) Michalson, Jr., read draft chapters of this manuscript and offered insightful comments. He brought to this reading not only a keen eye for articulate expression but also a broad training in religious studies that enabled him to question my assessments and force me to defend the points of view I expressed. I owe Mike a great deal.

Special thanks must be extended to the dozens of Krishna devotees who consented to be interviewed and who gave of their time to make my life inside the various Krishna temples both pleasant and informative. From the gurus such as Rameswar, Satsvarupa, Kirtananda, and Hridayananda, who shared their understanding of Krishna theology and institutions, to the many devotees, like Laksmana, and Sitarani, who gave of their time and talents or shared their homes with me, I express my sincere gratitude.

Most of all, I am obliged to Subhananda dasa, who encouraged my project from the beginning, traveled with me to facilitate my entrance to many of the Krishna communities I visited, and read this whole manuscript to offer an insider's perspective on its content and my interpretations.

To my new friends and colleagues at Bucknell University, I express my sincere appreciation for their understanding and assistance during the period of my transition from Oberlin College to Bucknell University.

My daughters, Robyn and Christie, have been supportive throughout the writing of the book, and Christie assisted me in the completion of the final draft of the manuscript. Hence, to the three special women in my life I will remain completely obliged.

1

The Great American
Cult Scare

During the last week of June 1981, a hot Santa Monica courtroom was filled
with spectators who had come to witness a cult trial. The litigation that had
attracted so much pretrial attention involved a twenty-three-year-old woman,
Rebecca Foster, who was a member of the Hare Krishna movement. Unlike
most cult trials, which involve an angry parent or ex-member suing a cult for
damages, this trial was initiated by Rebecca, who was suing her mother,
brother, and sister for kidnapping, false imprisonment, and conspiracy.

As the testimony in the Foster trial unfolded, a not too uncommon description of a middle-class American family emerged. The father had been a
Marine fighter pilot in World War II who had difficulty adjusting to society
upon his return. He was respected by his son, Matt, who wanted to emulate
him, and by Rebecca, who felt especially close to him. Five children were
born into this family before the father's drinking became a serious problem
complicated by recurring nightmares of his war experiences. Lengthy stays
in a veterans hospital took the father away from the family for long periods
of time. The mother, who was described as a hardworking and faithful wife,
had to become the sole head of the household when the father's drinking and
personal problems finally resulted in a divorce.

Rebecca soon developed a supportive and close relationship with her
mother. Though the family was poor, it was close-knit. A friendly neighbor
described the Fosters as a "normal" family that had developed a home with
a certain "peacefulness" about it. But all of this changed in the fall of 1976
when Rebecca rejected a scholarship to go to college and joined the Hare
Krishna movement instead.

According to her mother's testimony, Rebecca was "gentle, outgoing, and
enthusiastic" when she joined the Hare Krishnas. She had been a Krishna
devotee less than two years before the mother felt she had to act because "I
thought her mind was going to deteriorate. I was also convinced that she
didn't know right from wrong." Matt felt that his sister's religious chanting
was a form of self-hypnosis and became convinced that his sister "wasn't
thinking," wasn't "capable of making decisions." Consequently, all the de-

fendants viewed their dramatic actions as a "rescue" of a cult victim and not a "kidnapping" of a young adult daughter and sister.

The family had sought help in trying to understand Rebecca's new faith. They tried reading some of the Krishnas' books but couldn't make much sense of them. Then Rebecca's mother found a helpful friend in a professor from a nearby Oregon community college who taught a course on the cults. The mother expressed concern over her daughter's vegetarian diet, her lack of sleep, and the "deception" she felt was associated with the Krishnas' bookselling activities. She was convinced that Rebecca had lost her ability to make a "free choice" in deciding whether to stay or leave the Hare Krishnas. All that her professor friend told her about the cults and the Krishnas supported her fears. Furthermore, the professor encouraged Rebecca's family to read certain anticult books.

And read the family did! When they read Ted Patrick and Tom Dulack's book *Let Our Children Go!* the family became convinced that the Hare Krishnas were a dangerous cult. They felt that Flo Conway and Jim Siegelman's book *Snapping: America's Epidemic of Sudden Personality Change* confirmed their worst fear that Rebecca was unable to think for herself or to leave the Krishnas of her own volition. In Jack Sparks's book *The Mind Benders: A Look at Current Cults,* the Foster family were told that the Krishnas' bookselling was simply a crass form of "begging and peddling." But, worst of all, Sparks argued that the Krishna teachings are demonic and that their chanting is a "dangerous ritual." Sparks advised, "These people offer their words to a false god and the endless repetition of the sounds throws them into a trance."[1] Melanie Foster's view that her sister Rebecca had become a "mindless robot" seemed to be borne out by what the family read. The family agreed that they had to act to "save" Rebecca.

After consultation with the deprogrammer Ted Patrick, the Foster family planned and executed a kidnapping of the twenty-one-year-old Rebecca. To gain her daughter's confidence, Rebecca's mother had stayed with her in the Los Angeles Temple the night before the kidnapping. Then, in the early-morning twilight of June 12, 1979, Rebecca's mother enticed Rebecca over to a parked car, where her brother waited. After a brief scuffle, during which Rebecca's knee was injured, the frightened family drove off with Rebecca in their car, believing they were saving her from a destructive cult.

After two and a half days of strenuous deprogramming in a heavily guarded home in Lake Tahoe, Ted Patrick appeared to have achieved the desired breakthrough. Having placed Rebecca under the heat of several strong lamps and the watchful eye of a video camera, Patrick had bombarded her with quotes from the Christian Bible and refutations from anticult literature of her Krishna beliefs. Repeatedly, Patrick had encouraged Rebecca to rejoin her natural family and return to a normal way of life. On the third day Rebecca broke down in tears and embraced her family. From the family's point of view, Rebecca's mental slavery to the Krishnas had been broken and the rescue appeared to have gone as planned. Ted Patrick returned to his San Diego home to await other such requests from frightened parents.

Meanwhile, the police arrived at the Lake Tahoe house where Rebecca was being held with warrants for the family's arrest on charges of kidnapping and false imprisonment. Realizing she was free from her captors, Rebecca immediately denounced her family's and Ted Patrick's harsh treatment and returned to the Hare Krishnas. Having deduced from Patrick's deprogramming style what he expected to happen, Rebecca had feigned her "return to normalcy" and tricked Patrick and her family into believing she had denounced her new Krishna faith and accepted theirs.

Rebecca now sat in a tension-filled courtroom, having filed a suit against her family for kidnapping, false imprisonment, and conspiracy. She hoped that the minimum she would achieve in court was freedom from her family's interference with her right to practice her maturing Krishna faith. To the family's bewilderment, their fearful and well-intended actions, designed to bring Rebecca back into the family fold—even if by force—had instead driven her farther away. When the trial drew to a close with the family's acquittal, there were no victors or celebrations. Rebecca left the courtroom unsure whether her family would once again try to interfere forcefully with her chosen life and faith. The Foster family left the courtroom having lost Rebecca's trust as well as her companionship.

The Foster trial reveals that there is in America today a pervasive fear that can cause parents and families to take drastic measures in their well-meaning attempts to "save" their children from "cult" groups. What the Foster trial also reveals is that the Hare Krishnas are lumped into that collection of nascent religious groups that sprang up in the late 1960s in America and are labeled cults. This book explores the images and stereotypes associated with the cults that have fueled the fires of cult fears. There is a set of images evoked by the word "cult": stereotypes that include greedy gurus, brainwashing, deceptive life-styles, and the specter of impending violence.

This book discusses cult images and stereotypes in the context of the Hare Krishna tradition in America to acquaint the reader with one alternative religious group and to demonstrate the danger of lumping all such groups together. The Hare Krishna movement is known formally as the International Society for Krishna Consciousness, or ISKCON. The group is an excellent one for examination of cult stereotypes because it is so well known for its ocher-robed and shaven-headed devotees dancing in the streets or distributing books in airports. Their differences in appearance, life-style, and practice and their formation in America around an old guru from India seemingly fit the cult stereotype perfectly. However, the Hare Krishnas and their religious faith are worth studying in their own right as a Hindu missionary venture into the English-speaking world.

To acclimate the reader to the two primary focuses of the book, this introductory chapter will ask, first, what we mean when we use the word "cult." Second, we will examine briefly the nature and extent of the fear and suspicion that is commonly attached to cult discussions. Third, we will see how general cult images and attributes get attached specifically to the Hare Krishna tradition. And finally, we will show how the book's organization unfolds a discussion of cult stereotypes while at the same time presenting the Hare Krishna tradition as an intrinsically interesting test case.

A Naming Game: "The Cults"

The old folk adage, "Sticks and stones may break my bones, but words will never hurt me!" seemed a good protection against name-calling when we were children. However, that childish trust in immunity from the sting of unkind words or ugly and derogatory phrases has long since been replaced by the realization that words, especially when used to incite mistrust or violence, *can* result in emotional or physical harm—or even death. The power of the words *"Heil Hitler!"* still rings in the ears of those who experienced the horrors of World War II Europe. Today, a new set of terms is linked to the specter of Nazi youth camps, S.S. brutality, and slavish obedience to a power-hungry leader. Who among us can say that the words "Charles Manson," "Jonestown," or simply "the cults" do not have emotive as well as cognitive significance for us? Dusty Sklar in her book *Gods and Beasts: The Nazis and the Occult* makes explicit the similarities that she feels exist between the horrors of Hitler's Germany, Manson's "family," and the contemporary American "cults" (such as the Hare Krishnas, the Moonies, and Scientology).

But what is a cult? Who has decided that some groups belong to this pejorative social category and some do not? Are all cults the same? A quick glance through a selective six-month sampling of recent articles on the cults sheds some light on the elusiveness of this term. Rather than providing discriminating examinations of a single cult or a comparison of a variety of cults, most popular media and literature simply assume that the reader knows what cults are and spend their time telling atrocity stories that serve to heighten the reader's fear of "the cults" in America.

For example, in February 1983 the *Denver Post's Empire Magazine* reported the liberating deprogramming of DeAnn Reher in an article entitled "Battling the Cults." In March 1983, the *Phi Delta Kappan* carried an article entitled "The Urgent Need for Education About Cults." In that article all cults are lumped together and their techniques of conversion are compared point by point with those of Hitler. The author, Shirley Hale Willis, has a daughter who is a member of the Crossroads movement within the Church of Christ.

In April 1983, the *New York Times* in its "New Jersey Opinion" column published an anonymously written essay whose title warned, "Cult Syndrome Has Claimed Another Victim." That same month, *Teen* magazine reported "The Truth About the Cults" in an article by Aurora Mackey. We learn in that essay how Kathy Mackey was lured into a cult by the love and support of cult members who "all had a glow about them, as though they'd discovered the truth." Utilizing extensive references to anticult psychiatrist John Clark and other such "experts," Ms. Mackey recites the litany of cult abuses—sleep deprivation, poor diet, trance-inducing chanting—and then ends her article by reminding her readers of the Jonestown atrocities, the high-caliber weapons found in an unnamed cult's warehouse, the drug smuggling and killing associated with another unnamed cult, and the rattlesnake that was placed in an anticult lawyer's mailbox.

The two basic assumptions that these articles make are that all cults are the same and that they are equally dangerous. The inaccuracy of this material (and of virtually all anticult books) resides not so much in the "facts" reported about a particular religious group as in the assumption or assertion that what is true about one person or group (e.g., Hitler and the Nazi movement or Jim Jones and Jonestown) is also true of *every* cult leader and cult (e.g., Rev. Sun Myung Moon and the Unification Church). Yet this process of undifferentiated name-calling, which leads to guilt-by-association and equal fear and hatred of any and all cults, persists in the general media, in anticult publications, and even in some sympathetic essays and books.

Who among us who simply reads the daily newspaper cannot recognize the familiar list of the cults: the Moonies, the Hare Krishnas, Scientology, the Divine Light Mission, and the Way International? This list occurs with only a few alterations in virtually every anticult publication. It was precisely the attribution to the Hare Krishnas of the destructive features that are assumed to be common to all the cults that made sensational reading in the books by Patrick, Conway, and Sparks and that influenced the Foster family to attempt a forceful and dramatic "rescue" of Rebecca. Because of the fear aroused by the association of groups like the Krishnas with the specter of Jonestown, irate parents and a suspicious public refuse to listen to the reasonable pleas of young people, like Rebecca, who insist that their life of faith is something different or special.

Despite the pervasive assertion of the homogeneity of cults in America, one will not find any two lists of characteristics that agree exactly on what constitutes a cult. Nonetheless, a representative list of cult characteristics can be found in Lita Schwartz's "The Cult Phenomenon," which includes, as identifying markers, a charismatic leader, submission to authority, communal life-style, rigid ideology, restricted communications, isolation from one's family, active recruiting, physiological deprivation, hate and/or fear of outsiders, and the relinquishing of one's personal assets to the group.[2] These identifying characteristics finally constitute the core images or stereotypes associated with the cults and are assumed to be equally descriptive of any group called a cult. Other lists include the types of salvific beliefs that some cults promote, the threat of violence a cult poses to its members or outsiders, the cults' systematic use of deception, their excessive stress on fund-raising, or their subversive political designs.

One difficulty with such sets of criteria is that when applied equitably they also describe many mainline and accepted religious and political institutions. A second problem is that some cults exhibit only a few of the stated characteristics, while others fit other features better. A third observation is that when cult criteria such as those above are applied to anticult groups, it would appear that many of those groups could themselves be considered cults. Finally, which groups get included under the label "cult" often depends more upon the biases and prejudices of the critic than upon the offensive characteristics and activities of a particular group. That is, cult stereotypes are often more prescriptive accusations than they are descriptive assessments of any unpopular religious group on the margin of American society.

Gordon Melton and Robert Moore characterize the popular conception of a cult in their book *The Cult Experience* this way: "A cult is a cult. That is to say, cults are religions that espouse an alien belief system that deviates strongly from the traditional faiths with which most people have grown up."[3]

In the end, using the term "cult" is a naming game. Just as with a woman being called a witch in the eighteenth century in America, being called a cult is sufficient to brand a marginal religious group as dangerous. Finally, because of the genuine diversity of such groups, all objective attempts to lump the cults together fail unless very general definitions are used that include more groups and situations than anticult groups intend. As we will see in the next chapter, even the charismatic leader is not unique to the cults, nor do all charismatic leaders of cults claim the same kind of authority.

Melton and Moore's solution to the definitional problem is to use the term "alternative religions" for the groups commonly known as cults. These authors make a convincing case for their thesis that contemporary cults are but part of a traditional American phenomenon, the alternative religious quest. They point out that the Mormons, the Seventh-Day Adventists, the Jehovah's Witnesses, and the Theosophical Society all arose in the nineteenth century as alternatives to the mainline American faiths. Each exhibited social features similar to those of the contemporary cults, and all suffered many of the same kinds of persecution. Hence, today's alternative religious and mental health groups exhibit less the characteristics of social movements unique to contemporary America than of a fairly predictable social pattern of "deviant religion" well known throughout our history.[4]

"New religious movements" is a phrase used with regularity by many scholars to connote the new content (Asian religious beliefs in particular) and new context (religious and nonreligious pluralism) of cults in contemporary America. These scholars note the "new religious consciousness" made explicit in the counterculture of the 1960s and 1970s in America as a further indication of the cults' "newness." A representative of this point of view is the academic clearinghouse for information on cults in America that is located in Berkeley, California, and is called the Center for the Study of New Religious Movements. Still other writers have used terms such as "emergent religions" or just plain "sects" to circumvent the negative connotations of the word "cult."[5]

Mindless Robots and the Specter of Jonestown

When some anticult writers encountered dead ends trying to list social or religious characteristics common *only* to the cults, they began to assert a common malevolent process of indoctrination as the basic identifying feature. Flo Conway and Jim Siegelman, who wrote the best-selling exposé *Snapping: America's Epidemic of Sudden Personality Change*, are representative of this new tack. They say, "In the course of our research, we came to the conclusion that America's cults and mass therapies should be viewed together because they use nearly identical techniques of manipulating the mind and because, in this decade, many of them have become impossible to categorize."[6] Conway and Siegelman identify the largest and most dangerous cults to be the Moonies, the Way, the Divine Light Mission, the Hare Krishnas, Transcendental Meditation, and Scientology. Predictably, the list of destructive cults doesn't change, even when the reason for their inclusion together does.

Many anticult writers place at the heart of their proclamation of the dangers of the cults the assertion that the cults *are* different from legitimate religions because of their use of "brainwashing." The euphemisms for this now imprecise and overused term include mind control, coercive persuasion, instant hypnotism, mind-bending, and snapping. Conway and Siegelman describe the process of "snapping" as "one of shutting off the mind, of not-thinking. . . . In all the world, there is nothing quite so impenetrable as a human mind snapped shut with bliss. No call to reason, no emotional appeal can get through its armor of self-proclaimed joy."[7] At the base of this claim is the expressed fear that no one is immune from the ability of the cults to convert innocent victims *against their wills*.

Not only have the terms for the *process* of mind control gained popular use, so too have the terms that describe the *state of mind* of the victims. As her sister reported, Rebecca seemed to be a "mindless robot." James Alle, lawyer, warns, "There's thousands of robots walking around this country and it's terribly dangerous."[8] Margaret Singer, a psychologist often quoted by anticult writers, says, "Indeed some cults can reduce their followers to a kind of 'robot-like functioning.' "[9]

What is used by some cult critics as the defining characteristic of a cult becomes also the emotional lever they use to engender fear of the cults. The phrase "mindless robot" was used more than a dozen times in just one day of testimony in the Foster case. The negative effect of using this terminology to sway the jury was achieved without anyone once defending these terms as descriptive of Rebecca's state of mind during her deprogramming when she clearly had the reasoning ability to assess her situation and outthink her captors. The imputed characteristic of robotlike mind control seems designed to create fear of the Hare Krishnas, not to describe Rebecca's mental condition.

In the anticult literature, "robot" is rivaled by "zombie" as the favored pejorative label for a person who has been brainwashed.[10] The term "zombie" conjures up in the minds of most readers the image of ghostly creatures who have been resuscitated by a master of voodoo. If pressed to describe the physiological or psychological characteristics that constitute a zombie, most users of this term could not. Furthermore, many who use this term would deny that they really believe in a person's rising from the dead. Yet Ted Patrick includes not only the followers but also the leaders of cults in his characterizations: "Most of the leadership . . . are themselves robots, zombies, incapable of rapid thought."[11]

Regardless of the credibility of their use of descriptive terms, anticultists insist there is a common state of mind among all cult devotees. The cult person is humorless, lacks free will, and exhibits no distinguishing individuality. Each is marked by "the thousand mile stare." But even more important, the cult member is judged guilty by the perception and proclamation of outsiders. Distressed parents, anticult antagonists, and deprogrammed ex-members make up the usual chorus of expert witnesses lined up against the cults.

Contemporary cult members are viewed as being incapable of rational thought or truthful testimony. There is no self-defense. The foreman of the jury in the Rebecca Foster trial commented to the press: "Her testimony was quite plastic. She was like a puppet with strings being pulled by someone else."[12] Consequently, it is not simply the phrase "the cults" that colors the thinking and response of the general public to such groups as the Hare Krishnas, but so too do terms such as "brainwashed," "robot," "zombie," and "puppet" which are used to describe members of *every* cult.

The other side of the coin of the fear of the cults is the conviction that "brainwashed" devotees will do anything their cult leader commands, including doing harm to others. The link between "brainwashing" and the threat of violence in what he calls the "destructive cults" is made explicit by John Clark. He writes, "A member of such an organization must not only bend his will to the group and its leaders but must yield control of his mind as well. Failure to do so is punished or corrected; banishment is the ultimate sanction in some groups, death in others. . . . [Thus] in groups organized in the ways I have been describing, there is an inherent danger . . . that they can become destructive for the sake of destruction."[13] Like all of the other anticultists, Clark includes the Moonies and the Hare Krishnas in his grouping of what he calls "destructive cults."

What makes assertions like Clark's plausible is the example of Jonestown. The initial media reports on November 18, 1978, said that Congressman Leo Ryan had been assassinated and more than four hundred persons in Jonestown had committed suicide along with their leader, Jim Jones. Later investigations revealed the dead to number more than nine hundred and murder as well as suicide to be the cause.[14] Who among us can say that such frightening memories and images have not been kept alive by television shows (e.g., *Lou Grant* and *The A-Team*) and the print media which constantly compare current cult leaders or cults with Jim Jones and Jonestown? It is precisely this connection which the anticult antagonists try to keep alive and which the often uncritical media frequently report.

James and Marcia Rudin in their book *Prison or Paradise?* best exemplify this tactic. They first lump all familiar cults—the usual list—under the heading "hard-core cults" and then connect these groups to Jonestown. They assert, "Following the People's Temple massacre, some optimists believed the cult phenomenon would come to an end. Clearly, this has not happened; indeed, it is our belief that the cults are stronger than ever."[15] At the end of their first chapter, entitled "The Cult Boom," they ask three questions: "Is another Jonestown possible? Are there other Jim Joneses, perhaps unknown to anyone now? Do these cult leaders hold such power over their followers that they can persuade them to kill themselves—and perhaps others—at their command? Many observers of the cult scene fear the answer is 'yes.' "[16] They close the chapter by quoting John Clark, who states that these cults train adherents like armies willing to kill "their parents or themselves" or, if necessary, outsiders.

In chapter after chapter, the Rudins equate the leaders, life-styles, and practices of the cults with Jim Jones and Jonestown—often by innuendo, by rhetorical questions, or by the quoted words of others. The message is clear: "Fear the cults. They are dangerous and potentially violent." Furthermore, the Rudins are not alone in their attempt to sound this indiscriminate alarm to the general public. The Rudins appear to agree with Ted Patrick's conclusion: "[There is] not a brown penny's worth of difference between any of 'em."[17]

As the reader will come to see, there *is* a difference between the cults, especially in their inclination toward violence. Quite often it is the very small, localized sectarian offshoots from mainline Christianity (which describes the People's Temple as well) that commit acts of violence—*not* the well-known cults. For example, on July 13, 1983, a small Midwestern newspaper reported the death of two children. Both children had been beaten to death while undergoing punishment that was religiously motivated. One death had occurred in Michigan in the House of Judah sect and the other in West Virginia in the Stonegate Christian commune.[18]

Anticult writers and speakers never say that the dozens of deaths associated with "the cults" that they report nearly all arise from Christian sects that no anticult law could touch without abolishing mainline religion in America as well. Consequently, anticultists do not distinguish between those groups willing to use violent tactics against their critics (like Synanon and Manson's Family) and those whose communities have never been found guilty of such systematic and purposeful violence (like the Moonies, the Divine Light Mission, or the Hare Krishnas). Instead, all cults are simply lumped together as potential perpetrators of the "Jonestown Syndrome."

What are the symptoms of this Jonestown disease? Simply put, the same characteristics that were earlier used to define a cult also are employed to define a group assumed to be capable of violence as well. The leader is (or becomes) possessed with power. The followers are brainwashed robots or puppets that will do anything the leader commands. Because the cult's ideology cuts off communications with the outside world, the cult becomes isolated and both the members and the leader become paranoid and fearful of their detractors. Violence against oneself and/or others is the final consequence. This is the "Jonestown Syndrome." Bound up in the image of Jonestown are the primary stereotypes that led to the Foster family's dramatic action. It is also these primary cult images which the various chapters of this book will discuss.

The Hare Krishnas and the Cults

The Hare Krishnas exhibit all the stereotypic features usually attributed to a cult. The movement was founded in America by a charismatic Indian guru. The Krishnas insist on absolute submission to the guru. Their ideology can appear to be totalistic and rigid as it divides the world into two groups: devotees of God and those outside the pale of God's grace. They practice a communal life-style and are required to alter their name, their dress, and their life-style. They actively recruit young outsiders to their membership.

Anticult writers have made the further claims that the Krishnas brainwash their adherents through six or seven hours a day of repetitive chanting. Moreover, the Krishnas have been accused of stockpiling guns in their American temples and of teaching their devotees to hate (and kill if necessary) their parents or others who oppose them.

In the first place, the Rudins, Conway and Siegelman, Ted Patrick, John Clark, and a host of other "cult experts" insist that chanting mantras in the Krishna context leads to mind control. For example, the Rudins report that ISKCON's chanting practices "discourage rational thought" and "lead to a complete dissolution of the mind."[19] Ted Patrick says of the Krishnas' chant-ing, "They're simply into self-hypnosis."[20] For verification, the critics point to a common sight in many American cities of a group of Krishnas chanting ecstatically on a street corner with heads askew and eyes glazed.

In the second place, of all the accusations made against ISKCON, none has been so persistent as the charge that violence is accepted and taught by the Hare Krishnas. Sporadic outbreaks of local antagonism between the Krishnas and the general public have occurred since ISKCON's inception in America. Most of the early incidents centered around child custody battles, parents trying to get their children out of the movement, or harassment of Krishna temples by local youths "having fun" with these foreigners. But the tone of public concern changed in 1977 and the years following. The Krishnas were accused in California of being involved in a gangland style murder and in other states of hoarding large caches of guns.

For example, a *New York Times* November 2, 1977, article entitled "Cali-fornia Slaying Case Involves Ex-Mafia Figures and Krishnas" reported that three former Mafia men and a twenty-eight-year-old Krishna devotee, Alex-ander Kulik, were arrested for the drug-related murder of Steven Bovan. The story goes on to report that Mr. Kulik, a "member of the Hare Krishna sect, lived in a $450,000.00 ocean front home and drove a $100,000.00 Stutz-Blackhawk. He was arrested with an estimated one million dollars' worth of heroin in his possession."

In a longer, more thorough article, Evan Maxwell of the *Los Angeles Times* reported on December 18, 1977, that the only relationship Kulik had with the Hare Krishnas consisted of a $25,000 contribution to ISKCON's book publishing enterprise. Further, Maxwell reported that three other Krishna devotees implicated in the drug-running (but not the murder) had actually been "expelled" from ISKCON a year earlier and had used their Krishna connections as a facade for their illegal drug business.

Newspapers throughout the United States picked up this sensational story. The articles simply stated that the Krishnas were engaged in drug-smuggling as anticult critics had asserted and now this involvement had led to blood-shed. Few of these accounts ever picked up the obvious discrepancies in the New York and Los Angeles stories. If Kulik were a shaven-headed devotee, brainwashed to give all his possessions to Krishna and run drugs illegally for his "masters," what was he doing with a half-million-dollar home and a fancy car? Further, why was he not living in the confines of the closed-off com-mune? The answers to these questions reveal a whole different story from the one the media originally announced.

Alexander Kulik had *never* been initiated by ISKCON's guru, nor had he *ever* lived in a Krishna temple. He had used three dissident Krishna members, who *had* been discredited in the Laguna Beach Krishna temple a year earlier, as operators in his international drug-smuggling business. The three dissident members had kept up their connections with the Hare Krishnas by giving money to ISKCON publishing ventures and occasionally coming to services in the temple. Hence, they could be called fringe Krishna devotees, but in no way could their activities be viewed as supported or approved *by* ISKCON. Most important, the accused murderer of Steven Bovan was not, nor had he ever been, a Krishna devotee. Yet the worrisome headlines and stories incorrectly linking the Krishnas to this violent act had already made their impact.

A Tale of the Dark Lord

This book purposely accepts the double entendre of the title, *The Dark Lord*. On the one hand (see chapter 5), Krishna is the name of the deity at the center of ISKCON devotion and is presented quite often in dark-blue or black images. The name Krishna in Sanskrit literally means "black," and this deity has been worshiped in India for more than two thousand years without any pejorative meaning being attached to his color. In fact, the scriptures of India extol Krishna's color as the beneficent expression of the God who chooses to enter our bleak period of history in a form that will be most beneficial to the salvation of humankind. On the other hand, the anticult writers have painted Krishna and the movement that bears his name as dark and demonic blots on the recent religious history in America. Claiming violence to be at the very heart of the scriptures of ISKCON (namely, the *Bhagavad Gita*), cult critics have accused ISKCON devotees of teaching parental hate, promoting societal disharmony, and developing an "army" of robots willing to do anything for the success of ISKCON. These are among the images that will be tested against the realities of ISKCON's teachings and practices.

In the pages that follow, the generalizations that all cults are the same and that they are all equally dangerous will be strongly contested. These tendencies to exaggerate the similarities and the dangers of all the cults have been two major forces in promoting public suspicion and fear of such groups. Rather than accepting these stereotypical assumptions, this book will test the appropriateness of the images against one primary group that is labeled a cult. As Melton and Moore appropriately remark, "Global generalizations about religious individuals or groups . . . become increasingly difficult in direct proportion to the degree of familiarity with the scholarly literature. . . . In sum, the need for reliable information on diverse religious traditions and practices will increase."[21] This book will provide just such particular information on one group, the Hare Krishnas.

Each chapter will begin with an abridged story of one devotee's life that can add nuances to the images and issues to be discussed in that chapter. The names and the identifying geographical details of the stories have been changed to protect the persons interviewed from embarrassment, since very explicit personal details are often retained to ensure the integrity of the stories. Otherwise, the stories have not been edited to save the devotee or ISKCON any discomfort. In short, the stories serve as part of the evidential record regarding ISKCON that this book makes available to its readers.

After the introductory story (and sometimes before), a basic anticult stereotype will be presented through the words of the antagonists themselves. Then information about the Hare Krishnas from the relevant literature, interviews, and current practices within ISKCON will be presented to test the cult image or stereotype. Finally, alternative explanations will be offered for many of the anticult interpretations in the light of the evidence presented.

Throughout the book an attempt will be made to interweave the presentation of primary anticult images with a discussion of the historical and theological underpinnings of the Hare Krishnas as a religious movement. However, in some chapters (e.g., chapter 7 on brainwashing) the anticult image will determine the primary agenda for the discussion. In other cases (e.g., chapter 3 on the transmission of charisma) the inner logic of the history of ISKCON will dictate the focus of the presentation.

The outline of the book follows the essential thread of the anticult thesis: A greedy or power-hungry guru (chapter 2) or his successors (chapter 3) seduces new converts into a completely submissive (chapter 4) faith (chapter 5) and life (chapter 6) by brainwashing them (chapter 7). The only avenue out of the cults for a member, therefore, is to be deprogrammed so that the cult spell can be broken (chapter 8).

Nonetheless, this book is not written simply to debunk anticult stereotypes and rhetoric. Rather, the reader will find that there persists throughout this presentation an interest in understanding why some people find the full-time and demanding religious life of ISKCON attractive. Why do some American youth feel compelled to worship the Hindu god Krishna in a cultural setting so dramatically different from ISKCON's Indian homeland? Why do well-educated and economically advantaged youth renounce the comfortable world of their parents and don the Krishna's ascetic clothes and way of life? In short, what *is* the attraction of the dark Lord Krishna?

2

Godmen and Gurus

While of average height and build, Govinda Dasa[1] makes a forceful, immediate impression upon entering a room. He has a head of thick blond hair which he let grow out for his job as the leader of a mobile fund-raising team that sells Asian art reproductions. He is a rather quiet person who nonetheless gives the impression of being capable of taking strong stands and defending them. Unlike the hesitancy of speech punctuated with nervous mannerisms that is common to many persons who are being interviewed about their ticklish personal history, Govinda is very forthright about his remarkable past and how he came to be a disciple of ISKCON. Here is the story that he tells.

Now from my current perspective as a devotee, I can see traces of my past lives. They were very present when I was young. For example, from a very young age I wanted to sit on the floor to eat like Indians do. My parents refused to let me, so I used to stand at the table to eat, not using a chair. Also, I hated the sight of meat and eggs. I would get nauseous looking at them and would vomit night after night when my parents forced me to eat meat. I would sometimes stuff the meat in my jeans to avoid eating it. It took several years of conditioning before I could eat meat and hold it down. I was also kind of fanatical about cleaning myself after going to the toilet. I used to put water on the toilet paper and felt really dirty when I had to use the paper alone. As you know, this is a Vaisnava [Hindu sect, with Krishna or Vishnu as highest god] practice, to be so concerned with cleanliness. These things couldn't have rubbed off on me from anyone around. Everyone thought these behaviors were strange.

Otherwise, my childhood was pretty normal by most Western standards. I was born in November 1954 in a suburb of Washington. My father was an insurance salesman but never was very successful financially. I had two brothers, one older and one younger, and three older sisters. My parents were not practicing Catholics, but had very strong sentiments about learning the rituals and taking first communion. They couldn't afford to send me to a Catholic private school, so they sent me to the Saturday classes of a local Catholic church to learn the doctrines and prepare for the first communion. So I went to the priest and his school and learned a few prayers and some scripture.

In school, the teachers always liked me because I was always quiet and obedient. And I used to get really good grades, especially in high school, where I was always on the honor roll. I also was a wrestler on the varsity team in high school as a freshman and won most of my matches. But I was also kind of a hippie. By the end of the junior high school years I had let my hair grow long and had tried pot. I sympathized with the countercultural movements that questioned American society and its practices, but was never actually active in them. In the summers I used to hitchhike to California and stay with the kids who slept on the beaches. I smoked pot to find deeper meanings in life than normal consciousness could give. But when I returned in the fall, I was still obedient to my teachers and parents and didn't give them any more trouble than a teenager normally does.

After I graduated from high school, my parents moved to southern California. I took menial jobs like working in a car wash and occasionally dropped acid [LSD] or smoked marijuana. I didn't like drugs that much, but saw them as a way to expand my mind and find a deeper purpose to life. I attended a junior college in the fall and got all A's that first year. I was particularly interested in philosophy and read many books on Eastern religions. During this first year on my own, I just stood back and watched our society at war in Vietnam, and hungrily seeking material values at home. I saw that the whole idea of society—get a good education, get a nice job, have a nice family and that would mean life was successful—I saw that those people who had all these things were as miserable as anyone else. I realized that what I had been brought up to believe in was not true! . . . I just knew that there must be something more.

During this time, I got deeper and deeper into religious books. The Bible made a very deep impression on me. And also the books of the East (J. Krishnamurti, Evans Wentz, etc.). I became initiated into TM [Transcendental Meditation arising from Maharishi Mahesh Yogi] as I sought to find deeper spiritual avenues to truth. I realized such a journey would be very difficult alone and wanted to find a spiritual master to help lead me. So I sold my car and, along with a friend, bought a ticket to Europe.

In Europe I traveled with my friend, living on one meal a day and staying with people who would take us in. When things got really bad, I sat down on the street and played my harmonica, with a hat in front of me. A loaf of bread and some cheese was often our only meal for the day. But during all our travels in Europe, I was reading several books on Eastern spirituality as well as the Bible I had brought with me. We quite often visited Christian cathedrals and monasteries and talked with the leaders of them. I was less into the hippie goals and carefree life-style than into preparations for my spiritual quest. It was on the top of a mountain in Switzerland after a day of meditation and prayer to God that I decided to journey to India in search of spiritual truth. My purpose in going to India was to find a spiritual master, a guru, and to dedicate my life to spiritual purposes. My friend was unwilling to go to India with me, but I linked up with another young man and set off for India overland.

Before I ever met my guru, I was already strictly adhering to the four regulative principles (no intoxicants, no sex, no meat eating, no gambling). I never had gambled, and each of my vows to renounce one of the remaining three pleasures came out of an important experience I had on the trip to India. For example, one night while smoking some really good hashish I got real stoned and thought, This is the essence of getting stoned, this is the high point, and where is this getting me spiritually? Right then I made a heavy vow that I would never take drugs again.

While in Amsterdam, I met a beautiful hippie girl who took me to her place to spend the night. . . . Well, this Dutch girl was really lusty and here I was meditating on going to India to find a guru. She was doing everything to get me going, and she knew all the tricks too! Although I had had sex before, I finally resolved as we lay in bed that if I wanted spiritual life, I must give all of this up. So I got up out of bed and while she was begging me to come back, I walked out the door. It was about midnight, the streets were cold and I had no place to go, so I walked around the streets all night . . . thinking, I'd rather do this than be in there. . . . So I made a vow not to have a sex life.

Upon arriving in India, I again hung out with the hippie crowd. One day as I watched a herd of cows, I asked an Indian why the cow was so sacred. "She is your mother, she gives you milk," he said. Not long after that conversation, a hippie friend bought me supper and when I was half through eating, I asked what the little chunks were on the rice and he said beef. I vomited violently, just as I had when I was a kid, and vowed never to eat meat again.

As winter began to approach, I traveled north to begin my search for an authentic guru. I went first to Hardwar and then to the famous retreat town of Rishikesh in the foothills of the Himalayas. There were no Westerners there, since it was wintertime. Only sadhus [ascetic holy men] and their committed disciples were in the ashrams [religious retreats] that sprinkle the town and mountains there. I went from ashram to ashram, finally settling in Vendantaniketin Ashram, where I was given one of ten cavelike, clay-mud rooms along the Ganges River. A Nepali ascetic who thought I was a sincere seeker gave me a lungi and chader [loincloth and shawl]. I was ready to begin my quest.

I decided first that I needed to purify myself. So I began by arising at sunrise and then, after eating a few nuts and a bit of fruit, headed for the Ganges to meditate until sunset. I used to sit on a rock in the middle of the river all day, meditating while the river gurgled around me. I would meditate silently most of the time. Sometimes I would chant mantras I had learned in my reading and even chanted the Hare Krishna mantra which I heard many holy men chanting. One day as I sat on my usual rock in the river, my mind returned again and again to the harmonica tunes I loved so well. Since this attachment was hindering my progress, I threw my expensive harmonica into the Ganges.

I was introduced to a cave sadhu who spoke no English. He saw that I was sincere and taught me his meditation techniques on my frequent trips to his hillside cave. I was beginning to look like him with his matted hair and thin ascetic's body. But I had to move on, since I wanted to experience more masters so I could decide whom I should follow.

After some travels in the north of India, I traveled to Banaras just like all other sadhus do—riding free in the crowded third-class compartments of trains. In Bombay I saw Prabhupada [founder and guru of the Hare Krishna movement] for the first time and was impressed with his sincerity. He gave a whole week of lectures, and I arrived early so I could sit right at his feet to hear all that he said. Though the Krishna devotees preached really hard to me, I was not ready to listen.

Many months later in Vrindavan [a small village near Mathura, where Krishna is said to have grown up], I headed to the Jumna River as was common practice in each city I came to. On the way I met an Indian devotee who said, "Anyone who comes to Vrindavan is a guest of Krishna." He offered me a place to stay and food to eat. As the days passed into weeks, I came to appreciate the subtle but real difference living in a holy city or village makes. You wake up to the sounds of devotees praying, singing, or chanting and go to bed to the same sound. The whole atmosphere is purified. I came to be more and more impressed with the devotion of the people of Vrindavan.

After a while, I set off to visit some of the many temples and ashrams there, wanting to learn more about Krishna. I came one day to the ashram of a godbrother of Prabhupada. After studying and living there for some time, I was told that I would have to become a disciple if I wanted to stay in his ashram. I responded, "I have already spoken to and lived with so many gurus. . . . One thing I found is that so many Americans take gurus so cheaply. They surrender to one guru and then they want to check out another one. If ever I surrender to a guru, I have to stay with him for the rest of my life. I have to never give up his order. So I cannot surrender to somebody unless I can be sure that he is a person I can actually surrender to."

While at the ashram I got typhoid fever. When I left I needed assistance just to carry on normal functions. Person after person took me in, sheltered me and treated me like a son. I lived with the people of Vrindavan and drank deeply from their devotion to Krishna for six months. Then one day a busload of American and European Krishna devotees arrived in a new bus. They were disciples of Prabhupada and were coming to Vrindavan to hear Prabhupada speak. I was put off by their opulence: shiny new bus, tape recorders, cameras, and their holiday attitude. But I was attracted to Prabhupada.

One morning I went to the house he was staying in and he was giving *Bhagavatam* class [morning scriptural reading and preaching session preceded by a period of devotional singing]. He was chanting, and just by the sound of his voice I could see this person really loves God. . . . When he spoke, I was listening to him on a higher platform of interest than I did in Bombay. And everything he said just made so much sense that I was thinking that this philosophy puts all other philosophies in perspective. I really felt in my heart that this man is very old and truly is the greatest saint I ever met, and I should surrender to him. But because I was very cautious, I wouldn't do it. . . . I had examined and learned from so many gurus. Though I was attracted to Prabhupada, I wanted to remain in Vrindavan; so I did not go with him.

My visa ran out and I was forced to leave after two years in India. On the way home to visit my parents, I stopped in Amsterdam. I was completely shocked by the materialism and sinfulness. In India I usually stayed in villages that were sacred places. And here I was in this big city where there were drugs, sex, red-light districts. . . . It seemed so degraded. Then I found there was a Hare Krishna temple there, and it was like I was back in Vrindavan again. So I lived there about a month before returning home.

When I arrived at my parents' home in Washington they were delighted to see me but shocked beyond belief at my long matted hair (highly prized in India but seen as "filthy" in America). My habits simply blew their minds. I would sleep on the concrete patio outside the house. I sat on the floor to eat my meals and wouldn't take part in their television watching and other frivolous activities. They thought I was really strange and said, "Why don't you be just like a normal person?" They'd be watching television and it really seemed disgusting to me to have left Vrindavan and just to see these habits of Westerners . . . how they waste their time so much in these useless kinds of things. They are so forgetful of Krishna. They are so forgetful of God. But it was nice to see them, because naturally I had great affection for them.

I soon began to long for association with devotees again. I heard that Prabhupada was going to be speaking in New York City, so I went there. After a few days, Prabhupada set off for India again, and I went to the Pennsylvania Krishna farm community instead. I planned to stay only a few months until I could get a new visa for India. . . . I hadn't accepted Prabhupada as my guru yet. I really wanted to make sure. So I read the books of Prabhupada and other gurus when I was not milking cows or doing other farm work. I really wanted to see how genuine the life-style of these devotees was and what this movement was really like.

In other words, I was making an experiment. I would live with the Hare

Krishnas just like I had lived with so many other gurus to see what philosophy they were actually following. After I was there three months they wanted to give me initiation, but I refused. I said, "Until I am one hundred percent positive that I'm never going to leave this person, I don't want to accept initiation. . . . I'm not going to cut off my hair until I accept my guru." And I was there a year before I shaved my head.

What was the final proof for me? Well, Prabhupada was giving me something that I had experienced already in India: he was presenting an ancient Indian system of faith that is based on the authority of the scripture. He wasn't concocting something on his own. So the authority by which he spoke was actually one of the most impressive things to me. . . . I was accepting the word of the *Bhagavad Gita* and the *acaryas* [teaching sages] because they were all speaking through him and he was the perfect example of it. His disciples were also dedicated to the service of the Lord Krishna twenty-four hours a day, not just a half hour morning and night . . . and that's what I wanted. All my doubts just gradually disappeared; the process was definitely gradual.

Also I never thought this path was the only path. Prabhupada never said it was the only path. I could see that what was being presented here was really pure and genuine. . . . Gradually, Prabhupada's greatness became revealed in my heart. I became satisfied, and though being a "black sheep" for having refused initiation months earlier, I now asked for initiation. Basically it had been the philosophy which had satisfied me. All other philosophies I could now understand in very proper perspective through the philosophy of Krishna consciousness. . . . Krishna consciousness just explained it so nicely. I was convinced that this was a genuine path back to godhead . . . not the only one, but a genuine one.

The Guru as Deceiver

Who are these modern gurus and holy men who attract our youth? What motivates them to build communities cut off from the mainstream of life? How can they be so effective in gaining the submission of intelligent and capable young people who are sons and daughters of our most affluent and educated citizens? Most important, how do we stop these cult leaders from stealing our youth who many times are barely into their teens before being snatched up by these cults and taken out of their natural families?

These were some of the questions asked by men and women of the elite classes of sixth century B.C. India as their sons and daughters abandoned the privileged life of the court or the marketplace to join the Buddha and his assembly of monks and nuns. Furthermore, this disruptive threat to the family came not only from the Buddha and his mendicant band of devoted followers who sought release from the ephemeral world of suffering and rebirth. There was the even greater fear of one's child joining the radical ascetic Mahavira and his followers, called Jains. These monks and nuns performed self-mortifying fasts, blinding sessions of gazing into the sun, and other such extreme bodily penances.

To become a member of the Buddhist or Jain sects were but two of the many options for youth seeking spiritual guidance in India twenty-five hundred years ago. Clearly, the fear, anxiety, and questions expressed by parents in ancient India are not much different from those of their American counterparts twenty-five centuries later. And as in ancient India, it is not just parents who are concerned. The success of new or unusual religious movements was and still is a challenge to all of society's institutions—political, economic, social, and religious—and to the persons who would protect or defend them.

Negative images of the gurus and cult leaders in America typically revolve around two basic themes. First, gurus are thought to be greedy for monetary and/or political power; and second, gurus presumably attempt to control the thought and actions of their devotees through deception, mind control, and insincere claims of divinity. Andrew Pavlos states in his book *The Cult Experience,* "Many of the messiahs and gurus, or Gods in a Rolls Royce, are getting richer and stronger despite the mounting criticism."[2]

The charge that gurus seek political power for themselves is not as easy to demonstrate, since only a few of the leaders of cults in America have ever engaged in politics either directly or indirectly. While the Rev. Moon and his followers did engage in political speeches and activities in the mid-1970s, his movement has never been primarily focused in the political arena. Most gurus who have come to America have stayed aloof from political activities altogether.

The second claim of those opposed to the leaders of the cults charges that gurus manipulate their young followers by an appeal to divine authority. For example, Lowell Streiker in *The Cults Are Coming!* says, "To worship a human being, to treat him as a god, . . . requires a considerable change in consciousness. And that is exactly what the cults offer."[3] The guru thus depicted is an authoritarian personality who needs to control others. Ronald Enroth in *The Lure of the Cults* confirms this stereotype: "Rigid, charismatic, authoritarian leadership is the keystone of all cultic movements. . . . Such a leader exudes certitude, self-confidence, and self-importance. . . . Jim Jones was the epitome of the charismatic leader."[4] The specter of Jim Jones and the tragedy at Jonestown become standard scenarios, the bases for the so-called "Jonestown Syndrome," that Enroth, Rabbi Rudin, and others warn is possible with *any* cult leader or group.

The founder of the Hare Krishnas, Bhaktivedanta Swami Prabhupada (called Prabhupada throughout this book), is less often listed by anticult writers as a dangerous cult leader; nonetheless, he has occasionally been attacked in precisely the terms outlined above. Speaking before a PTA audience in Glendale, California, Chad Hughes, the brother-in-law of a Krishna devotee, described Prabhupada this way: "The power he has over these kids is obvious. He has one of the most lucrative printing presses in the country, a good incense business, and all of the money that the kids give him. . . . I suppose these vices lurk in all of us. Some men know no bounds in their lust and they will use your children for it."[5]

Hughes claims that Prabhupada and the leaders of the Krishna movement are motivated by "power, money, and sex." Furthermore, the Jonestown syndrome lurks behind Hughes's absolutely false assertions: "The Krishnas are taught that it is not wrong to kill their families. They think that by killing someone, they liberate him from his body."[6]

Given these widespread negative images, is it any wonder that families of new cult converts, newspaper journalists, lawyers, mental health professionals, and citizens who sit on the juries that must hear Moonie or Hare Krishna cases are afraid of the cults and their leaders? The problem that persists is that individual instances of vice and abuse are so often generalized to include all cults; for example, in the popular imagination, the extreme wealth of Rajneesh, the sexual abuse of disciples of Moses David, and the violence of Jim Jones or Charles Manson are all attributed equally to *all* gurus or cult leaders. All gurus, like Hitler, are mad with power, greedy for wealth, and firm believers in their own delusions.[7] The guru from this perspective is a deceiver.

The Guru as Spiritual Master

One can appreciate the public's difficulty in making critical distinctions between types of cult leaders who are known by a bewildering array of titles and claims to divinity. For example, does the title "Reverend" mean the same thing when applied to Billy Graham, Jim Jones, and Sung Myung Moon? Is it true that the disciples of the gurus Maharaj Ji, Maharishi Mahesh Yogi, and Prabhupada all view their spiritual masters in the same way? Do these disciples attribute to their masters the same divinity? Why does the controversial guru Rajneesh insist on the title "Bhagawan" (literally, "Lord" or "God") while Meher Baba, who also claimed to be God, used the title "Avatara" (literally, "descent" or "manifestation" of God)? Merely, to raise questions such as these should make it clear that one cannot comfortably collapse the roles of all the above religious leaders into a single, vague category such as "cult leader."

One obvious distinction to be noted when naming religious leaders is that some titles signify institutional roles—for example, Christian priest, bishop, and abbot, or Muslim mullah and imam. Other forms of address are honorific or spiritual designations—for example, reverend, master, bhagawan, and guru. Some titles—such as rabbi, which literally means "teacher"—refer to both an institutional role and a religious status.

A more elusive and important distinction that most cult critics fail to take into account is the distinction between the "holy person" or *"man-god"* (like saint, prophet, guru, or sage) and the divine descendant or *"god-man"* (like messiah, incarnation, or avatar).[8] The essential difference between these two basic types of religious persons lies in their respective claims to authority. Members of the first group claim authority on the basis of an elevation of their human life to divine or near-divine status through election by the divinity (prophet), achievement through discipline (saint), or appointment in a disciplic line (pope).

The "god-man," however, is understood to have been born as a direct manifestation of God. Consequently, the words and the deeds of the "god-man" *are* the words and the deeds of God! Whereas the "man-god" is a holy person who speaks *on behalf of* God or the Divine and therefore is not the highest authority, the "god-man" by contrast *is* the highest authority, since he or she is the Divine in human flesh. The Buddha in the Mahayana Buddhist traditions and Jesus in the Christian tradition are obvious examples of the "god-man" type.

Most of the gurus in India, as well as those who have come to the United States, do not claim they are a Jesus or a Buddha, that is, a god-man. Most are examples of the "man-god" and not the "god-man," and therefore they claim to be perfected men or representatives of the Divine and not gods themselves. Consequently, if we are to understand Prabhupada as the guru of the Hare Krishnas, we must take seriously his own strong warning when he says, "God is God. The Spiritual Master is His representative. . . . Is that clear?"[9] In many places in his writing, Prabhupada stresses this point by saying that a guru should not be confused with God even though he does act as a conduit between God and the devotee. For example, in a 1973 speech on the importance of surrendering to a guru, Prabhupada explained: "The spiritual master will never say, 'I am God—I can give you mercy.' No. That is not a spiritual master—that is a bogus pretender. The spiritual master will say, 'I am a servant of God; I have brought his mercy. Please take it and be satisfied.' "[10]

"Spiritual Master" and "Pure Devotee" are the two titles most often used with reference to Prabhupada. Both designations clearly associate Prabhupada's status as guru with his functions and attributes as a "man-god," that is, one who has achieved perfection in his own spiritual life and can thereby lead others in theirs. The devotional bias that Prabhupada passes on from his native Bengali (northeast India) Cantanyite (chan'tanyīt) faith can be seen in its criteria for an authentic guru. The Krishna tradition of Caitanya (chītan' yə) (sixteenth-century Bengali reformer) says that the tests of a true guru are that: (1) he must be able to extinguish the seeker's anxiety; (2) he must always be engaged in chanting the names of God; (3) he must engage others in the worship of God; (4) he must encourage the distribution of God's "blessed food," or *prasadam;* and (5) he must always be thinking of the Lord Krishna and his lifetime on earth.

To the above list of five characteristics of a spiritual master, Prabhupada adds the traditional Indian requirement that says the guru must be ordained in a disciplic line (guru succession, or *parampara*) in order to give formal initiation to others. The guru from this perspective is a perfected human ("man-god") who is able to lead others (as a "spiritual master") in their religious quests because of his spiritual achievement. Furthermore, his initiation into an authorized, institutional lineage secures his claim to traditional authority in the Caitanya line of Krishna spiritual leaders. Thus Prabhupada traces his own initiation and lineage back through Caitanya to the Lord Krishna himself (the supreme God of the Caitanya Krishna faith).

Consequently, a spiritual master in the Bengali Krishna tradition conveys a received tradition that limits and corrects what he says and *can* say. In Prabhupada's words, "I should approach someone . . . who has heard from his guru perfectly. . . . This is called guru-parampara, disciplic succession. I hear from a perfect person, and I distribute the knowledge the same way, without any change. Lord Krishna gives us knowledge in the Bhagavad-gita —and we are distributing that same knowledge."[11]

Peter Brent in *Godmen of India* says, "For almost all who embark on the long and rigorous disciplines of Sadhana [spiritual discipline], the guru is mentor, judge . . . [and] the glass which pulls together the disparate rays of the sun into a single burning shaft. Their need for him is total, their devotion to him is absolute."[12] Thus there is more to a guru than his claim to authority and the teachings that he inherits. He is, above all, a guide into the very mysteries of the Divine by virtue of the success of his own spiritual odyssey.

In America, the notion of a person needing a spiritual guide seems more than a bit foreign. Few persons see their minister, priest, or rabbi as a spiritual guide. Rather, such religious leaders are seen as teachers of tradition and ritual officiants—seldom as holy persons. Yet even within the Christian and Jewish religious traditions there have always been a select few who have been considered to be "spiritual directors."

In his book *Soul Friend*, Kenneth Leech unfolds the often forgotten heritage of the spiritual director in the Christian tradition. He notes that the practice of submitting oneself to a spiritual guide was primarily a monastic or elitist one in both the Jewish and Christian traditions. There was the zaddik in later Hasidic communities and the abbot in the Roman Catholic monastery. For example, in the writings of the Christian desert fathers, the advice is given, "Go, attach yourself to a man who fears God, . . . give up your will to him, and then you will receive consolation from God."[13]

The contemporary Trappist monk Thomas Merton describes the Christian "spiritual father" or "spiritual director" as one who was set on fire by the Holy Spirit. According to Merton, such a person should be, above all else, a charismatic leader marked by complete devotion to God. Second, he should be a man of experience who has struggled with the realities of prayer and devotion in the midst of worldly life. Third, he must be a man of learning who is steeped in the scriptures. Fourth, the spiritual guide must be a man of discernment who has special perception and insight into the world and its limitations as well as into his pupil's soul and its particular needs. Finally, such a guide must always be open to the direction of the Holy Spirit as the channel of God's love and grace. Only a person marked with these special attributes can hope to help others "read the breathings of the Spirit."[14] The similarity of these criteria to those for the Krishna spiritual master is obvious.

The problem of understanding and differentiating various types of spiritual guides is compounded in our contemporary American setting by the emergence of secular substitutes for the spiritual adviser, such as the psychiatrist or the psychological counselor. In a powerful book called *Guru: Metaphors from a Psychotherapist*, Sheldon Kopp says, "A spiritual guide [i.e., the therapist] who helps others move from one phase of their lives to another is sometimes called a guru. He is a special sort of teacher . . . [who] introduces his disciples to new experience, to higher levels of spiritual understanding, to greater truths. . . . The guru, however he appears at different times and places, is always that member of the community who understands the 'forgotten language' of the myth and the dream."[15]

Much of the fear of the gurus and other charismatic leaders who have come to America from foreign lands has arisen because even our religious leaders are perplexed, skeptical, or threatened by these persons who claim special religious insight.

From the perspective of world religious history, the spiritual master is a guide for the troubled religious seeker, a master swimmer in deep spiritual waters who can teach others to swim. We have already seen that popular views of contemporary gurus are often simplistic and one-sided. A good way to rectify these distortions is to pursue the example of the founding guru of the Hare Krishna movement. How and why did Prabhupada come to America? What exactly was the message he brought with him? Why did he wait until the age of seventy to come? The answers to these and similar questions will lay the foundation for a more balanced and informed assessment of the phenomenon of the guru in our modern age.

The Profile of One Indian Guru

The turning point in the life of Abhay Charan De, later known as Prabhupada,[16] occurred when his friend Naren Mullik insisted that they stop at a Krishna devotional center to meet a visiting guru named Bhaktisiddhanta Sarasvati. Abhay was reluctant because his father, Gour Mohan, had hosted hundreds of gurus and holy men in his home and Abhay had learned how inauthentic many of them were. Some pretended to be holy men but were merely beggars living off of the generosity of others. Some even smoked ganja (hashish). Others were arrogant and proud men who enjoyed a debate but imparted little sense of spiritual achievement. Furthermore, was not he, Abhay, a college graduate now employed by the prestigious Bose pharmaceutical company? What need did he have of a guru?

Naren persisted and, virtually dragging Abhay by the arm, entered the small building where the devotees of a Bengali sect of Krishna worshipers housed visiting speakers and dignitaries. A young boy escorted Naren and Abhay to the rooftop where guru Bhaktisiddhanta was entertaining the questions of several devotees. Abhay immediately recognized the thin yellow clay markings on the forehead of this guru to be those of his own family's tradition. He also knew that this man had renounced the worldly life, since he was dressed in the saffron robes of the *sannyasin* (an ascetic who forsakes all social and worldly ties and comforts) and held the rosary beads used for daily prayer rounds.

Using the time-honored Indian custom for showing respect, the two young men prostrated themselves before the visiting guru. While Abhay and Naren were rising and preparing to sit cross-legged before the guru, Bhaktisiddhanta said to Abhay, "You are educated young men. Why don't you preach Lord Caintanya Mahaprabhu's message throughout the whole world?" Abhay was shocked by the boldness of this guru's question and skeptical of its relevance to him at this time in his life. Little did the twenty-six-year-old Abhay know then that he would in fact be the person to bring this reformed Hindu tradition to the West—and at the age of seventy![17]

Abhay was born on September 1, 1896, in Calcutta to the Gour Mohan De family. His father was a cloth merchant of moderate means. The De family lived on the wealthy Mullik family properties in the midst of their shops selling gold, salt, and cloth. Directly across the street from the De home was a small temple devoted to the worship of the god Krishna and his consort Radha. This temple was supported by the Mullik family's prodigious wealth, and each day Abhay would join his mother, father, or servant in worshiping the Krishna and Radha deities there.

Abhay's father, Gour Mohan, was a very religious man who read the Vaisnava (Krishna) scriptures regularly, prayed on his rosary beads, and observed the strict vegetarian diet prescribed for all devotees of Krishna. He took every opportunity to invite venerable sadhus, or religious sages, into his home to discuss scripture with them.

Abhay mimicked his father's religious activities from a very young age. He begged his father to provide him with his own festival carts so that he could act out the most famous of Krishna festivals, the Ratha-yatra, an annual festival of carts made famous in Puri, Orissa (northeast India). Gour Mohan always was more concerned that his son be religiously faithful than economically successful. Nonetheless, Abhay was provided with the best education his father could afford.

Abhay had private tutors in Sanskrit and Bengali from ages five through eight and was eventually sent to a highly respected Vaisnava private school. There he studied mathematics, sciences, history, and geography as well as his own Krishna religion. He began college in 1916 at Scottish Churches' College, a prestigious Christian school in Calcutta, where he studied English, Sanskrit, philosophy, and economics. The study of the Bible and Christian doctrine was compulsory.

Like many young persons who go to college, Abhay allowed his own religious practice to lapse. Only after a dream in which his old childhood Krishna image appeared to him to protest being placed in a box and hidden away did Abhay take that image from its resting place and begin to pray daily again.

In Abhay's third year of college, his father arranged his marriage to an eleven-year-old girl named Radharani Datta. Radharani, daughter of a wealthy Vaisnava family, remained at her parents' home until Abhay could set up a home for both of them. This he did when he graduated from college and as he began his career in the pharmaceutical field by becoming a department manager in the Bose laboratory.

During the early years of his business career, Abhay's interest in his childhood faith became rekindled. Wherever his active business life took him, Abhay began to make contacts with the Gaudiya Vaisnava community. His business associates and his family began to complain that his religious activities were interfering with his business responsibilities. Nonetheless, though he had been a reluctant visitor the first time he met Bhaktisiddhanta, he received formal initiation as a disciple of this Krishna guru in 1932 (at age thirty-six).

After his initiation as a disciple of Bhaktisiddhanta, Abhay donated significant amounts of his money and time fulfilling his guru's desire to publish books about Krishna. Bhaktisiddhanta told Abhay, "If you ever get money, print books." Each time Abhay went to a new city, he sought out Bhaktisiddhanta's disciples and offered monetary assistance to fulfill his spiritual master's wishes. These religious activities often interfered with his business responsibilities. It is clear that his family—especially his wife—did not share his increasing enthusiasm for spreading the Krishna faith, and family tensions arose.

Because of his generosity, scholarship, and devotion, Abhay was honored in 1939 with the title "Bhaktivedanta" or "One who has devotion and knowledge." His spiritual master had died only two years earlier after sending him a letter that reaffirmed his first charge to Abhay that he should turn himself "into a good English preacher." Following his guru's command, in February 1944 Abhay created a new English magazine called *Back to Godhead.* In the first issue of this publication, Abhay wrote that God was light but most of civilization was living in utter darkness. He continued, *"Back to Godhead* is a feeble attempt . . . to bring up a real relation of humanity with central relation of the Supreme Personality of Godhead."

After only two issues, Abhay had to stop publishing his magazine because of the wartime shortage of paper and higher printing costs. He revived this magazine four times over the next twenty-one years before leaving for America, but each time he had to cease publication because of lack of funds. His guru's own publication, *The Harmonist,* had suffered a similar fate at the hands of devotees who fought over control of their master's movement after his death and could not sustain the publishing momentum.

While his concentration on his business ventures seemed to ebb and flow, Abhay turned more and more to activities associated with his growing faith in Krishna. However, in 1948 Abhay lost his last profitable factory in Lucknow and came to another turning point in his life. During the next two years he tried to establish a new pharmacy in Allahabad, where his first business had failed, but his heart seemed to be elsewhere.

In 1950, Abhay's wife moved with her sons back to her father's home, since she felt she could not depend upon Abhay to support them. Abhay viewed his economic losses and his wife's actions as a fulfillment of his scripture's *(Srimad Bhagavatam)* pronouncement: "When I [Krishna] feel especially merciful towards someone, I gradually take away all his material possessions. His friends and relatives then reject this poverty-stricken and most wretched fellow."[18]

For several years, Abhay tried to keep his various business ventures afloat to provide for his family, but he actually spent most of his waking hours writing religious tracts and discussing religion with his godbrothers. There is a venerated Indian tradition of leaving one's home and wife after the children are raised in order to devote full time to spiritual advancement. This parting is usually marked by a ritual in which one becomes a *sannyasin,* but Abhay never made this formal break. He just seemed to drift away from his family as he became more and more engrossed with the religious life and its demands.

In 1952, for instance, he went to the city of Jhansi on business but ended up giving a public lecture on his Krishna faith at the invitation of a business associate who had read a copy of his *Back to Godhead* magazine. His next trip to Jhansi was spent organizing a League of Devotees which was intended to fulfill his guru's dream of a "league of preachers" to spread consciousness of Krishna throughout India.

Abhay spent much of 1953 in Jhansi away from his family devoting virtually all of his time to the new League. He wanted to enlist forty young men and train them to be missionaries "throughout the world." Late in 1953 he learned that his Allahabad business had been burglarized by his own servants, who stole all the available money and chemicals, leaving him bankrupt once again.

Early in 1954, his League of Devotees failed also, and Abhay returned to Calcutta to his family. But it was now clear that his heart was set on spreading the message and love of Krishna around the English-speaking world. The once skeptical young businessman had become a religious evangelist for his traditional Krishna faith to anyone who would listen.

There also was no doubt that his wife was weary of his habitual neglect of business activities due to his obsession for preaching and writing. One day in 1954, his wife took a Krishna scripture which Abhay used for daily devotions and traded it in the market for some cookies for her to eat with her daily tea. Earlier, Abhay had said his wife would either have to give up drinking tea, an "intoxicant" forbidden by strict Vaisnava practice, or lose her husband. Not realizing how serious he was, Radharani chose her tea, and on the day that Radharani bartered his scripture for tea cookies, Abhay left home for good.

When Abhay left home at the age of fifty-eight, he went immediately to Vrindavan, the birthplace of Krishna. During the next eleven years until he departed for America, he spent as much time as he could living in various Krishna temples in this holy city in order to strengthen his faith. He arose at two thirty or three in the morning to translate the Krishna scriptures or write articles for *Back to Godhead*. He then chanted his daily rounds of prayers (the Hare Krishna mantra or prayer) and fixed his simple breakfast. The rest of the day was then spent on devotional or preaching activities.

He lived in the cities of both Old Delhi and New Delhi at various times while he was overseeing the printing of his magazine or translations of scriptures. During these times he went from shop to shop and door to door trying to sell copies of his writings. Abhay was now fully engrossed with fulfilling his spiritual master's wishes to print as many books as possible and to spread devotion to Krishna in English-speaking lands.

By the fall of 1959, Abhay decided formally to commit his whole life to spreading Krishna consciousness. The traditional Indian way of fully committing oneself to the religious life is to renounce the worldly life formally as "one who casts off" *(sannyasa)* all worldly interests and responsibilities. Consequently, on September 17, 1959, Abhay Charan De was initiated as a *sannyasin* by a godbrother named Kesava Maharaja. Abhay was henceforth to be known by his spiritual name, A. C. Bhaktivedanta Swami Prabhupada —shortened by his disciples to Prabhupada. His godbrothers with whom he had stayed for the previous five years as well as many of his former business associates respected Abhay's role as Prabhupada, a God-intoxicated man who needed to devote his remaining life to Krishna.

Abhay had made many friends and contacts in the business and political worlds through his previous business successes and failures.

One of the persons attracted to him was Mrs. Sumati Morarji, head of the Scindia Steamship Company in Bombay. She had earlier provided the necessary money for Abhay to finish printing the third volume of his translation of the Krishna scripture, the *Srimad Bhagavatam*. Now in mid-1965, Abhay pleaded with Mrs. Morarji to give him a free passage on one of her ships going to America. Both Mrs. Morarji and a godbrother tried to persuade Bhaktivedanta to be content with his expanding preaching mission in India. But Abhay insisted that he must fulfill his spiritual master's command that he bring the Krishna tradition reformed by Caitanya to the English-speaking peoples of the world. And America was among the neediest of those places.

On August 13, 1965, Abhay, now known as A. C. Bhaktivedanta Swami Prabhupada, embarked on the Indian ship *Jaladuta* on a journey to America. While on shipboard, he wrote a prayer that read in part: "Although my Guru Maharaja ordered me to accomplish this mission, I am not worthy or fit to do it. I am very fallen and insignificant. Therefore, O Lord, now I am begging for Your mercy so that I may become worthy. . . . If You bestow Your power, by serving the spiritual master one attains the Absolute Truth—one's life becomes successful."[19]

On September 17, 1965, the *Jaladuta* docked at Boston's Commonwealth Pier. Prabhupada accepted the captain's invitation to spend part of the day visiting Boston before the ship set off for its final destination, New York City. Upon returning to the ship, Prabhupada wrote a second prayer-poem in Bengali. This poem reveals Prabhupada's first impression of America: "My dear Lord Krishna, You are so kind upon this useless soul, but I do not know why You have brought me here. . . . But I guess You have some business here, otherwise why would You bring me to this terrible place? Most of the population is covered by the material modes of ignorance and passion. Absorbed in material life they think themselves very happy and satisfied, and therefore they have no taste for the transcendental message of Vasudeva [Krishna]. I do not know how they will be able to understand it. But I know that Your causeless mercy can make everything possible, because You are the most expert mystic."[20]

Another Indian guru had thus arrived in America—not an uncommon occurrence after the new immigration law of 1965. But unlike many of his counterparts, Prabhupada did not bring a watered-down Yoga or meditation practice to sell to Americans. Rather, he came to fulfill the request of Bhaktisiddhanta made at their first meeting that he be a preacher of Krishna to the English-speaking West.

Consequently, Prabhupada brought a devotional form of Hinduism not previously known to the American public. Unlike most other gurus and holy men, the movement he founded in the United States did not bear his name. Even after his remarkable preaching success in North America and around the world, few laypersons still know his name. What Prabhupada brought to America in 1965 was a deep faith that he was being led by Krishna to spread this venerable Indian devotional belief and practice.

The story of Prabhupada's next twelve years in America is a tale of success no one could have predicted. Previous attempts by Bhaktisiddhanta's disciples to establish Krishna outposts in England and Europe had predictably failed. Given the lack of financial, personal, and institutional backing common to most missionary ventures, Prabhupada's mission seemed destined to follow that of his unsuccessful godbrothers. Yet from his initial storefront apartment/temple in lower Manhattan, with mimeographed pamphlets, *Back to Godhead* magazines, and only a handful of hippie followers, Prabhupada slowly built a religious organization with more than forty temples or farms worldwide, an impressive religious press to disseminate his more than fifty books of translated scriptures and teachings, and over nine thousand initiated disciples—all in the span of twelve years. And throughout all the difficult first years and later years of success, Prabhupada continued the same arduous schedule of writing and devotion that he had begun in the solitude of his temple room in Vrindavan, India.

The International Society for Krishna Consciousness acquired property and financial resources throughout the world and Prabhupada could have retired in regal comfort—as have many gurus who have come to America—but he did not. Though his disciples tried to treat him with the honor and comforts accorded renowned gurus in India (e.g., the New Vrindaban Palace which he never lived to see completed), Prabhupada still devoted himself to his translation of Krishna scriptures into English and his own spiritual life. His whole life-style—the simple monastic dress, the sparse vegetarian diet, and a single-minded orientation to his religious activities—remained constant throughout the bad and good years.

By 1970, when the movement began to put heavy demands for management upon his religious schedule of activities, Prabhupada turned over the primary management of the movement to a Governing Body Commission made up of advanced devotees. Even on his sickbed before he died in the fall of 1977, Prabhupada continued to translate Krishna texts as his guru had instructed him. He viewed that as his special mission.

Charismatic Authority

As one talks with American Krishna devotees, it becomes increasingly clear that Prabhupada was a special man. He did not attract devotees by his spellbinding sermons or flashy life-style. Several devotees even said they found his lectures and sermons boring and nearly unintelligible the first time they heard them. For example, a Harvard M.B.A. graduate said of his first encounter with Prabhupada, "I didn't have any emotional experiences. Prabhupada was very much an ordinary person, until you developed a relationship [with him]. He never put on a show . . . with his logic, argument, belief, the way he holds himself, everything. He was extremely ordinary to the ordinary eye."

Still, the religious sincerity and piety of Prabhupada clearly made a deep impression on most of the persons he met. We have already heard Govinda Das tell us, "He was chanting, and just by the sound of his voice I could see this person really loves God." Another devotee, now an initiating guru himself, said on hearing Prabhupada's lecture on the Berkeley campus, "So when I went to see Prabhupada the first thing I hoped was that this man would not be simply another of these silly Indian gurus. But when he walked in, I thought, 'He is different.' . . . He had that bearing, that gravity, that dead seriousness that you associate with a military leader, a commander. . . . The *kirtan* [dancing and chanting/singing] began and Prabhupada became immediately ecstatic. . . . I was stunned, because at that time he was a little over seventy years of age, . . . so that immediately shattered all my previous conceptions about a spiritual master."

It was not only devotees who were impressed with the personal piety of Prabhupada. Stillson Judah, the author of a book on the Krishnas in the early 1970s, said of him, "I was struck by his humility."[21] Judah then went on to say that Prabhupada obviously *lived* the life of faith that he expected of others.

As one longtime devotee who has now moved to the fringes of the Krishna movement said, "Guru means always being a guru; it's not a nine to five job. Every moment he was a guru . . . he never forgot his position." George Harrison, a former Beatle, said of his contact with Prabhupada: "The thing that always stays [in my mind] is his saying, 'I am the servant of the servant. . . .' A lot of people say, 'I'm it. I'm the divine incarnation.' But Prabhupada was never like that. I liked Prabhupada's humbleness. . . . He always had a childlike simplicity."[22]

It would appear that Prabhupada profited from two intertwined sources of authority. In the first place, he had been initiated by Bhaktisiddhanta into the disciplic line (*parampara*) of Caitanya and therefore had what sociologist Max Weber calls "traditional authority." Weber says, "The object of obedience is the personal authority of the individual which he enjoys by virtue of his traditional status."[23] Traditional authorities, according to Weber, are bound by traditional laws and can modify those laws only when the innovation does not conflict with tradition. It is clear that Prabhupada claimed such traditional authority, with the traditional Krishna scriptures as his limiting authority. It is also obvious that Prabhupada was constrained by those same scriptures to interpret his new American home and its values from this traditional Vaisnava orientation. To this extent, Prabhupada was an orthodox Krishna devotee acting out a role and offering a theology that are centuries old in India —though startlingly new to America.

In the second place, Prabhupada's authority was that of a charismatic prophet. Weber says, "We shall understand 'prophet' to mean a purely individual bearer of charisma, who by virtue of his mission proclaims a religious doctrine of divine commandment."[24] The authority of the charismatic prophet derives from his personal qualities, not inherited status.[25] Weber defines charisma as "a certain quality of an individual personality by which he is set apart from ordinary men and treated as endowed with supernatural . . . or exceptional powers or qualities."[26] Jesus was such a charismatic prophet whose authority as a "god-man" was supported by his miraculous powers. But even those disciples of Jesus who were of the lesser, "man-god," status were viewed by the Christian apostle Paul to be capable of *charismata*, or "spiritual gifts," such as wisdom, faith, healing, prophesies, and tongues (e.g., 1 Corinthians 12 and 14).

It is into this second category of the "man-god" that Prabhupada falls, according to his own accounting. The difficulty for the outsider to ISKCON —as well as for some devotees *in* ISKCON—is in recognizing that Prabhupada saw himself as a man trying to be a perfect conduit to God (Krishna) and not as God himself (i.e., as a god-man). When this important distinction discussed earlier is not remembered, statements made by the Krishnas will be misinterpreted.

Prabhupada's disciples did see in him a man whose faith was perfect. Consequently, his disciples speak effusively of Prabhupada's "exceptional qualities" of faith and devotion to explain his charismatic aura. For example, one exceptional quality his devotees remarked about again and again was the depth and breadth of his scriptural knowledge. He could in any situation recite from memory and in Sanksrit a scriptural verse that would apply specifically to that occasion (though he obviously exercised his right to translate and to interpret "according to time and circumstance"—a right claimed by Caitanya some three centuries earlier). It is here that his role as *acarya* (teacher) became enhanced by his scriptural erudition that made him stand out among other traditional Indian authorities.

Furthermore, what becomes obvious to any careful observer of the Krishna movement is that this man who founded it was not charismatic because of his electric personality or his dazzling speaking ability. Instead, it appears that it was the depth of his piety and his level of personal integrity that constituted the "exceptional qualities" that made Prabhupada appear to be a perfect devotee. One well-educated devotee in his mid-thirties said, "One's heart would melt, one's mind change before his awesome piety. . . . It was a profound sense of his integrity, that he was not a greedy guru on a power trip, that made him appear to be so special." As I listened to the "Prabhupada stories" that devotees loved to tell, the constant themes of Prabhupada's full-time commitment to his faith and his ability to exemplify that faith were repeated consistently. His disciples experienced him as a perfect devotee who lived what he preached.

In sum, Prabhupada was the embodiment of both traditional and charismatic authority. He was at the same time one who stood within an age-old Indian Krishna scriptural tradition and yet one who was able to translate new meanings and initiate new applications of his received scriptural heritage on the basis of his own accomplishments. His imperfect English, his naiveté about American customs, and his vacillations regarding fund-raising strategies all paled in the eyes of his devotees before his sincere desire to share his deep faith in Krishna with the English-speaking world.

To critics outside ISKCON, Prabhupada may be viewed as being all too human to be considered "perfect." He was impatient at times with his new "hippie" disciples and could become very angry at tasks not done. He encouraged marriages blessed by Krishna that were destined not to endure. Prabhupada was so caught up in spreading his Krishna faith that he allowed experimentation with certain fund-raising tactics—such as the "Santa Claus Krishnas"—that were actually counterproductive to his intent. In short, he made both tactical and programmatic decisions he later would have to retract.

Yet regardless of his errors in judgment about how to spread Krishna consciousness, Prabhupada was faithful to the life of devotion he demanded of his disciples. As Govinda Das said of his reason for finally accepting this man from among all the other gurus he rejected, "So the authority by which he spoke was actually one of the most impressive things to me. . . . I was accepting the word of the *Bhagavad Gita* and the *acaryas* [teaching sages] because they were all speaking through him and he was a perfect example of it." His authority was both institutional and personal, traditional and charismatic.

As Weber asserts, charismatic prophets come at times of social upheaval and unrest. Clearly, what made the gurus and self-proclaimed messiahs who came to America in the 1960s even more threatening was largely a matter of timing: the United States was in turmoil, with the controversial Vietnam War and race riots occupying our media's attention, and with divisive sloganeering (e.g., "God is dead") and disagreements over social and political action preoccupying the mainstream Christian churches. Meanwhile many youth simply turned from traditional religious and political authorities to charismatic ones.

Charismatic prophets are not evil or good as a group; rather, they represent an alternative in times of social and personal stress. David Bromley and Anson Shupe summarize the situation this way: "There is a danger in charismatic authority, as it is a form of leadership usually emerging when great change is in the making. . . . To those who are not part of that effort, the whole affair may look extremely risky and absurd. Surely the parents of the men who left behind their jobs and families to follow Jesus of Nazareth must have been worried and fearful. From our current perspective it was worth the price."[27]

While history will finally judge the guru Bhaktivedanta Swami Prabhupada and his movement, it should record that he was a sincerely religious old man who came to the United States to spread his faith in Krishna much in the pattern of Christian missionaries to India and the third world. Because Prabhupada was the driving force in the origin and development of the International Society for Krishna Consciousness, his death posed a stark threat to the continuation of his missionary movement. Consequently, in the months preceding his death in 1977, Prabhupada named eleven of his advanced disciples to carry on his spiritual role of initiating guru. While this fulfilled the traditional requirements of disciplic succession (*parampara*), he could not ensure that his personal piety and attendant charisma would in fact be transferred. It is to this issue we shall turn next.

3

The Transmission of Charisma

Nestled in the hills of central Pennsylvania is a Krishna dairy farm called Gita Nagari. The way of life in this ISKCON center is distinctly pastoral and will be described in some detail in chapter 6. This center was bustling with activity in mid-January 1981 in anticipation of the formal initiation of new devotees into ISKCON's traditional form of Bengali Krishna devotionalism. This was also the occasion of the following interview of one of the most respected new gurus in ISKCON, Satsvarupa dasa Goswami. Satsvarupa was one of the earliest disciples of Prabhupada and has come to be known throughout ISKCON as one of the most pious and respected of the eleven successors appointed by the founding guru.

In a small cabin on the farm are the living quarters and study of Satsvarupa. It is not unusual for one to have to wait for the guru to finish his devotions and chanting before gaining his audience. Upon entering Satsvarupa's office, one encounters a thin, saffron-robed man who looks far younger than his forty-plus years of age. He has the ubiquitous Krishna ponytail (*shika*) cropping out of a short stubble of blond hair that covers his head. His brow is marked by furrows that are undoubtedly deepened by the various religious, administrative, and publishing responsibilities he assumes. As Prabhupada's official biographer, he had just finished in the winter of 1981 the third of six volumes of the life of his spiritual master.

From Disciple to Spiritual Master

A two-hour interview with Satsvarupa revealed that he had been born in New York City to Irish immigrant parents as the second of two children.[1] Raised as a staunch Catholic, Satsvarupa spoke of his family as being "middle-class Americans with moral values to match." His father was not particularly involved in his Catholic religion, but his mother was. It was from her that Satsvarupa heard the Christian message of Jesus' love being a model for all children and adults. And his mother prayed regularly and urged him to follow her example. His father spent most of World War II in the U.S. Navy and returned to join the local fire department. He rose to the rank of captain before he retired.

It was when Satsvarupa went to Brooklyn College in the 1960s that his comfortable worldview was challenged. There he read Nietzsche and Dostoevsky, met professors and students who were religious skeptics, and was attracted to their existential philosophies. Like many of his peers, Satsvarupa underwent a rapid transformation during his college years that made him feel a stranger in his family's home. Nonetheless, near the end of his college career, he acceded to his father's urging to join the Navy and on graduation spent the better part of two years on aircraft carriers touring the Mediterranean. But by now his heart was in his quest for meaning in a godless world.

On being discharged from the Navy in 1963, Satsvarupa settled on New York City's Lower East Side and became part of the drug culture. Eventually he got a job with the Welfare Department and moved into an apartment near that of Prabhupada. For six months he attended Prabhupada's lectures, ate with this old Indian guru, and helped support his work economically. By then he was a firm believer, but he did not join Prabhupada's fledgling movement until the second group of initiations in September 1966.

Satsvarupa described the nascent ISKCON as a group of devotees who did little in common. There were no standard dress codes, regular rituals, or street singing and proselytizing, and no shaven heads unless one chose to get shaved. The lectures by Prabhupada and the power of chanting were two strong attractions for Satsvarupa, but it was his relationship with Prabhupada that was the key. Satsvarupa remembered, "After six months in San Francisco where he set up a new temple, Prabhupada returned to New York. With Prabhupada there, everything was completely fulfilled; he's the spiritual father of your spiritual life. Those were beautiful days."

After a near-fatal stroke in May 1967, Prabhupada decided to return to India. Satsvarupa was still a young disciple who knew the Krishna philosophy only in a basic way. Yet on Prabhupada's request, Satsvarupa went to Boston to open a new preaching center as his guru left for India. The Boston center was a success, and Satsvarupa remained there until 1971 serving most of that time as editor of the newly established ISKCON Press. In January 1974, Satsvarupa was called to be the personal secretary of Prabhupada. In that capacity, he traveled for six months with his spiritual master through India and Europe.

In July, Satsvarupa became the leader of the ISKCON Library Party which traveled around the United States selling ISKCON books to college and university professors and libraries. In 1976 he published a book of scriptural readings that set him apart as an advanced disciple. In 1977 Satsvarupa's religious life came full circle when he, a disciple of Prabhupada, was elevated to the role of initiating *acarya* (i.e., guru) who would have his own disciples to nurture and protect.

We pick up the interview at the point of Satsvarupa's description of the process of Prabhupada's selection of his successors and his interpretation of this critical juncture in ISKCON's history. Prabhupada puts his action in the context of Caitanya's tradition. Satsvarupa's reflection on his acceptance of the mantle of guru reveals the real hurdles that religious movements face when the founder dies.

LARRY SHINN: What were the circumstances that prompted Prabhupada's appointment of his successors?

SATSVARUPA MAHARAJA: When Prabhupada fell ill in May of 1977, he thought he was going to die then. At that time he composed his will. The Governing Body Commission [GBC] was together with him then and we thought we should ask him some questions about publishing new Sanskrit books and how the initiation process should continue in his absence. So we went to see him and I asked, "What will be the process of initiation?" He said, "I will name some people, and they will initiate." But it was understood that any persons they initiated were not their disciples but Prabhupada's. And then I asked, "Prabhupada, after your disappearance, whose disciples will they be?" He said, "They will be the disciples of the gurus I have named. As Caitanya said, 'When I name them, I order that they are at that moment gurus. Regular gurus.' " So what Prabhupada confirmed was that upon his death, those men whom he had named to initiate on his behalf would then initiate on their own behalf. This is the age-old system of *parampara* [disciplic succession]. The disciple of the guru will someday become a guru.

Prabhupada had not initiated any new disciples for a long time during his illness. So several weeks after our discussion, he decided that he would take some more disciples, but through intermediaries who would pick out the new spiritual names and chant on the new disciples' beads. So he then named the persons who would help him. He gave out eleven names. So then after his disappearance, those eleven persons assumed the responsibilities of regular gurus.

L.S.: Describe for me, if you will, what you understand your position to be as a guru to your disciples in reference to your experience as a disciple of Prabhupada.

S.M.: My responsibilities to my disciples are all in the Sastras [scriptures]. The guru is supposed to make his disciple follow the four regulations of Krishna consciousness and then help raise him to the platform where he is always engaged in thinking of Krishna. The complete success will be that his disciple becomes a pure devotee.

L.S.: Must a guru be a pure devotee?

S.M.: Yes.

L.S.: Can one assume, then, that all eleven disciples who became regular gurus on the eleventh of November 1977 were at that point considered by Prabhupada to be pure devotees?

S.M.: The term "pure devotee" can be used in different ways. Prabhupada has used it to mean someone who is fully surrendered to Krishna. That may mean just a devotee who comes and joins the temple, gives up everything, and is engaging his whole life in Krishna consciousness. And if there is anything that's not perfect in him, it will become perfect in time. . . . For example, if a rod is put in a fire and stays there, it finally becomes like fire. Prabhupada has said, "As long as devotees are engaged in Krishna consciousness from morning to night, they are completely pure."

L.S.: Even if your intentions are pure as a guru, will not your inevitable mistakes in judgment or actions have negative consequences for your disciples?

S.M.: Our scripture, the *Bhagavad Gita,* says, "Even if one commits the most abominable actions, if he is engaged in devotional service, he is to be considered saintly, because he is properly situated." The disciples' mistake would be not to follow their guru. The *Gita* warns that because of an accidental fall-down, a devotee of Krishna should not be derided. The mark of a spot which may be seen on the moon does not become an impediment to the moonlight. Similarly, the accidental fall-down of a devotee from the path of a saintly character does not make him abominable.

L.S.: Has working on Prabhupada's biography rekindled your memories of your spiritual master and the time you spent with him?

S.M.: Yes! I think mostly there is a lamentation that I was not a good enough devotee of his, plus the lamentation that he's gone.

L.S.: What would you say your greatest loss is with Prabhupada gone?

S.M.: Well, the feeling is there that I wish I had another chance to serve him in a pure way. I appreciate better now what he really was, and wish I had been more surrendered and had taken more advantage of his personal association. That regret is there. When he was here I did not take good enough advantage of him, and now that he is gone there are strong feelings of inadequacy in respect to his greatness. . . .

L.S.: What impact has his being gone had on. ISKCON?

S.M.: Well, I see that we have lots of trouble. But in one sense, I am preoccupied. I'm just holding my own trying to be a spiritual master, and not listening to the voice of lamentation that would say, "You're not a real guru," or "This movement is going to pot," or "What about all these news reports?" I tend to be a bit callous toward all those doubts and disturbances and just keep my mind on the *parampara*. It's not good for me to start lamenting. I know what's happened, and everyone can see it. We [ISKCON's leaders] don't have the single direction we did, and there's fighting and everything. But there are such immediate demands. I have so many disciples, and the question is how to become a pure devotee, how to deliver them? . . .

There are real problems to consider. Whether the movement will splinter; what different gurus will do; how the GBC will conflict with various gurus. But I feel that the solution has to come not by better law and law-abiding devotees and a stronger management [of the GBC], but we have to start becoming saintly and loving towards each other. . . .

It was simpler, when Prabhupada was alive, to think of oneself only as a disciple of Prabhupada. I think as you go around ISKCON and hear different unrest expressed, it is partly just a lament that things are not like they used to be. Now there are many gurus . . . even if they are not as great as Prabhupada. I also sometimes feel that this [complexity] is disturbing to my being a disciple, and here I am a spiritual master! But I finally resolve it because I am convinced that the job must be done.

L.S.: Will there be more gurus appointed in the future?

S.M.: There is an assumption in ISKCON, just by reading the texts, that any disciple, when he becomes ready, can become a guru. So that means potentially that every disciple can become a guru and take disciples. We have an institution [GBC] that says one cannot become a *sannyasin* [renounced, full-time preacher] until he's qualified. The GBC selects him to preserve the integrity of our movement. So why not with additional gurus? The real controversy is more like, why only eleven?

The Death of the Founder

As we saw in chapter 2, the stereotype of cult gurus and messiahs as authoritarian charletans whose real motivations are money and power has only occasionally been applied directly to ISKCON's founder. However, stereotypes function by including all named members of a class or group— in this case "cult gurus"—under their generalized aura. Therefore, even the critics who exempt Prabhupada from direct criticism clearly implicate him through their depreciation of his teachings on guru veneration and the chanting of Krishna's name as primary acts of faith. These two spiritual practices are usually assumed by critics to be the basis of Prabhupada's authoritarian control of his disciples.[2] Consequently, ISKCON has been viewed by critics and students of the cults as a movement that was created and sustained by a charismatic founder and whose future depended upon a successful transmission of the founder's authority.[3] This is an assumption commonly made by students of charismatic movements.

The death of a top religious or political leader usually occasions uncertainties regarding the transfer of leadership to his or her successor(s), but the death of a charismatic founder threatens the very survival of his or her group. At the very least, the death of a founder requires a transition from the more spontaneous and charismatic leadership of the prophet to a more institutionalized form of leadership. In early Christianity, for example, the death of Jesus led to an initial disillusionment and defection of his most mature disciples (see Mark 14:27ff.). Only after their experience of Jesus' presence (resurrection) after his death did his appointed disciples take up his mission as their own. And even then, the early record of the Christian community is spiced with controversies and conflicts such as disagreements among the apostles Peter, James, and Paul over the place of non-Jews in the Christian fellowship and whether they had to be circumcised or could eat at the same table as Jewish Christians (see Acts 15).

The prophet Muhammad left no heir or designated successor, and Islam survived only through the able leadership of the four successive Meccan caliphs (political and religious leaders) elected by the eldest disciples of Muhammad. But conflicts over the rule of these elected successors led to the assassination of three of them and, eventually, to a permanent schism between the Sunna and Shi'a branches of Islam.

Likewise, the Buddha left behind his teachings (*dhamma*) and disciplined monastic community (*sangha*) to be guides for future generations, but in less than one hundred years after his death there were more than a dozen sectarian Buddhist communities. Such a history of conflicts and schisms over community leadership and spiritual direction is often the legacy of ecstatic or charismatic communities after the death of their founder.

One critical factor in the confusion and disillusionment that follows the death of a charismatic community's founder is the sense that the founder simply cannot be replaced. For Krishna devotees, it was each disciple's direct link (guru) with Krishna that was disrupted when Prabhupada died. More personally, however, it was that a man whom disciples felt to be really special in his spirituality, piety, and knowledge (a pure devotee) and thus revered as specially endowed by God (charismatic) was now gone. One temple official likened Prabhupada's death to dying a little himself: "We felt that our whole life was about to end. . . . It felt like the end of the world."

For many of Prabhupada's disciples, the death of their guru *was* the end of ISKCON and their dreams of spreading Krishna devotion throughout the English-speaking world. By the best estimates of senior devotees, fewer than two thousand of the more than nine thousand disciples initiated by Prabhupada are still living in ISKCON centers anywhere in the world. And many of those who defected did so in the months immediately following their spiritual master's death.

What is even more notable, however, is that ISKCON did not dissolve with the death of Prabhupada. Unlike the case of Islam or Buddhism, where no spiritual successors or institutional governing structures were appointed by the founder, Prabhupada did name eleven spiritual successors and left behind an institutional governing structure, the Governing Body Commission, that could make overarching institutional decisions and provide a sense of unity. To a great extent, both the traditional and the charismatic authorities of the founder as described by Weber *are* embodied in current ISKCON roles and governing structures. However, the simplicity of both types of authority being located in a single person died with Prabhupada.

The Routinization of Charisma

The January 1978 edition of the *Back to Godhead* magazine reported to Krishna devotees, and the general public, around the world:

> At 7:20 P.M. on November 14, 1977, His Divine Grace A. C. Bhaktivedanta Swami Prabhupada, the Founder-*Acarya* of the International Society for Krishna Consciousness, departed from this world. At the time, he was in his quarters at the Krsna-Balarama temple in Vrindavana, India, surrounded by loving disciples chanting the Hare Krsna *mantra*. The chanting continued throughout the night as devotees performed the last ceremonies for their revered spiritual master. The following morning, the devotees took Srila Prabhupada's body on procession to the main temples in Vrindavana, the holy city most sacred to Lord Krsna, and finally they performed the burial ceremonies in the temple's outer courtyard.[4]

What lay behind this simple announcement was more than met the eye. During the twenty-four-hour daily chanting sessions organized to soothe their spiritual master whose life had been dedicated to spreading his love of Krishna to English speakers, little thought had been given to what ritual procedures had to be followed when Prabhupada actually died. So in their state of shock the senior devotees turned to a respected Indian Krishna devotee outside ISKCON to seek advice on the proper ceremonial etiquette for the burial of a saint.

Following the guidance of Narayan Maharaja, a disciple of one of Prabhupada's Indian godbrothers, the mostly American and European young disciples of ISKCON followed age-old Indian customs designed for special holy men. The ceremonies began with a dressing and garlanding of the dead body. The body was then placed in a seated position on a palanquin (ritual carrier). Next, the palanquin was taken into the temple and presented to each of the three altars there before several ritual processions around the temple were completed. The dead guru's body was then seated on his "preaching seat" (*vyasasana*), and the disciples stayed throughout the night singing songs of lament and chanting according to Narayan Maharaja's directions. The next morning the body of the dead guru was paraded through the streets of Vrindavan on a final journey to the eight major Krishna temples in this pilgrimage city, allowing the public a final view of their highly respected spiritual son. The body was finally buried (holy men are not usually cremated in India) just outside the front entrance to the Krishna-Balarama temple.

For our purposes, the noteworthy feature of the above account is that, even though Prabhupada had spent twelve years educating his followers in proper Krishna worship and chanting, dress and cleanliness rituals, cooking and eating habits, and so on, he had not really prepared them to bury him. His devotees had to rely on other Indian devotees of Krishna to conduct the final rites. Furthermore, Prabhupada's instructions over the last months of his life gave slightly conflicting notions of how he intended his authority to be transferred and institutionalized so that his mission would be carried on in his absence.

The same January 1978 *Back to Godhead* that announced Prabhupada's death also ended with an editorial note called "What Now?"[5] The editor, a longtime and respected devotee, reflected on the matter of succession and authority in ISKCON in the absence of the founding guru and unintentionally revealed the difficulty of transmitting to the next generation not only traditional authority (i.e., disciplic succession) but also the founder's charisma (his knowledge and piety). In that short page the editor reminded devotees that Prabhupada had, several months previous to his death, named eleven senior disciples to be "initiation *acaryas*" and thereby to stand in the disciplic line of Caitanya but that Prabhupada had also said that *any* of his disciples could become a guru if they perfected their Krishna devotion. Yet the editor had begun his essay with the words, "First of all, *no one* can replace His Divine Grace A. C. Bhaktivedanta Swami Prabhupada. You cannot simply elect a person to the post of the most exalted sainthood." Put in the terms of Max Weber, Prabhupada could appoint successors to his traditional role as initiating *acarya* but not to his status as charismatic leader.

To add to the confusion about whether anyone could really replace Prabhupada's spiritual and governing roles, the editor also pointed out that "as early as 1970, Srila Prabhupada created a Governing Body Commission (GBC), which now consists of twenty four senior devotees, all personally selected by His Divine Grace to supervise ISKCON's missionary activities in various zones around the world. . . . The GBC meets yearly in India, and together its members plan how to execute the will of His Divine Grace."

The fact that the will of Prabhupada is to be found in his teachings on the Krishna scriptures complicated matters even more: "If I depart, there is no cause for lamentation. I will always be with you through my books and my orders."[6] In other words, the guru lives on in his teachings even after his body is gone. But who is to be the final authority in interpreting the founder's teachings and their intentions? Who are the real inheritors of Prabhupada's mantle? The new gurus? The GBC? All the disciples of Prabhupada who have the capacity to be gurus? No easy answers emerged in the years following Prabhupada's death.

Thus we are presented with a classical instance of the problems associated with the transfer of religious authority. As we saw in the previous chapter, however, Prabhupada's authority was both traditional (i.e., he was an initiated disciple of Bhaktisiddhanta) and charismatic (i.e., it was based upon his scriptural erudition, personal piety and integrity, and his mission's seeming ordination by Krishna himself).

Consequently no one could fully replace Prabhupada. Weber confirms this when he says that "in its pure form charismatic authority may be said to exist only in the process of originating. It cannot remain stable, but becomes either traditionalized or rationalized."[7] According to Weber, in its pure form charisma is strictly personal and based on the qualities of the individual. Consequently, if the movement begun by such a charismatic figure is to continue, the charisma must somehow be "routinized" or transferred to surviving institutional roles or structures. Therefore the burning issue for ISKCON in the aftermath of Prabhupada's death was not that of succession; there was a traditional disciplic line into which his own designates and gurus appointed later could fit. Rather, the problem was how his personal authority to interpret scriptures, to decide future courses of action for the society, and to solve personal and institutional problems could or would be institutionalized.

One answer that some devotees gave was that each of the eleven "new gurus" had the traditional authority Prabhupada and his godbrothers all exercised. Yet the Gaudiya Math (ISKCON's predecessor in India) had failed in India precisely because the successors appointed to continue the work of Bhaktisiddhanta each went his own way. The guru's perspective took precedence over the collaborative setting of goals in the Gaudiya Math.

A second answer that some ISKCON leaders offered was that the GBC, which was established in 1970 for managerial oversight of ISKCON, could provide a unifying authority. The problem here was that such a solution seemed to grant spiritual authority usually located in the guru to an institutional body that included all eleven gurus.

The third answer that some disciples suggested was that Prabhupada alone was capable of providing sufficient spiritual insight to secure ISKCON's future and thus his "words and orders" contained in his writings must serve as the highest authority. And in the end it would appear that it is the writings of Prabhupada that have become the primary institutional embodiment of his charisma. Consequently both the new gurus and the GBC have continually based their own decisions and claims to ultimate authority on the words of their founder, even when those words were ambiguous or contradictory.

The New Gurus and Prabhupada's Legacy

Each of the eleven appointed successors to Prabhupada was given a geographic zone, and these zones, along with the zones managed by general secretaries not elevated to the status of guru, covered the whole world. Rameswar Swami, a recently deposed guru who resided primarily in Los Angeles, said Prabhupada considered this territorial factor in naming his successors: "The process was simply that Prabhupada envisioned how the society would practically go on expanding after his disappearance. So he picked leading men, his leading disciples, thinking in terms of their level of spiritual advancement, and also thinking in terms of the geography of the world. . . . We took it that Krishna was dictating. . . . Prabhupada would be that much in touch with God."[8] While there was sometimes a GBC general secretary also appointed to oversee the fiscal and organizational health of the ISKCON centers within a particular zone, the responsibility to initiate new disciples and to teach them the rituals, beliefs, and ethics of Bengali Krishna devotion belonged to the new gurus. Thus in some zones the managerial responsibilities fell mostly upon general secretaries and in others upon a guru, but only gurus could initiate new disciples.

Early in 1978, only a few months after Prabhupada's death, some new gurus began to adopt fully and enthusiastically the role that Prabhupada had occupied. This included encouraging worship of themselves as guru (*guru puja*) that is traditional in India. However, one of the eleven gurus who was responsible for the Texas and India zones demanded that even his own godbrothers (also disciples of Prabhupada) must join new disciples in prostrating themselves before him as they had done before Prabhupada. Clearly, such examples as this one suggest that at least one of the new gurus saw himself as *replacing* Prabhupada. Just as Prabhupada had been the channel to Krishna when alive, some new gurus saw themselves serving that function for their disciples and their godbrothers.

Though the two overzealous gurus were censored by the GBC for overstepping their bounds with regard to their godbrothers, the March 1979 GBC meeting confirmed the new gurus' authority to receive guru adoration from their own disciples if their succession powers were to mean anything at all. This decision and subsequent ones like it gave the new gurus essentially the same position with their disciples as Prabhupada had with his. This is the way of disciplic succession. However, the seeming haughtiness of some of the new gurus has angered some of their godbrothers and continues to sow seeds of discontent. One outspoken GBC member who is not a guru said to me, "Attachment to the position of guru—or any other position in ISKCON—has nothing to do with spirituality. . . . Such attachment has another problem attached to it. . . . Just by definition, it makes you arrogant; it makes you absolute; it makes you sound like you've started to love the sound of your own voice."

Two of the six new gurus I interviewed appeared to fit the description of the critical GBC member. During an interview with one of these gurus, most of his wordy responses to my questions emphasized his power and prestige. He indicated that, as Prabhupada's successor, he was now charged with setting the course of ISKCON in his zone, which he saw in the forefront of the movement. During his morning lecture on the Krishna scriptures, he responded sharply and critically to questions he had encouraged devotees to ask. The constructive tone I had seen other Krishna gurus and leaders set in their morning devotional period was absent here. In my presence, he spoke to his "servants" with a harsh disdainful tone and appeared to relish his lordship over them.

Critics of the new gurus within ISKCON also argue that to give complete authority to the new gurus weakens the place of Prabhupada in the movement. In a letter addressed to his godbrothers (Prabhupada disciples), Panchadrivida Swami, a recently appointed guru responsible for Latin America, said:

> There is a great need in our society for putting Srila Prabhupada back in the center. . . . Actually there is only one real Acarya for ISKCON, and that is our

Founder-Acarya A. C. Bhaktivedanta Swami Prabhupada. . . . It is quite obvious
to almost all that despite so much glorification of the new gurus, they are quite
different from Srila Prabhupada and not at all on the same level as him. We
should be quite candid: we are young men endeavoring to advance.[9]

Panchadrivida's letter reflects the ambivalence many of the new gurus have
felt in trying to take Prabhupada's mantle upon themselves. The fact is that
most new gurus know they have the traditional authority but are equally
aware that the charismatic authority Prabhupada had can only be earned, not
bestowed. Hence, Prabhupada's translations, purports, letters, and direct
personal instructions ("orders") become the substitute for his presence and
have remained guiding forces in ISKCON since his death. Put in Weber's
terms, Prabhupada's charisma has become routinized.

For example, many disciples of Prabhupada view their role in ISKCON to
be forever set by special instructions from their guru. Tripurari, a *sannyasin*
who has now broken away from ISKCON to form his own sectarian expression
of ISKCON, was told once by Prabhupada that he was "the incarnation of
book distribution." Consequently, Tripurari sees his special spiritual task as
being the promotion of ISKCON's religious texts. Furthermore, many devotees in the movement accepted this special confirmation by Prabhupada and,
for several years after Prabhupada's death, called upon Tripurari to instruct
their devotees in techniques of book distribution.

Kirtanananda Swami, the guru who is building the palace and temple
community in New Vrindaban (Moundsville, W.Va.), was given a special
commission by Prabhupada to build an American replication of Krishna's
Indian birthplace. In a letter to Kirtanananda in 1969 Prabhupada said,
"Build this New Vrindavana to your heart's content."[10] And that is exactly
what Kirtanananda is doing and will do as long as he lives. Such specific
instructions from the guru have kept certain people in ISKCON in the same
job or the same place for more than a decade. In Kirtanananda's case, this
sense of ordination has led to his settlement's virtual independence from
ISKCON's GBC control. Prabhupada's words have set a course of action that
Kirtanananda believes he alone is authorized to determine.

While the codification of his teachings and instructions is the primary way
Prabhupada's charisma has been institutionalized in ISKCON after his death,
as Thomas O'Day has noted, "routinization of charisma . . . also involves the
containment of charisma."[11] That is, Prabhupada is not alive now to alter his
instructions or apply his teachings in new ways to new situations. Consequently, the legacy he gave to ISKCON was not only *his* words but also
appointed disciples who could make new disciples, apply his teaching to new
situations, and give ISKCON personal leadership. This legacy of passing on
Prabhupada's traditional authority has created *new gurus* in ISKCON with very
different styles of leadership and authority.

Satsvarupa dasa Goswami is a good example of a new guru. As I spent
several days in the Potomac, Maryland, temple and several more in the Gita
Nagari farm in Port Royal, Pennsylvania, I saw Satsvarupa in action. At the
farm, I witnessed an initiation ceremony that was taken verbatim from the
religious rituals of sixteenth-century Bengal. Satsvarupa kindled the traditional Vedic fire and, in Sanskrit, led the initiates through the required

prayers and vows. At the celebration that followed, Satsvarupa clearly was treated with the deference due a guru (e.g., a sumptuous meal served in silver utensils and a special seat to sit upon while watching children present a play). However, he seemed uncomfortable with all the attention directed to him and ate very little of the food that had been especially prepared for him and his guest.

Throughout ISKCON, Satsvarupa is respected for his integrity, his humility, and his piety. His complete devotion to the task of writing Prabhupada's biography is a clear confirmation of his respect for and adoration of his guru. Nonetheless, Satsvarupa publishes a newsletter for his disciples and the temples of his zone (which includes parts of New York, Pennsylvania, and Maryland) in which he makes it clear that he views his role as initiating *acarya* in quite traditional terms—namely, as a direct representative of Krishna and therefore one who conveys Krishna's teachings completely and one to be honored "as if he were God."

In a letter published in response to a request for initiation by a young non-initiate, Satsvarupa spells out the proper position and attitude required by the disciple in the master-disciple (*guru-sisya*) relationship:

> I am sure that before too long the temple authorities there will recommend you for initiation, and I will be glad to accept you as my disciple. Please consider the matter very seriously in the meantime. It is not a matter of simply being in the temple a certain amount of time; it is a matter of realization. You have to agree to become thoroughly submissive to the orders of the spiritual master, which are especially fixed up in faith and practice of chanting Hare Krsna and following the regulative principles. Whatever personal instructions he gives has (*sic*) to be taken as coming from Krsna. So before one agrees to such a relationship, he should be certain.[12]

In another letter to a disciple, Satsvarupa agrees with the disciple's conclusion that "the checks and balance system of *guru, sastra* and *sadhu* is used to find out who is a bona fide *guru*. But once we find out a bona fide *guru* and take initiation from him, . . . we are not in the position to make any more check on him."[13]

Of the new gurus I have met and interviewed, Satsvarupa stands out as one of the few who appears to balance well the responsibilities of being a guru who has traditionally absolute authority over his disciples with a sense of his own need for future growth. Those new gurus who balance well their authority with humility stand out, even to the outside observer.

It is clear not only that the new gurus I interviewed were at various levels of religious maturity but that they varied also in the extent to which they insisted upon the absolute authority of their new role. On the one hand, there are those who clearly have kept Prabhupada at the center of their devotion through their stress placed on *his* teachings, *his* instructions, and *his* role as their avenue to Krishna. On the other hand, a few new gurus appear to me, and others in ISKCON, to have placed *their* words, *their* instructions, and *their* traditional connection to Krishna above that of Prabhupada's. Several such gurus who placed themselves above any scrutiny were finally expelled from ISKCON. These guru controversies also resulted in the GBC's assuming some of the spiritual authority previously reserved only for gurus.

The New Gurus and the GBC

Prabhupada had learned from his own experience of the fragmentation of his guru's organization that there must be some overarching governance system in order for a multiple successor system to work. His guru, Bhaktisiddhanta, had tried to create a governing commission to hold together the sixty-four Krishna centers in India, but he died before such a structure was in place. Prabhupada, however, was successful in creating a Governing Body Commission for ISKCON partly because he initiated it only four years after ISKCON had begun its mission in America. It was on July 28, 1970, when Prabhupada's travels to ISKCON's international centers and his lengthy stay in India required his absence from his fledgling American centers, that the GBC was established as a nuts and bolts governance structure.

The GBC was made up initially of twelve (and expanded gradually to twenty-four) of the most advanced devotees who also held positions of authority in ISKCON (e.g., temple presidents and book editors). In the dictated document that established the GBC, Prabhupada said of these twelve disciples, "These personalities are now considered as my direct representatives. While I am living they will act as my zonal secretaries and after my demise they will be known as Executors."[14] This document goes on to say that each GBC secretary should travel throughout his zone to ensure that every devotee in ISKCON is chanting the sixteen rounds each day and adhering to the ritual and moral life that Prabhupada had prescribed. Prabhupada's idea was that the GBC could relieve him of the day-to-day management of ISKCON and allow him to focus his full energies on his translating and preaching.

From its first year, the GBC has met annually in Mayapur, India, to decide ISKCON-wide policies. At these annual meetings, economic, political, and religious issues and problems were discussed and institutional policies and strategies set. Personnel decisions were made and new centers staffed. Prabhupada's word was final, but much of the decision-making process rested in the hands of the GBC members. Consequently, when Prabhupada died in 1977 the GBC already had experience in exercising a leadership role for all of ISKCON. Furthermore, all but one of the new gurus were already members of the GBC, making a natural, if sometimes uncomfortable, link between the role of the new spiritual masters and the institutional role of the GBC.

The institution of a central authority such as the GBC posed no difficulties for ISKCON as long as Prabhupada was alive, because his word was final. However, after Prabhupada's death, the question arose almost immediately, "Who *is* the ultimate authority for ISKCON?" Of course, every devotee would say immediately that Prabhupada's teachings and instructions were the final authority (as his institutionalized charismatic word). But since he had appointed eleven successors, were they not the authoritative interpreters of Prabhupada's teachings and the creators of new interpretations as well?

However, what would happen if the various gurus disagreed on a point of doctrine or management practice? Was the GBC to adjudicate such disputes, and if so, was not the GBC the final authority? It did not take long for the inherent tensions to surface that were produced by Prabhupada's dual transmission of his authority to individualist gurus and the centralizing GBC.

The tenure of Hansadutta Swami, a new guru located in Berkeley, California, forced ISKCON to face the issue of the limits of a new guru's authority head on. Hansadutta had been considered an individualist even before his appointment as a new guru by Prabhupada. Born in Brunswick, Germany, on May 27, 1941, Hansadutta was raised a Catholic. His parents brought him to America in 1949, and it was in New York City that Hansadutta met Prabhupada and became one of his earliest disciples. He describes his joining ISKCON this way:

In 1967, having exhausted all my attempts at finding some basis for my activities, I came to read Srila Prabhupada's little book, *Easy Journey to Other Planets.* Immediately on reading this book, I put it down and walked to the temple. I was so impressed by this little book that I knew at once that this is what I had been waiting for; so I decided to become a devotee.[15]

He rushed home and told his wife what he had decided, and within a week's time they both had joined ISKCON.

After helping to establish new temples in Canada, Hansadutta went to Germany to proselytize there. He founded a successful center in Hamburg and, in July 1970, was named to the first GBC. Hansadutta spent most of his early career developing the German ISKCON mission (temples, German translations of Krishna scriptures, etc.). He was next located in India and South Asia for two years prior to being named one of Prabhupada's eleven successors. As a new initiating *acarya*, Hansadutta was placed in charge of the northwest United States (Berkeley, Portland, and Seattle) along with parts of Southeast Asia.

To his new spiritual status, Hansadutta brought this view of the guru's role:

The main function of the guru is to preach the conclusions of the *sastras* and to demonstrate them in his personal life, and to establish new centers, to publish books, and to distribute books, and, of course, to initiate new disciples. Just as our spiritual master did, so we should follow his footsteps as far as possible.[16]

The difficulty for Hansadutta throughout his stormy tenure in Berkeley was that his actions often did *not* reflect the orthodox teachings he knew so well.

For example, Hansadutta's godbrothers believed that his fund-raising tactics violated even the most liberal ISKCON interpretations of accepted practice and, if known, could bring about public condemnation of ISKCON. In one specific instance, correspondence between Rameswar in Los Angeles and Hansadutta expressed concern that if Berkeley disciples were to engage *only* in selling secular goods (e.g., records and buttons), such practices could put that temple's tax-exempt status in jeopardy.[17] Finally, Hansadutta's personal preoccupation with fast, fancy sports cars and with guns evidenced a life-style that hardly emulated the example set by Prabhupada.

The media and the police became more and more suspicious of Hansadutta's temple activities and got their chance to put him on the spot in the early months of 1980. On February 2, a longtime devotee named William Benedict reported to Berkeley police that his checkbook and some credit cards had been stolen while he was at the Berkeley temple for prayers. On March 4, police raided the Berkeley temple's farm community, called Mount Kailasa, looking for Benedict's stolen credit cards and the guns they had been used to purchase. The police searched the Krishna farm and, according to one newspaper report, "they uncovered several thousand rounds of ammunition, a grenade launcher, three rifles and four short-barrel shotguns."[18]

Because most of the media accounts of the Kailasa farm raid greatly exaggerated the amount of arms and ammunition that had actually been found and were slanted with an anticult interpretation, the worst fears of a public with Jonestown on its mind were confirmed. "Hare Krishna Revealed" and "Have the Krishnas Turned Violent?" were the types of headlines that announced the farm raid.

On March 27, papers throughout the country reported that "nine tons of gunpowder and bullet-making equipment" had been found at the gun shop of Roy Walters, another Krishna devotee. And even though papers such as the *New York Times* published corrections that said it was nine *pounds*, not nine *tons*, of gunpowder that had been found, media throughout the United States began to proclaim: "Krishna sect taking up arms." Then on May 14, Hansadutta himself was arrested. Although Hansadutta was finally exonerated of the illegal arms charge, his godbrothers thought it was time to put a stop to the damage he was doing to ISKCON and its mission.

The three separate public Berkeley gun incidents gave the persons in ISKCON who already criticized Hansadutta's style of leadership a reason to act. Hansadutta's arrest was only the final blow to his already tarnished image. The GBC quickly gathered in a special meeting and decided to relieve Hansadutta of all authority in his zone and, according to one devotee I interviewed, "send him back to India for spiritual rest and recuperation." Another new guru, Hridayananda, was sent to Berkeley to assume Hansadutta's responsibilities and put that zone back on good spiritual footing.

This action of the GBC, however, raised to the fore the question of ultimate leadership over ISKCON that had been simmering only slightly below the surface since Prabhupada's death. Are the individual successors to Prabhupada's traditional authority *really* independent agents in ISKCON, or is the institutional council, the GBC, the ultimate "direct representative" of Prabhupada's spiritual legacy? The action of the GBC in relieving Hansadutta from his position of authority in Berkeley seemed to settle this debate, when in actuality the debate was just gaining momentum.

On the one side were those who insisted that ISKCON's spiritual mission was best represented and protected in the guru/disciple relationship. Consequently, the guru's authority should not be superseded by that of *any* person or group. Those who held this view got authoritative support on October 21, 1980, when Sridara Maharaja, a godbrother of Prabhupada, was consulted. In this consultation, several members of the GBC went to India and put their dilemma clearly before this respected sage of the Indian Krishna movement.

Sridara left no doubt about what he considered to be the correct resolution of the debate when he said, "To the disciple, the *acarya's* [spiritual master's] position is supreme. . . . In all the scriptures we find this. The guru is more near and affectionate than God. God has many [devotees] to deal with, but the guru is always careful of his disciple's welfare."[19] His understanding of institutional law (e.g., the GBC's proclamations) was that it was there "to promote faith, to make room for faith to develop." Consequently, Sridara urged each new guru and all their godbrothers to respect each other and to work toward harmony by *voluntarily* accepting the rules and directions set down by the GBC. Still, he argued, no person or group in ISKCON has any final authority over the guru's relationship with his disciple.

On the other side of the debate were those who reminded their godbrothers that such individualistic assumptions as those which Sridara expressed had led to bickering among Bhaktisiddhanta's successors (of whom Sridara was one) and fragmentation of the Gaudiya Math's missionary efforts in India. Rameswar Swami (the Los Angeles-based new guru) was an outspoken proponent of this view as he argued that the GBC was the legitimate heir of Prabhupada's missionary legacy. During an interview in June 1980, Rameswar said, "Our society has a governing body which is the ultimate authority within this whole movement worldwide." Rameswar reminded his godbrothers that the GBC was Prabhupada's "direct representative." He also pointed out that the GBC was the legal heir to all ISKCON properties and assets. The will of Prabhupada said plainly, "The Governing Body Commission (GBC) will be the ultimate managing authority of the entire International Society for Krishna Consciousness."[20] Hence, Rameswar argued, the GBC was required to intervene wherever Prabhupada's mission was being thwarted.

An intermediate position was articulated by Kirtanananda Swami. He argued that the guru/disciple relationship is inviolate because of its spiritual status but that all new gurus had been instructed by their guru Prabhupada to cooperate with the GBC decision-making process. And with this attitude prevailing in the early months of 1981, Hansadutta was reinstated to his position in the Western Zone.

Meanwhile, throughout ISKCON there were disenchanted disciples of Prabhupada who criticized both the new gurus and the GBC for taking all the power for themselves and forgetting that Prabhupada had said that *all* his disciples were potential gurus and therefore responsible for ISKCON's future. One such critic was the Los Angeles temple president, Dheera Krishna. He claimed that ISKCON was being diverted by the GBC and the new gurus from its primary spiritual mission. He suggested that all the leadership of ISKCON should spend more time gaining personal piety and less time trying to build a successful religious institution. After being dismissed from his position as temple president, he left ISKCON to found a competing Krishna temple.

A second critic was Adi Kesava Swami, the Northeast Zone's GBC and later New York City temple president. He felt that the new gurus' godbrothers were being overlooked by both the GBC and the gurus in the decision made at the annual GBC meeting in Mayapur not to add any more gurus. In a lengthy letter to the GBC, Adi Kesava argued that the only two courses of action for a spiritually mature and administratively successful godbrother of the new gurus was either to submit to the authority of one of them or to "fade into oblivion." In Adi Kesava's case, his arguments were deemed to be self-serving and his attitude one of confrontation with the guru in his zone, Satsvarupa. He finally resigned his positions and moved out of the temple, although he continues to be a household member of ISKCON.

Dheera Krishna's defection and Adi Kesava's resignation were among the early signs in ISKCON that a third force, those initiated by Prabhupada and located in high institutional positions (e.g., temple presidents), would challenge the GBC and the gurus' authority when circumstances required such a challenge. While neither Dheera Krishna nor Adi Kesava attempted to form a political alliance of Prabhupada's disciples (i.e., the gurus' godbrothers), such a movement would occur four years later in New Vrindaban. In the intervening time, ISKCON had to face several more crises occasioned by the misconduct of the new gurus.

Early in 1982, Jayatirtha, a new guru who was located in London and had Great Britain and South Africa for his zone, occasioned the first actual, though short-lived, schism in ISKCON. Accused of taking drugs, sleeping with some of his female devotees, and aligning himself with Sridara Maharaja against ISKCON's leadership, Jayatirtha was called on the carpet at the GBC's meeting in Mayapur in April 1982. He was told that he must abide by the new decision of the GBC not to seek solace or advice from Sridara any longer. Jayatirtha was told that he would be removed from his zone if his political and immoral behavior did not cease.

Jayatirtha immediately called his disciples in the London temple and urged them not to admit any devotees not loyal to Sridara. He then fled across the river from Mayapur to Navadvip, the home of Sridara. He took those of his disciples who were in India with him to Sridara's religious retreat and claimed Sridara to be the real spiritual leader of ISKCON. The devotees back in London boarded up the doors to the temple and, at first, refused to admit any of ISKCON's officials. Some of the London devotees fled to India to join their spiritual master. Thus, ISKCON had to deal with its first potentially major schism. Jayatirtha was a charismatic hero to many of his disciples, and the threat of losing one of ISKCON's oldest temples was great.

The GBC, however, acted swiftly to stabilize Jayatirtha's zone. Some of the most respected godbrothers of Jayatirtha were sent to London to try to persuade the London devotees that Jayatirtha was acting against Prabhupada's will. Throughout Jayatirtha's zone, GBC members carried the message that Prabhupada's teachings were the highest authority and that the GBC was acting to protect those teachings from individual contamination. Representatives of ISKCON were finally successful in isolating Jayatirtha's influence to just a few devotees who either stayed with him or simply left ISKCON altogether. Jayatirtha ceased to be a threat to ISKCON and became the first of Prabhupada's appointed successors actually to leave ISKCON.

A year after Jayatirtha's departure, rumors of illegal activities persisting in Hansadutta's zone occasioned a special meeting of GBC leaders in Miami. At that meeting, Hansadutta was excommunicated from ISKCON, and the debate over the ultimate authority for ISKCON was settled—at least in practical terms. The news release that made Hansadutta's ouster public said in part, "The GBC is ISKCON's highest ecclesiastical body and maintains the Hare Krishna religion's spiritual standards, guarding against teachings and practices contrary to those of the religion as determined by its scripture and Founder-Acharya."[21]

The GBC had named three new initiating *acaryas* or gurus at its Mayapur meeting in the spring of 1983. In making such appointments, it clearly had acted as though it was the "direct representative" of Prabhupada. Thus, in acting to discipline Jayatirtha and to remove Hansadutta, the GBC was being consistent in exercising the kind of authority that only Prabhupada could when he was alive. Nonetheless, what should be apparent to the reader is that there is considerable room for individual initiative and decision-making, within broad limits, for the individual gurus. And it is the tendency toward individualistic and authoritarian rule by the new gurus that led to a major crisis in ISKCON in the fall of 1985.

In August and September of 1985, two emergency meetings were held in New Vrindaban that fundamentally altered the shape of ISKCON's guru structure for the future. These meetings were occasioned by a rising tide of concern and protest that came primarily from the American temple presidents and frustrated godbrothers of the new gurus. At these meetings, some of the current gurus were accused of deviating from the spiritual practices they were obliged to live and to transmit to their disciples. They were also accused of placing themselves on a par with Prabhupada when, in fact, their spiritual maturity and actions belied such arrogance.

These extraordinary meetings of ISKCON's senior disciples and leaders resulted in a series of proposals that were transmitted to the regular GBC meeting in Mayapur, India, in the spring of 1986. While toning down the recommendations of the gurus' godbrothers, the GBC decided (*a*) to democratize its own voting by allowing a majority vote (instead of two-thirds) to determine ISKCON policy matters; (*b*) to encourage gurus to demonstrate their proper place in ISKCON by lowering the height of their special guru seats below that of Prabhupada (or removing them altogether); and, most important, (*c*) to increase significantly the number of gurus who are authorized to initiate disciples (to offset the individualistic stamp of a single guru upon any ISKCON zone).

One tangible result of the fall 1985 crisis and spring 1986 GBC meeting was the rapid initiation of over two dozen new gurus, more than doubling the number of ISKCON gurus. A second consequence was the decision by several gurus to remove guru worship from their temples in America. However, there was also a backlash from some gurus, like Kirtanananda in New Vrindaban. Accused of intemperate and exaggerated claims for a special status for himself and his community, Kirtanananda made only one grand entrance and formal speech at the fall 1985 meetings and then did not attend further meetings. Since that time he and his community have, for all practical purposes, though not formally, seceded from ISKCON. Nonetheless, in many zones of America, ISKCON's successor gurus have accepted, or even welcomed, new gurus and their initiates as a revitalizing and reforming influence in their temple's spiritual life.

One thing this recent crisis reveals is that the godbrothers of the gurus (i.e., Prabhupada's disciples) are an additional voice of authority in ISKCON along with the GBC and the gurus. What the events of the past two years also reveal is how difficult it is to transmit charisma institutionally and personally.

The Containment of Authority and Charisma

Now that the dust has settled a bit from the intense guru-GBC-godbrother authority debates, it is clear that the tensions arising from assertions of primacy by the nearly autonomous gurus within the context of an institutionalized GBC will continue into the foreseeable future. This should not be surprising, since the histories of religious movements throughout the world reveal a tendency for sectarian, theological divisions to occur after the death of the founder. Clearly, ISKCON is not immune to these centrifugal forces. However, the impressive fact for any careful observer of ISKCON's history is that it has been able to evolve in a very short time from a charismatic movement to a relatively stable institution in the face of a hostile external environment and a volatile governance structure within.

Even the most casual examination of ISKCON communities throughout the world today reveals complex and differentiated communities led by often individualistic gurus that are somehow held together by the dream of Prabhupada for unity among his disciples and by the institutional force of the GBC. Still, it is surrender to a single guru that remains the mode of access to ISKCON faith for a new initiate. Consequently, we must take seriously the claims of anticult critics that the surrender of an individual's will to the guru/disciple relationship is complete and debilitating. Therefore we now turn to the question of what constitutes "surrender" to a guru.

4

Surrender and Authority
Among the Krishnas

The authenticity and subtlety of taste of the daily Indian vegetarian cuisine eaten in Krishna temples vary considerably from place to place. At most temples, however, visitors to the temple are served more elaborately prepared food, which is tastier and usually reserved for the temple president, the resident guru, or any visiting dignitary in the movement. Consequently, the best cooks are assigned this task.

During the summer of 1981, Mahema was the specialty cook at the Miami temple; her meals were indistinguishable from the best that one could expect of her Indian teachers.

At first meeting, Mahema appeared shy and reserved and spoke with a quiet voice and nervous laugh that bolstered that impression. She was of medium build, with dark hair and a round, attractive face. Mahema was dressed in a white sari, marking her as one of ISKCON's few "widows." Her husband was one of the newly appointed gurus who succeeded Prabhupada and he had just taken *sannyasa* (the ritual that ends all worldly ties and commits one to a celibate religious life). Consequently, Mahema had just moved with her young son from her husband's temple in Europe to the Miami Krishna community. As with other ISKCON "widows," money had been set aside for the material needs of Mahema and her young son.

Other devotees indicated that Mahema was highly respected in ISKCON for her personal warmth and piety. She had been in the movement for more than seven years and had often served as a counselor for new women devotees. She had listened to the spiritual autobiographies of many young women and now she relayed hers.

I went to the Catholic church and knelt before the altar and prayed to Jesus, "I'm not going to turn my back upon you." I sort of took Jesus' permission to join the Hare Krishna movement because I felt close to Catholicism; but I also felt that this was a path that could lead me even further. On a spiritual level, in my heart, I felt that the link was still there to my Catholic upbringing. But it was like I had kind of gone through Catholicism and was continuing on another path. I was not turning my back on my faith, nor was I rejecting Catholicism.

I sensed that I had gotten permission to join ISKCON, and the next day I was initiated.

I saw my joining ISKCON as a natural extension of my Catholic spirituality. I had been born in a suburb of Detroit in 1948, but my parents moved to California, where my father had bought a small orchard. My mother had six children in five years and, since I was the oldest, I ended up taking care of my brothers and sisters a lot. My mother spent a lot of time in the fields with my father, which increased even more my child-rearing responsibilities. I never minded making meals and taking care of the household chores, because I enjoyed serving the needs of my family.

My father had been raised in a Jewish home and had converted to Catholicism during the Second World War. He met my mother while he was a Marine and she was working for the Navy. I remember them as devout Catholics who went to Mass every Sunday and tried to follow the principles of the Catholic Church. My mother prayed a lot and used to say, "Never underestimate the power of prayer." She used to pray all the time.

When I was fifteen we moved back to Detroit and I immersed myself in the life of a middle-class parochial school student. My high school career was uneventful, as I did well scholastically and participated fully in school social activities. I even considered becoming a nun.

However, when I went to a Catholic college, I hung out with friends who had a very different response to their Catholic backgrounds. They smoked dope, drank, and smoked. They were active in the anti–Vietnam War movement and were much more activists than I was. I was still living at home but was beginning to feel stifled by my parents' strictness. Likewise, my friends' dependence on drugs seemed silly to me. I liked to be more in control of myself than they did. You know, it actually frightened me to see how people were becoming speed freaks and dope addicts, and I didn't find that attractive at all.

By the beginning of my third year in college I was beginning to feel the need to return to the simple life in the country. So I dropped out of school and shortly thereafter went to the Woodstock Festival with some friends. I met some people at Woodstock who lived in a tepee and who offered me a job working in their leather shop. I accepted and moved to Woodstock for a while. While there, I began to search for alternatives to the Catholic religious life.

From Woodstock I joined a group of traveling hippies who were going to New Mexico in an old bus they owned. We stopped at several hippie communities that were practicing American Indian paths to spiritual growth. I came to appreciate the Hopi's and Navajo's simple ways of life. I never had been into the violent antiwar protests nor the heavy drug scene, so this rural way of life really agreed with me. Most of my friends were flower children who were more into nature than drugs and demonstrations. After a while, I traveled with them from New Mexico to a farm in Oregon. I stayed on that farm for nearly two years.

The farm commune was like a big family where everyone was like a brother or sister. I ended up cooking for everybody . . . just being the mother like I had been to my real brothers and sisters. I indulged very little in sense gratification, though I would occasionally smoke some dope. My friends were not into abusing the body, since most were vegetarians and believed that the body was the temple of the spirit. I had deep friends, but most of my friendships were platonic.

Because we were using outhouses and drinking water from a nearby river, I contracted hepatitis at the end of my second year on the farm. Luckily, I had returned to Detroit for a visit with my family when the hepatitis made me violently ill. While I was in Detroit recuperating from my illness, I began to read

English translations of the Indian Krishna scriptures called the *Bhagavad Gita* and the *Srimad Bhagavatam*. I didn't know who wrote these books or what community used them. Then one day on the street I met a Krishna devotee. He said, "You got the right book, but you got the wrong guru!" While I had met the devotees on the streets of San Francisco and had enjoyed dancing with them in public, I had not been to a Krishna temple until invited by the Detroit devotees. A friend and I went to the Detroit temple and he felt they were fanatics, while I just thought they were real nice, if a bit too exuberant. Nonetheless, they seemed to be really blissful and really pure-hearted. They had given up everything, completely dedicated themselves to serving God, which was something I really respected. One devotee was really kind and would engage me in dialogue on the *Gita* or some other Krishna scripture. For the next month I came daily to the temple.

I was also attracted to the chanting and the *kirtan* [dancing and singing praises to Krishna]. Kirtan was especially blissful and reminded me of the communal chanting we had done on the farm. . . . You really felt a spiritual high from singing, which also was attractive to me. These religious occasions reminded me of my childhood when I would feel chills go up my spine while praying or singing in the church. Though I found the association of the devotees and the life of the temple to be attractive, I decided to return to the Oregon farm.

When I went back to the farm I took a picture of Krishna with me and followed most of the basic precepts [i.e., no drugs, no sex, etc.]. I would offer my food to Krishna before each meal. I did daily *pujas* [worship] before the image of Krishna and chanted the Krishna mantra frequently. Consequently, the farm just didn't seem the same. My friends there simply were not as serious about the spiritual life as I was and they enjoyed their sensual activities too much.

I felt I needed more direct spiritual guidance and the Krishnas I kept in contact with urged me to accept Prabhupada as my guru. But by this time I was twenty-three and I didn't know if I could surrender that much. I didn't know about giving up my independence by moving into a temple. I wouldn't be able to take a walk in the ocean whenever I wanted. I just didn't think I could ever be a devotee who would give up so much.

Nonetheless, I was reading the books and I was attracted to the philosophy. The *Bhagavad Gita* was my main attraction. I was convinced by the *Gita*'s argument that the soul is eternal and that there was a purpose for every life. And the *Gita* showed how one could come to a higher level of consciousness in the spiritual life. When I was on the farm I believed that love was the motivation for the world, that love tied the world together. But I knew that pure love was something that had to be cultivated. So I felt that the *Gita* was right when it said that pure love was love of God—not just each other. Consequently, in reading the *Gita* I felt that all that I believed as a Catholic was being confirmed and that the *Gita* was going further because it was telling you *how* to love God . . . step by step.

It took me about a year to assimilate the philosophy. I visited the Oregon and Berkeley temples for short stays during this time. I was reading the *Gita* and I was chanting, though not consistently. I tried to cultivate the spiritual life and was actually, in my heart, thinking about the devotees and Prabhupada. I would say to myself, "Oh, someday I will surrender."

I came south to Santa Barbara, and the devotees there encouraged me to go to the Los Angeles temple. When I arrived I was shocked at the activities and excitement surrounding that temple. The devotees were preparing for a festival and asked me to stay for two months and help prepare for it. I stayed for a while but then began to say, "I left all of my material belongings at the farm. I need to return there to get them." The devotees replied that I would never return it

I left. They said, "It's so much nicer here; and you should just surrender to Krishna now! You don't need all that stuff. . . . You need to just search here for Prabhupada."

So then I went to the temple and I said [in prayer before the Krishna images], "Srila Prabhupada, make me surrender! . . . Srila Prabhupada, I have no intelligence; I just want to be spiritual. . . . I want to know love of God and maybe you can help me." At that point I felt actually an inner strength, from Srila Prabhupada. Some reciprocation. The next day I went to the Catholic church to ask for Jesus' permission. And I actually sensed that my joining was authorized.

I didn't fully understand what it meant to surrender to a guru. As time goes on, you understand more. But at that time I felt that I could really learn something from Prabhupada, and I really felt that he was my spiritual teacher. . . . Before, I would perform all kinds of service for my friends, but now, after coming to the temple, my service was to Krishna and my spiritual master.

Total Surrender of the Self

More than three decades ago and before the burgeoning of current cult fears, Eric Hoffer asserted that no matter how gifted the cult leader, "he cannot conjure a movement out of a void."[1] Though a charismatic leader is "indispensable," according to Hoffer, he needs a fully committed and loyal following. To get this devoted following, there must be a group of persons willing to surrender themselves completely to the innovative leader. In short, followers must grant a "total surrender of their distinct self" to promote group unity and self-sacrifice, and "blind obedience" to a leader is a common way of accomplishing that goal. Hoffer concludes, "The true believer . . . is basically an obedient and submissive person."

Lowell Streiker agrees with Hoffer when he asserts that ISKCON's guru Prabhupada exercised complete authoritarian control over the thought and behavior of hundreds of young Americans.[2] He argues that the young cultist is "desperate for structure, order, authority" and finds a solution in surrender to a charismatic authority.[3] Streiker goes on to say that, after having undergone traumatic and emotional upheaval in their personal lives, cult adherents like the Krishnas sublimate or misdirect the real cause of their feelings by projecting them onto the cult leader. The result is a sense of relief and purification and a feeling of being reborn into the new world to which one has surrendered.

In speaking of a Krishna devotee, Streiker says, "This devotee has neither been hypnotized nor kidnapped. . . . His conversation is shallow, revealing a one-track mind. . . . He is annoyingly immature. But no one is holding him against his will."[4] From this point of view, the convert's surrender *appears* voluntary, though it is made in a context of personal stress. Rabbi Rudin concurs. "Bewildered, frightened, unnerved by the world as it is, the potential cult member, in desperation, makes a total surrender, a fanatical commitment to the cult in hope of overcoming the uncertainties of life."[5]

Not all observers of the Krishnas and other such groups agree that surrender to the guru or leader even appears to be voluntary. Psychiatrist John Clark, in his testimony before a Special Investigating Committee of the Vermont Senate in 1976, said in his opening remarks, "I will state that coercive persuasion and thought reform techniques are effectively practiced on naive, uninformed subjects with disastrous health consequences."[6] Clark asserted that cult joiners tend to come from "intact, idealistic, believing families" who protected the victim from the vicissitudes of life. And when their attempts to cope with the worldly crises common to all adolescents and adults was ineffectual, "they became covertly depressed."

Clark continues: "For individuals in this state of vulnerability to be converted, a series of circumstances, techniques and events must occur to bring about the complete subjugation of mind and person." The techniques often include those of chanting, singing, and being barraged by the cult's rhetoric —all of which Clark elsewhere identifies with Krishna practices. The result is *involuntary* surrender. Clark puts it this way: "This state must be described as a trance. From that time there is a relative or complete loss of control of one's mind and actions which is then placed in the hands of the group or of individuals."

Some social scientists have likewise come to the conclusion that surrendering to a religious group or authority is a psychologically unhealthy and regressive act. Francine Daner in *The American Children of Krsna* places her discussion of surrender in the context of Erik Erikson and Erving Goffman's identity theories.[7] Viewing the conversion process of Krishna devotees as products of personal identity crises, Daner claims that modern society fails to provide youth with identity models, ideology, and rituals that allow their incorporation into traditional roles and activities.[8] Daner views the guru Prabhupada as a father figure with whom the homeless seekers can identify.[9] Consequently, to surrender to Prabhupada is to accept him completely as one's identity model and authoritarian guide. She says, "The struggle and surrender to this spiritual master is harsh. . . . To disobey, mistrust, or betray him is rejection of the love and mercy he has offered them."[10]

Daner concludes that the initiatory rituals of ISKCON in which the head is shaved, monastic clothes are adopted, and new Sanskrit names are assumed serve to strip the new devotee of his or her "identity kit."[11] Krishna ideology which stresses such self-negating concepts as "You are not your body; you are an eternal soul" supports the surrender of a devotee's previous attachments to self and family, says Daner. She observes, "The devotees readily admit that they are engrossed in material attachments [i.e., in *maya*] and that they are helpless unless they can seek a spiritual master."

According to Daner, "The complete surrender to Prabhupada and to Krishna is evidenced in the statement that 'we are very small and can do nothing for ourselves, but must be completely dependent on Krishna for everything.' Prostration before the deities and Prabhupada are symbolic of these feelings."[12] Daner concludes that such surrender makes the Krishna devotees "totally dependent" on the temple for all necessities of existence and results in devotees "begging on the street" for ISKCON.

Whether their analyses are couched in popular jargon for the lay audience or in quasi-technical language for an academic one, most persons who write about the nature of surrender to a guru or spiritual leader agree that Krishna devotees have relinquished both their power to reason and their ability to exercise their own will to make decisions for themselves. In short, they have become intellectual and emotional vassals of their guru.

Surrender in the World's Religions

The religious tradition that most obviously recommends surrender and submission as primary spiritual values is Islam. The word *islam* itself comes from an Arabic root (*s-l-m*) that connotes surrender, resignation, and peace. That same root is embodied in the word *muslim,* which is usually translated "submitter" and refers to a person who has surrendered to Allah.[13] The theological justification for surrender is grounded in the preeminent place given to Allah (God) and his vehicle of revelation, Muhammad. The Islamic creed, or Shahadah, simply decrees, "There is no God but Allah and Muhammad is his messenger."

The sacred scripture of Islam, the Quran, is thought to be the direct "recital" by Muhammad of Allah's will and intentions, and what the Quran reveals is a transcendent God of judgment and mercy who demands complete submission to his will. The Quran makes it clear that submission to Allah is the foundation of the Islamic faith: "God bears witness that there is no god but He . . . the All mighty, the All Wise. The true religion with God is Islam [i.e., "surrender"]" (Sura 3.17–18).[14] Muhammad's role as prophet does not exclude him from those who must surrender completely to Allah. In fact, his authority comes from his being the *first* of the Muslims ("submitters") as he says, "My prayer, my ritual sacrifice, my living, my dying—all belongs to God, the Lord of Being. No associate has He. Even so I have been commanded, and I am the first of those who have surrendered" (Sura 6.163). The Islamic scholar Kenneth Cragg states the matter simply: "The crowning purpose of the Quranic affirmation of God is worship and submissiveness."[15]

Fear is the basic and natural mood of piety in Islam (e.g., Suras 76.7 and 39.24). Even the mountains quake before the sight of Allah! A Muslim scholar and disciple, Fazlur Rahman, says, "The Qur'an calls upon believers to undertake *jihad,* which is to surrender your properties and yourselves in the path of Allah."[16] Jihad requires that one be willing even to die while attempting to establish Allah's rule on earth. From this point of view, jihad means both "holy war" and total dedication by those who would bring unbelievers to their knees in submission. The battle cry of jihad is "Allahu Akbar," "Allah is Great," as many puzzled Americans learned during the Iranian hostage crisis of 1980–81. The believer is required to submit not only his heart and will but also his intellect and reason to Allah's revelation as contained in the Quran.[17]

No religious tradition places submission to God more at the center of its life and faith than does Islam. Furthermore, few religious traditions have publicly demonstrated both the strengths *and* the dangers of complete devotion to a totalistic religious ideology as has Islam throughout its history. Yet Islam does not stand alone in its demand for total submission by adherents. Most religious traditions of the world ideally require complete dedication to the life and worldview that their founders and sages have espoused.

By its grounding in a supernatural power or divinity, the vision of the religious believer stands over against that offered by live-for-today pragmatists, humanists, or other nonbelievers. Consequently, religious claims to "truth" or "reality" usually seem "unworldly" and incredible. What some religious traditions have done is to accommodate themselves to the secular world more adroitly than Islam and thereby either *appear* less threatening to secular institutions until they gain political clout (e.g., the religious Right in America) or *are* less threatening because they do not stress a world-denying reliance on a Divine Power (e.g., liberal Christian denominations and Reform Judaism in America). Consequently, to *surrender* to the Christian God in Methodist or Presbyterian institutions is not as disruptive to family or friends as being "born again" in a fundamentalist sect or in a Mormon mission.

In the earliest days of the Christian community, total surrender to God and the new life this surrender implied was a primary devotional motif. The first of the two great commandments of Jesus (Matt. 22:37–38 and Luke 10:27) says unequivocally, "You shall love the Lord your God with all your heart, and with all your soul, and with all your mind." This command was exemplified in the early Christian teachings regarding the necessity of a new, spiritual birth (hence "born again" disciples) which intended to orient one to living and viewing the world through devoted submission to God rather than through the materialistic vision of "the world" (John 3:16–21).

One early Christian writer puts this surrender to God over against acquiescence to the materialistic world in clear terms: "No one can serve two masters. . . . You cannot serve both God and the material life [mammon]" (Matt. 6:24 and Luke 16:13). Again and again early Christian disciples admonish their listeners to surrender to God and the spiritual life and reject the world and its sensual life (e.g., Gal. 5:16 and 1 John 2:15–17).

Though other motifs have been important to different segments of the Christian community in various places and times, the theme of surrender to God or the Divine has been present, if not practiced, throughout the whole history of Christianity. In our own time, evangelical Christians see themselves as guardians of this perspective. For example, Billy Graham in a crusade sermon in Rice Stadium on June 3, 1982, said bluntly, "Stop trying, give up, give in! . . . Come to Jesus Christ as a little child." Graham asserted, "Your mind is at enmity with God. . . . Stop thinking your way into faith." He then interpreted the first great commandment literally to mean that we must surrender our minds and hearts to God if we are to be true followers of the Christian way.

Not only have Christians emphasized surrender to God over against worldly possessions and authorities but this surrender has been extended in the monastic traditions of Catholicism to include spiritual guides and church officials. The monk should "for the love of God submit himself to his Superior in all obedience."[18] As we saw in chapter 2, surrender to a spiritual guide was not only encouraged but demanded in various Catholic monastic contexts. Thus Thomas Merton quotes favorably *The Rule of the Master* which defines a true monk as one who "walks by the judgment of his teacher and has learned not to know the way of his own will."[19]

Islam and Christianity are but two of the many religious traditions that demand unqualified obedience to a deity or representatives of that deity. Even in nontheistic traditions such as Theravadin Buddhism and Brahmanical Hinduism, surrender to the guru or master is the primary avenue to liberation. Therefore, to vow complete submission to the Buddha ("pathfinder"), his teachings (the *dhamma*), and the community of seekers (the *sangha*) is something every Buddhist monk or nun must do during their initiation ceremonies. And in the same spirit as the first great commandment of the Bible, the *Bhagavad Gita* instructs its devotees, "Whatever you do, whatever you eat, whatever you offer in oblation or give, whatever austerity you perform, do that as an offering to me [Krishna/Vishnu]" (9.27).

What seemed inconceivable to the wealthy citizens of ancient India was that their children would *willingly* give up a life of luxury to shave their heads, to adopt new names, and to live the austere life of a Buddhist monk. Such total commitment and surrender to an "otherworldly" or a "non-worldly" goal like Nirvana or "life-extinction" appeared to defy human logic. And it still does. But is such surrender as irrational and as total as it seems to those on the outside?

Who Really Is in Control?

Three months of living with Krishna devotees made clear to me that the stereotype of the mindless and passive cult submitter was inappropriate when applied to the persons I had encountered. Then again, it also became apparent to me why such a stereotype was applied to the Krishnas in the first place. All the behavioral trappings of surrender of the "old self" and adoption of a "new self" are present in Krishna devotees in their shaven heads, Sanskrit names, Indian dress, food, and hierarchical relationships, and in their shared, all-inclusive ideology. To an outsider, the Krishnas look as if they all have been cast in a single behavioral and ideological mold.

Yet to the person viewing ISKCON's devotees from the inside, it is obvious that instances of individual decision-making and willing abound. Just as in all monastic life, it is not unusual to find in Krishna temples personality conflicts, open disagreements on how the Krishna theology should be applied in a particular instance, devotees who disobey their spiritual master, individuals who place their own interests above the group's, and clear instances of some Krishna leaders setting policies at variance with those of other leaders. In short, it is abundantly manifest that many devotees are still thinking and willing for themselves and that their surrender is incomplete or only partial by *any* standard of judgment.

The persistent practice of most Krishnas to move from center to center at numerous intervals during their life in ISKCON reveals clearly the extent to which devotees march to their own drum as often as to that beaten by their leaders. Though it is said that each devotee has a particular "service" to do and must get permission from the initiating guru or temple leaders to alter his or her service or the temple or farm at which the service is performed, practice contradicts what outsiders may see as authoritarian servitude. For example, when the Denver temple vice president apologized for the tardiness of our breakfast one morning, he told me that his temple's renowned cook had picked up and left the night before after deciding to relocate to another temple. When I asked if permission had been given to the cook to make the move, the answer was no. When I asked if the new temple would receive the cook and his family and provide them with material support, the answer was yes.

Devotees I have interviewed are hard to find again because they have moved to another temple or left ISKCON of their own volition. Dozens of times during my four years of interaction with the Krishnas, I have learned of such self-motivated and unauthorized movement by devotees.

What is important to recognize is that an overly simplistic model of human willing and decision-making has been applied to cult joiners. Antagonists clearly assume that only when a person *independently* makes *all* decisions regarding his or her life can that person be said to be "in control" or truly "free." Consequently, even when a person willingly adopts a totalistic ideology and life-style that are dictated by a cult leader, it can only be concluded that the joiner has surrendered all of his or her will and reason to that outsider. Such persons are then perceived as captives, or victims of the cults. In short, it is concluded that cult joiners have lost *primary control* of their will, reason, and lives.

Exceptions to the above scenario are granted for accepted social groups that require surrender of personal decision-making. For example, Alcoholics Anonymous has a mutual support system that imposes desired behavior, but this external control appears to be both desired and limited to one sphere of the drinker's life. Military institutions often fill their ranks by conscription (i.e., involuntary joining) and require surrendering one's independent willing and thinking (i.e., involuntary submission) to a hierarchical decision-making structure in which behavior, dress, and even language are dictated by one's superiors. Absolute obedience to a "chain of command" is expected, as is acceptance of personal hardships and even the possible loss of one's life. What makes military life different in kind from the cults, say cult critics, is that people in the military are not consumed by a totalistic ideology or closed community that dictates all of one's waking hours.

David Bromley and Anson Shupe rightly suggest that many human interactions with institutions entail both coercive and voluntary dimensions.[20] For example, persons initially placed in mental institutions against their will may one day freely choose to remain, as they see their best interests being served by their hospitalization. Conversely, many young men and women who willingly join an armed service may be kept against their will when military life is not what they hoped it would be. Important as the issue of voluntary versus coercive is with regard to cult joining, such labeling is fraught with biased debates and is at best difficult to undertake.

Whether joining a cult is voluntary or coerced, what instills fear in parents and outsiders is the assumption that the reason and the will of cult "victims" are totally controlled by cult leaders. However, my research and experience among the Krishnas suggest that, regardless of the apparent coercion or freedom associated with the act of surrendering to an ISKCON guru or leader, it would appear that such surrender is very seldom total. Social-scientific studies that distinguish between primary and secondary control offer us some help in understanding how qualified or conditional "total surrender" can be.

In an article that surveys the social-scientific literature on "perceived control," Fred Rothbaum and his colleagues explore the often misunderstood area of "secondary control."[21] Rothbaum and his associates try to understand the "inward behavior" of those persons who are passive and submissive—that is, those who appear to relinquish all control over their lives. What is at issue is whether the only alternatives that people have for coping with their life crises and stresses is primary control (i.e., taking complete charge of one's life) or the abandonment of control to others in passive submission (i.e., giving up control of one's life entirely to another person or group).

After considering more than one hundred related sociological and psychological studies, Rothbaum and his associates conclude that "the motivation to feel 'in control' may be expressed not only in behavior that is blatantly controlling but also, subtly, in behavior that is not. . . . Inward behavior [i.e., surrender or submission] may be initiated and maintained in an effort to *sustain* perceptions of control."[22] If primary control is construed as an attempt to change the world to fit one's personal needs, then secondary control is more the attempt to align oneself to a world one has failed to change. Most persons use a combination of both types of life management which they perceive to be self-initiated.

"Secondary control is most likely to occur after attempts at primary control have failed," says Rothbaum.[23] Consequently, secondary control marked by passivity, withdrawal, and submissiveness is best understood as a late stage in a person's reaction to stress that is employed only after all attempts at primary control have failed. In other words, secondary control follows closely upon the heels of the anger, protest, and frustration that signal the end of a person's attempt to cope directly with life crises. Secondary control, therefore, can be considered an *indirect* way to control one's life that falls far short of the total surrender of one's will and reason.

There are four basic forms of secondary control, according to Rothbaum: (1) predictive control, (2) illusory control, (3) vicarious control, and (4) interpretive control.[24] Predictive control is the attempt by a person who has severely limited ability to control his situation by adjusting his expectations to avoid disappointment. For example, a political hostage may, after an initial period of resisting his captors, readjust his hopes for immediate freedom by expecting the worst each day (long captivity, torture, and even death). When his predictions of continued captivity and personal discomfort are realized, the hostage's perceptions are confirmed and he may avoid the debilitating disappointment that comes from unrealized positive hopes. Unable to gain freedom, the hostage expresses his interpretive command over his situation by adjusting his daily expectations in order to survive. He has gained predictive secondary control.

Illusory control is likewise the tack taken by persons who have a severely limited ability to change their life's circumstances but still need to feel "in control." This type of secondary control comes by aligning oneself with chance or luck so that one may share in the control exerted by that powerful, external force. Though recognizing the unpredictable element in this type of control, the participants in illusory control believe that "Lady Luck" or "fate" is "on their side" and to some extent controllable.

While illusory control may be a motivational factor at work in some participants in occult ideologies and groups, neither predictive nor illusory secondary control is particularly applicable to the behavior of the Krishnas whom I have studied. However, vicarious and interpretive control explanations are helpful in describing what is going on in the surrendering process of many devotees whom I interviewed or observed, and these explanations contradict the analyses of those who say that cult joiners have given up all control of their lives.

Vicarious control is exercised by a person when he or she aligns himself or herself with a powerful person (e.g., a guru or a powerful politician). As Rothbaum says, "This association is neither a means to an end nor a method of filling other objectives; rather, the association is desired for its own sake. By aligning themselves with more powerful others, individuals can share in their victories and in their accomplishments—in short, in their control."[25] In order to share in the primary control exerted on the world by the powerful other, the follower must appear to submit to the leader's demands and authority. In all societies, persons identify with individuals (e.g., politicians, movie stars, or religious heroes) and groups (e.g., sports teams, ethnic clubs, or vocational groups) and find personal gratification or loss in response to the fortunes of those revered or idealized persons or groups. So too does a Krishna convert find an ideal model in his or her guru. Moreover, the guru's piety and lineage are perceived to be the link between the devotee and Krishna (God) which permits the devotee's participation in the guru's achievements, power, and control.

Perhaps Erich Fromm was right when he concluded that most of us try to "escape from freedom." Fromm argues that freedom in the modern West has been so aligned with a rugged individualism (often expressed as a liberation from traditional family and religious ties) that a sense of isolation and power-lessness is often the experienced result. Such "free" individuals often seek to realign themselves with others through "compulsive conformity" to a chosen group or by submission to a political or religious leader precisely to escape their burdensome liberty.[26]

The personal odysseys of some devotees whom I have interviewed reveal the flight from freedom that Fromm describes. What these devotees have often done is to escape a free-spirited and undependable counterculture group or socially isolated life by their surrender to a guru who is perceived as a direct link to God's eternal law and stability. One devotee said of his previous commune's life-style, "There seemed to be no rules except one's own, and life was shallow and lonely even though I was a member of my group."

What I frequently noted in my interviews with devotees was that many only appeared to surrender while still reserving a great amount of control over their lives for themselves. Mahema indicated how difficult it was to surrender to a guru even when she wanted to. Another devotee I interviewed said, "No matter how hard I try I cannot surrender fully to my guru as I should." Yet a third devotee remarked, "Surrender is a lifelong process that one engages in. Our egos are too strong to permit easy surrender." Another indication of the conditional nature of their surrender was the recurring comment of devotees: "I thought I would try this Krishna life for a while and if I didn't like it, try something else." As a final example, remember that Govinda Dasa "experimented" by living in New Vrindaban for a year before shaving his head and being initiated.

Devotees whom I interviewed varied considerably in the apparent degree of their surrender, depending often upon the length of time they had been in the movement. "New devotees" who had been in ISKCON for fewer than three or four years often acted more submissive and dependent than did older devotees. This is not surprising when one considers the near-fanatical emotional and intellectual commitment of new converts to any group or ideology. But after the first wave of blind enthusiasm subsides, daily routines become habitually patterned, and increasing responsibilities are placed on the shoulders of the maturing devotee, submission to an authoritarian guru becomes something different from attempts at complete submission. Primary control begins to emerge as devotees make decisions for themselves, their new families, their temples, and their businesses. It is often the case among the Hare Krishnas that the follower who initially depended upon an association with a pious and powerful guru to give stability and structure to his or her life usually, after a period of maturation of faith, gradually begins to assert direct or primary control over important life decisions (marriage, vocation, etc.).

The fourth type of secondary control that Rothbaum describes is interpretive control. "Interpretive control refers to the search for meaning and understanding," says Rothbaum.[27] Following the lead of the psychologist Viktor Frankl (*Man's Search for Meaning*) and studies of other social psychologists, Rothbaum concludes that all human beings regard their search for a meaningful life as intrinsically important and rewarding. Whether their outward appearance is that of an authoritarian controller or a passive dependent, all human beings seek to interpret events and experiences that impinge upon their life situations in order to understand and accept them. Such understanding provides "interpretive control" over personal crises and chaotic events. Natural calamities, ill health, vocational failure, death, and other such seemingly uncontrollable life experiences are all events that cry out for meaningful interpretation.

In most persons, the perceived inability directly to control one's fate leads to a perceived secondary control over one's misfortune through explanations that provide a rational and emotional buffer from the full impact of the misfortunes that are experienced. My interviews with Krishna devotees confirm the claims of all of those (both friend and foe) who recognize that conversions to cults occur after a period of emotional stress or life crisis. Whether the crisis was academic, sexual, social, or religious, devotees usually experienced a failure of their old interpretive systems (religious, political, or otherwise) and were in search of "God," "new meaning," "answers," or "someone to lead me to truth" just prior to their joining ISKCON.

What Rothbaum and his associates show clearly is that the surrender of devotees to a guru and ISKCON may be understood as something other than simply a "giving up" of their will and reasoning ability. While a few devotees have made such a complete and self-rejecting submission, most have simply diverted their efforts at coping with a complex and troubling world from a primary to a secondary form of control. Certainly this understanding of the persistence of self-will and self-control best describes the conditional surrender of Govinda Dasa as well as the inability of Mahema to surrender completely.

My interviews and observations among the Krishna devotees confirm that, for many, acts of surrender and submission are actually vicarious and interpretive secondary attempts to continue personal responsibility for their lives. What is perceived from the outside as total surrender or mere helplessness is actually a circuitous road back to primary control.

Conclusive evidence of the power of secondary forms of control that can support primary ones is the high defection rate among Krishnas in America, which has kept their overall numbers stable for the past four or five years (i.e., there are as many defectors as new converts each year). Furthermore, it is clear that the greatest number of defections occurs during the first year of membership, when, to persons on the outside, new converts appear to be the most fanatically committed and totally surrendered.

A fact that most deprogrammers and cult antagonists don't choose to accept or to reveal is that more than 80 percent of the disciples originally initiated by Prabhupada have left ISKCON on their own initiative. Though there is much work to be done before we can understand all the factors that encourage defection among Krishna devotees, one thing is clear: such voluntary retractions of complete obedience to one's initiating guru evidence primary control being exercised where secondary control had previously sufficed.

Even for the persons who remain in ISKCON for several years and who do not defect, increasing reliance on primary forms of control emerges. In addition, those devotees who continue to utilize mostly secondary forms of control still perceive themselves to be in control. These conclusions drawn from my research are confirmed by the clinical study of the entire population of the Melbourne, Australia, Hare Krishna temple conducted by psychiatrist Michael Ross.[28] After administering four different personality and mental health inventories and examinations to all members of the Krishna temple, Ross concluded that recent joiners were not pathologically ill but appeared "healthy-minded" even though perceived happiness increased among those devotees who had been in the movement for more than three years.

The results of Ross's study substantiate my interviews that suggest that the preconversion stress and crises experienced by devotees are not usually pathological but rather well within the bounds of what most adolescents experience. Because there is an underlying need to find answers or solutions that will yield understanding and meaning to their lives, devotees' happiness or satisfaction with their lives increases as they internalize the new religious life they have adopted. Consequently, as devotees mature in their new faith and its ideology they not only gain interpretive control and perceived happiness but also begin to exercise primary control over their lives again. Rothbaum too concludes that submission to an authoritarian leader or group may eventually provide increased primary control for many individuals by increasing their confidence about their abilities in the context of such a protected environment.[29]

Whether speaking of submission to Allah or to Krishna through one's initiating guru, we would do well to remember "that persons perceive and are motivated to obtain secondary control in many situations previously assumed to be characterized by perceived uncontrollability and an absence of motivation for control."[30] The mistake made by many interpreters of religious (or cult) conversion is that they have generalized from a few cases of total surrender and subservient helplessness to claim a total loss of self ("ego," "identity kit," etc.) as the norm. Carroll Stoner and Jo Anne Parke assume this helpless submission in their definition of a cult, which says, "A cult has a living leader. . . . The cult leader is the sole judge of the quality of a member's faith and he enjoys absolute authority over the members."[31] This view is false. Absolute authority and control are often asserted or demanded but seldom enjoyed by cult leaders. The same is true of ISKCON's gurus and the GBC.

Regardless of how one argues the issue of coercive versus voluntary surrender in cult conversions, the surrender is seldom total or complete. As we saw in the last chapter, this fact has been nowhere more evident in ISKCON than during the transmission of authority from Prabhupada to his appointed successors. Eleven young men who were deemed by Prabhupada to be his most faithful and fully committed disciples quickly revealed to the outside world their quite individualistic and sometimes self-centered appropriations of his Krishna faith and practice. In seeing how the disparate lives and actions of the new gurus of ISKCON led ultimately to the defection of one and excommunication of several, we also observed how Prabhupada qualified surrender to the guru with his institution of a Governing Body Commission. From that tension-filled chapter of ISKCON's history we learned that the authority of the guru and surrender to a guru are both qualified and conditional.

What is clear to me after several months of observing Krishna devotees behind closed temple doors is that most of them are far more in control of their own personal destinies than even some of them realize. Surrender to a guru is neither so total nor so simple as it would appear to the casual outsider, and the new gurus themselves are outstanding examples of this fact.

Ironically, the totalistic beliefs and life-style of ISKCON that I heard preached in the temples and that are feared by parents and opponents are seldom to be found in anything like a complete or total form in the lives and practices of Krishna devotees. Rather, fully committed Krishna devotees appear to have just as much trouble living consistently according to their beliefs as did the Christian apostle Paul, who said, "I can will what is right, but I cannot do it. For I do not do the good I want, but the evil I do not want is what I do" (Rom. 7:18–19).

Furthermore, the faith and beliefs that Krishna devotees do attempt to follow are clearly more a product of rational, ideological processes of acceptance than psychological repressive ones involving total surrender. Thus if we are to understand *why* young persons have joined ISKCON and remain resolutely faithful to its mission, we would do well to understand *what* it is that ISKCON teaches and why those teachings are so attractive.

5

Why Worship
a Blue God?

Passengers who board buses in India are often greeted by a framed picture hanging in the center of the windshield. Such was the case the spring of 1973, in the South Indian city of Madurai, where the local bus to Singampunari was decorated with a large picture of Krishna that had been bedecked with fresh jasmine flowers. The devotional picture in the frame depicted a light-blue-skinned young man standing with his legs crossed and leaning up against a white cow while playing a silver flute. Both the cow and her calf which stood nearby were looking longingly with wide eyes at the handsome young man. The trees in the background bloomed luxuriously and were filled with colorful birds that were obviously enthralled with the music of the flute.

When the bus driver climbed onto the bus he placed fresh incense in a holder above the picture of Krishna Gopala (or the "Cowherd Krishna") as a token of his devotion to the blue-skinned Lord. Such are the popular signs of devotion to Krishna that are common throughout all of India—whether indicated on a picture calendar that depicts the young child Krishna, cherubic and with blue skin, sitting astraddle a large butter churn eagerly eating butter by the handful or on temple wall paintings that display Krishna dancing on the heads of a defeated serpent. Even in this South Indian city ruled by the goddess Minaksi and her consort Shiva, signs of Krishna devotion are ubiquitous. Though India is a land of many gods and goddesses, few are as widely recognized and revered as Krishna, the dark-skinned Lord.[1]

On the streets of America, however, and in the minds of ISKCON's detractors, the pictures and images of Krishna make no sense and often appear only as idolatrous icons. Consequently, if we are to understand the attractiveness of Krishna, we cannot skirt the story that is a stumbling block to so many angry parents and disbelieving critics of ISKCON and yet stands at the heart of this Indian devotional faith.

What follows is a greatly abridged story of Krishna that parallels closely the story in the revered Vaisnava scriptures of India, the *Bhagavad Gita* ("The Song of the Lord") and the *Bhagavata Purana* ("The Tales of the Lord").[2]

Five thousand years ago the world was ruled by an evil demon-king named Kamsa. Because Kamsa's rule was harsh, the earth, in the form of a white cow, along with a host of gods and holy men approached the eternal god Vishnu/Krishna, who was reclining in the milk ocean. The earth and the heavenly citizens pleaded with Vishnu/Krishna to help them, and he agreed to take an earthly form [*avatara*, or "descent form"] to restore righteousness on earth and rid it of the evil king Kamsa.[3]

Kamsa's sister was a beautiful princess named Devaki who was betrothed to Vasudeva, a handsome prince. On the day of their wedding, Devaki and Vasudeva rode together with King Kamsa in his chariot. Suddenly a voice from the heavens announced, "Kamsa, you foolish rogue, the eighth child of the woman you are carrying will kill you."

The shameless Kamsa at once drew his sword and, grabbing his sister by her hair, prepared to cut her head off. However, the coolheaded Vasudeva interrupted Kamsa with these diplomatic words: "It would not look good for a great warrior such as you to kill a woman, especially on the day of her marriage. I promise to bring to you all of our sons." Knowing Vasudeva to be a man of his word, Kamsa agreed, and the wedding procession continued.

Soon, however, and at the advice of his demoniac ministers, Kamsa imprisoned his sister and brother-in-law. He killed their helpless sons one after the other as they were born. But when the time came for the eighth child of Devaki to be conceived, Vishnu/Krishna himself entered the womb of the princess. As the time approached for Devaki to give birth, Vishnu appeared in his four-armed form and gave Vasudeva and Devaki detailed instructions to foil Kamsa's death-dealing plans.

On the night that Krishna was born, the prison doors suddenly swung open and exposed soundly sleeping guards beyond them. Picking up the beautiful dark-skinned child according to the divine instructions, Vasudeva walked out of the prison and proceeded to the Yamuna River. As Vasudeva approached the river, the waters mysteriously parted, allowing father and son to walk across on dry ground. Soon Vasudeva reached the village of Gokula. There he found Yashoda, wife of Nanda the village chief, and her newly born daughter just as he was told he would. Vasudeva exchanged his son Krishna for the baby girl and returned to the prison, where the guards were still fast asleep. He placed the girl baby beside Devaki, and the prison doors closed to hide this deception. Meanwhile, due to divine intervention, Yashoda slept deeply and did not recall whether she had given birth to a son or a daughter.

Upon hearing that Devaki had given birth to her eighth child, Kamsa came and demanded to see the child. Even though the child was a girl, Kamsa decided it must die. He grabbed the infant by its feet and was about to smash its head against the prison walls when the baby flew out of his hands and through the prison window and announced that she was Maya, the goddess of material nature and the creator of the illusion of life's permanency. She also reported that Krishna had appeared elsewhere and would soon kill King Kamsa.

Kamsa was stunned and frightened. He consulted with his ministers and decided that the only way to ensure his own safety was to kill all children under the age of two. Kamsa employed a succession of demons and demonesses to kill the children in his city and the surrounding villages. The first to reach Krishna [now the foster son of Yashoda and Nanda] in the village of Gokula was the demoness Putana. Appearing as a beautiful woman, Putana invited the young child Krishna to suck her poison-filled breasts. But Krishna, knowing her true identity, sucked out not only the poisoned milk but also the very life-breath of Putana. Though actions such as this revealed the divine power of this seemingly mortal child, the villagers of Gokula were swayed by God's mysterious power to think of Krishna as an ordinary, if a bit ornery, child.

Once while playing with his elder brother Balarama, Krishna appeared to grab a handful of dirt and eat it. Balarama reported to his mother, "Krishna is eating dirt!" While denying he had eaten dirt, Krishna invited his mother to look into his mouth. Yashoda took the child Krishna on her lap and, looking into his mouth, saw the whole universe—including all the planets, stars, and places on earth, including her village of Gokula. However, Yashoda's memory was immediately clouded, and as if awaking from a dream, she saw once again only her mischievous son on her lap.

A favorite prank of Krishna was to trick his mother or one of the village cow-girls [*gopis*] into giving him some of their freshly churned butter. Sometimes Krishna simply stole the butter. For example, one morning when Yashoda was churning butter, Krishna cried out that a pot of milk was boiling over on the kitchen fire. When Yashoda returned from the kitchen she found Krishna dipping up the butter from her churn with his hands. Exasperated, Yashoda finally tied Krishna to a large and heavy wooden mortar. Krishna gleefully rushed off through the yard with the mortar in tow and uprooted two close-standing trees, freeing two imprisoned souls who because of previous immoral behavior had been reborn in stationary trees.

Unnerved by the intrusion of the demons and demonesses into Gokula and by the unusual events and powers associated with Krishna's pranks, Nanda and his villagers decided to abandon their village and move to a new home. Packing up the whole village and herding their cows before them, the villagers of Gokula moved to the forests of Vrindavana [also transliterated Brindaban]. Nonetheless, the supernatural signs and demonic visits did not cease.

In their new home of Vrindavana, Balarama and Krishna were given charge of the calves. Once, when the brothers and their cowherd friends were playing in the Yamuna River, a demon named Vatsasura assumed the form of a calf and joined the herd. He intended to kill the brothers. Although the demon mingled well with the calves, Krishna immediately detected him. Krishna grabbed the demon by his back legs and, whipping him around forcibly, killed Vatsasura by throwing him into a nearby tree.

Not only did the people of Vrindavana take notice of the seemingly endless powers of the dark-skinned Krishna but so too did the god Brahma, the Lord of creation. Brahma decided to test the powers of Krishna to see just how mighty he was. Once when Krishna had gone off from the herds and his friends, Brahma stole them away and hid them in a nearby cave. When Krishna returned and found his herd and friends missing, he merely duplicated each animal and friend that was missing. So perfect were his illusions that not even the mothers of the calves and the boys could tell. Seeing the creative power of Krishna, Brahma returned the cows and boys he had stolen and offered prayers to the Lord Krishna, the supreme Lord in the form of a cowherd boy.

Krishna demonstrated his superior might over the traditional Indian gods one by one. He inhaled the most vicious fire the Vedic god of fire, Agni, could boast. He diverted a potential flood the king of the gods, Indra, attempted with his violent rains. He also humbled the proud brahmins [priests] who refused to share their food with low caste herders. As Krishna grew into young manhood, it became increasingly clear to the citizens of Vrindavana that he was no ordinary mortal. Furthermore, the wives and daughters of the cowherders [the gopis] were very attracted to Krishna.

All the gopis tolerated Krishna's pranks of stealing butter or of teasing them. At sunrise one morning the unmarried gopis came to the river to bathe and say their morning prayers. While the gopis were in the water, Krishna stole their clothes and climbed a nearby tree. As the gopis emerged from the water naked, Krishna commanded that they come one by one to pledge their love to him in order to receive back their clothes. Since only a husband is permitted to see his wife naked, Krishna promised to meet with the gopis as their husband in the next autumn season.

Later that year, on a beautiful autumn night, Krishna multiplied himself to provide a dancing partner for each of the gopis he had promised to wed. Forming a large circle in a secluded grove, the gopis each with their own Krishna danced throughout the night. This was the great *rasa* dance or dance of life which should be done only to the rhythm of Krishna's flute. The pure devotion and surrender of the gopis to Krishna identifies them as his greatest devotees and should not be confused with worldly lust. In previous lives, many of the gopis were great scholars and sages who desired intimate knowledge of Krishna. Krishna fulfilled their desires by becoming their paramour, although for him there was no question of lust. The relationship of Krishna and the gopis is, therefore, understood as the highest expression of the love of God. So intense was the gopis' attachment for Krishna that, when he took the cows to the fields each day, the gopis remained constantly absorbed thinking of him in separation.

Meanwhile, the evil King Kamsa had learned that Vasudeva had tricked him by hiding Krishna in the family of Yashoda and Nanda. After his demon emissaries had failed to dispose of Krishna, Kamsa sent a messenger to invite Balarama and Krishna to the capital city of Mathura. There, Kamsa thought, the two brothers would meet their death in the arena at the hands of Kamsa's wrestlers. Krishna and Balarama agreed to accept Kamsa's challenge and set off for Mathura with Kamsa's messenger. The gopis and the cowherders wept, since they now knew that Krishna would not return. He had to complete the mission for which he was born.

When Krishna and Balarama arrived in Mathura, they went straight to the wrestling grounds. The site was designated by a huge bow no mortal could string. Although admonished not to try, Krishna picked up the bow, strung it, and then snapped it in two with a *"Crraacck"* that filled the sky. Kamsa sent a small band of troops to punish Krishna for such impudence, but Krishna and Balarama killed them with the broken pieces of the bow.

Finally, Krishna and Balarama entered the wrestling arena. Kamsa's mightiest wrestlers, Canura and Mustika, stepped forward to challenge the smaller brothers. The crowd was anxious because the wrestlers seemed so mismatched. Assuaging the crowd's desires, Krishna and Balarama quickly killed their seemingly more powerful foes. The crowd cheered and the kettledrums rolled. But Kamsa was furious and ordered the crowd to stop cheering and proclaimed, "These two sons of Vasudeva should be driven from Mathura and their father killed!"

Upon hearing Kamsa's proclamation, Krishna leaped over the guards who surrounded the king and confronted Kamsa directly. Kamsa unsheathed his deadly sword, but Krishna simply grabbed hold of the king and threw him to the ground. Then, having straddled the powerful Kamsa, Krishna proceeded to strike the king until he was dead. Meanwhile, Balarama killed the eight brothers of Kamsa. Because these nine demons were killed by Krishna and his brother, they all attained salvation in heaven. Even Kamsa, because he thought of Krishna always (even if in hatred and fear), was liberated at the hands of Krishna.

After an interlude that included his building of the famed city of Dwarka, Krishna was drawn into the great epic war of India. The war started after the Pandava king Yudhisthira's successful sacrifice, when the king and his brothers enjoyed opulent feasts and merriment. Yudhisthira's cousin, Duryodhana, burned with envy at Yudhisthira's success and rule and conspired with the cousins of the Pandavas called the Kauravas to challenge their right to the throne. Krishna did not want to take sides in this pending war between cousins and thus agreed to let his army serve the Kauravas while he served as an adviser only to the Pandavas.

Duryodhana and his brothers massed an army ten times the size of that of the Pandavas. Yet on the day of the first battle, Arjuna, perhaps the greatest of the Pandava warriors, felt no fear. Krishna, Arjuna's friend, agreed to be his chari- oteer. Arjuna asked Krishna to drive his chariot between the two armies so that he could survey his foes. Then, however, seeing that his opponents were his cousins, friends, and teachers, Arjuna dropped his bow and declared, "I cannot kill my loved ones; I shall not fight."

At that moment, Krishna explained to Arjuna that only the body can be slain and that no one can slay the eternal soul. Krishna thus urged Arjuna to fulfill his warrior's duty and fight. In the brief, illuminating conversation that followed, Krishna explained to Arjuna—and by extension to all his devotees—how best to worship him and to attain salvation. Being raised from despair by the words of Krishna, Arjuna picked up his bow and fought the Kauravas. And thus it was that Arjuna and the Pandavas fought and won the battle of Kurukshetra and thereby established righteousness on earth.

The Krishna devotee who told me this abridged summary of the life of Krishna closed with these words:

Krishna's instructions to Arjuna on the plain of Kurukshetra are known as the *Bhagavad Gita* ["The Song to the Lord"], a sacred text that has provided spiritual inspiration and wisdom for millions of Indians down to the present day.

When Krishna finally departed to his eternal abode, he left behind the *Bhaga- vad Gita* for the enlightenment of all mankind. His superexcellent pastimes are recorded in such sacred texts as the *Srimad Bhagavatam* and the *Mahabharata.* These and other texts translated and commented upon by His Divine Grace Srila Prabhupada are the basis for today's worldwide Krishna Consciousness movement as well as for this brief summary of Lord Krishna's pastimes.

The Message of Prabhupada

This chapter will present three interrelated discussions of the Krishna faith: its basic *content,* the nature of its *plausibility,* and the different *styles* of its adoption. First of all, the central teachings of the Krishna faith that Prab- hupada brought with him from India will be summarized. This review of the basic assumptions of most Indian theology, and the Krishna theology of Prabhupada in particular, should make clear that part of the barrier to under- standing ISKCON in America is its genuine divergence from some traditional Western religious and historical assumptions. Second, against the backdrop of anticult accusations regarding the irrationality of the surrender that dev- otees must make to join ISKCON, an alternative view of the "logic" of the Krishna faith will be presented. This discussion will reveal a certain common rationality that ISKCON's faith has with that of every religious tradition of the world. Third, the issues of ideological totalism and religious fanaticism will be addressed by separating the matter of the plausibility of the content of the Krishna faith from the question of how strongly or inflexibly that faith is held. This last discussion of the chapter poses the same questions to the defenders of the Krishna faith as it does to the anticult critics of that faith. It is to a description of that faith we shall now turn.

When Prabhupada was growing up in India, the stories of Krishna's exploits just recounted were constantly heard in the temples, in his home, and on the streets where he played. Children in India still act out the various roles of the characters of Indian myths, and the stories of Krishna provide favorite personages for this game. In particular, the pranks of the baby or young child Krishna are enticing for children to mimic. However, his amorous adventures with the gopi girls are usually understood to be metaphoric expressions of the soul's love for God and never to be acted out by mortals.[4]

In the north of India where Prabhupada was reared and became a businessman, Krishna is quite often thought of as the enticing and lovable butter thief.[5] The many drama troupes that travel from village to village frequently act out episodes from the life of Krishna to the delight of large audiences of adults and children.[6] The story of Krishna, which can seem so incredible and alien to twentieth-century Americans, is an age-old favorite in India. So too are the lessons from this story which Prabhupada preached well known, if not universally accepted, in the India of today.[7]

It was important to Prabhupada, even in the earliest years of his mission to America, to link Krishna's *lila,* or story, to specific articles of faith articulated in his natal Bengali Krishna (i.e., Caitanya's) religion. Thus, in 1970, only three years after ISKCON was formally incorporated as a religious body in America, the society published a volume entitled *The Krsna Consciousness Handbook.* This small monograph briefly detailed the teaching of ISKCON, the qualifications for becoming a devotee, the meaning of Krishna symbols and ritual elements, the nature and purpose of chanting, an introduction to one farm community (New Vrindaban), an introduction to the basic literature, texts of some common prayers, a short description of the role of the guru, and a biographical sketch of Prabhupada.

While *The Krsna Consciousness Handbook* is now primarily of importance only to persons interested in the early history of ISKCON, this rehearsal by Prabhupada more than fifteen years ago of the "basic beliefs" of ISKCON still represents an accurate overview of the Hindu religious path he offered to those Americans who would listen. His final summary statement goes this way:

> The International Society for Krishna Consciousness is a bona fide religious society strictly following the principles described in the Vedic scriptures and practice in India for thousands of years. Our basic beliefs are as follows:
>
> (1) The Absolute Truth is contained in all the great Scriptures of the world, the Bible, the Koran, Torah, etc. However, the oldest known revealed Scriptures in existence are the Vedic literatures, most notably *Bhagavad Gita* which is the literal record of God's actual words.
>
> (2) God, or Krsna, is eternal, all-knowing, omnipresent, all-powerful and all-attractive, the seed-giving father of man and all living entities. He is the sustaining energy of all life, nature and the cosmic situation.
>
> (3) Man is actually not his body, but is eternal soul, part and parcel of God, and therefore, eternal.

(4) That all men are brothers can be practiced only when we realize God as our common father.

(5) All our actions should be performed as a sacrifice to the Supreme Lord: "... all that you do, all that you eat, all that you offer and give away, as well as all austerities that you may perform, should be done as an offering unto Me." (*Bhagavad-gita*, 9.27)

(6) The food that sustains us should always be offered to the Lord before eating. In this way He becomes the offering, and such eating purifies us.

(7) We can, by sincere cultivation of bona fide spiritual science, attain to the state of pure, unending blissful consciousness, free from anxiety, in this very lifetime.

(8) The recommended means to attain the mature stage of love of God in the present age of Kali, or quarrel, is to chant the holy name of the Lord. The easiest method for most people is to chant the Hare Krsna *mantra:* Hare Krsna, Hare Krsna, Krsna, Krsna, Hare, Hare/ Hare Rama, Hare Rama, Rama, Rama, Hare, Hare.

Our basic mission is to propagate the *sankirtana* movement [chanting of the holy names of God] all around the world, as was recommended by the incarnation of the Lord Sri Caitanya Mahaprabhu. . . .

It is not recommended that a Krsna conscious devotee go into seclusion to chant by himself and thereby gain salvation for himself alone. Our duty and religious obligation is to go out into the streets where the people in general can hear the chanting and see the dancing. . . .

It is hoped that the government authorities will cooperate with our *sankirtana* parties enabling us to perform *sankirtana* [chanting] on the streets. To do this it is necessary that we be able to chant the names of Krsna, dance, play the *mrdunga* drum, request donations, sell our society's journal, and on occasion, sit down with the *mrdunga* drum. As devotees of Lord Krsna, it is our duty to teach the people how to love God and worship Him in their daily life. This is the aim and destination of human life.[8]

Packed into this eightfold enumeration of primary ISKCON beliefs are numerous assumptions that are as much Indian as they are Vaisnava. That is, contained in Prabhupada's own faith are certain suppositions common to all native Indian religious traditions, whether Hindu, Buddhist, or other. It is there we should begin if we are to understand the attractiveness of ISKCON's teaching as outlined above.

The first assumption of Indian religions is that of *samsara* or the endless round of births and deaths of every living entity. Reincarnation is the English word most often used to translate this Indian conception. One dominant theistic formulation of this Hindu theological concept says that there is an essential self (*atman* or *jiva*) that undergoes one life after another in various living forms (human, plant, animal, etc.). Furthermore, the soul is of the same spiritual substance and character of God (Krishna), but is a distinct entity that maintains its independence even after liberation. It is this assumption that underlies Prabhupada's claim that "man is actually not his body, but is eternal spirit." According to Prabhupada, the deluded materialists—for him, atheists, historicists, and even most religionists fit this stereotype—

mistakenly believe that a person's identity is somehow linked to his or her body or at least to the time frame of that body. This is a basic form of spiritual ignorance and illusion from the point of view of Indian religious thinking. The real situation is that life follows life and death follows death in an endless chain that must be broken if the essential self (or "soul") is to be liberated.

One consequence of this teaching of the impermanence of this material world and the eternality of the spirit-soul and Krishna's divine realm is an antiworldly tendency that has characterized and shaped ISKCON's relationship to nondevotees from its earliest days in America. Stoner and Parke remark at the end of one interview with a Krishna married couple, "It seems only fair to note that this couple seems to carry some of the more notable Krishna traits, the anger and hostility to the world, for instance, to an extreme."[9] I would concur that especially up to 1975 or 1976, ISKCON's antimaterialist teachings produced a distinct distaste in devotees for the sensual world and all their past attachments to it (friends, family, etc.). However, a 1979 publication of the Krishna monthly magazine *Back to Godhead* qualifies this view with the reminder that Prabhupada had said that "this material world is zero. Bad. But if there is Krsna consciousness, then it has value. Then it has value."[10]

In recent years, then, some softening of relationships with *karmis*, or outsiders, has occurred as devotees have shifted their attention to developing ties with outside agencies and institutions and to establishing more broadly conceived Krishna communities than the more monastic model of the early ISKCON.

The establishment of the position of Steven Gelberg (Subhananda dasa) as ISKCON's person in charge of interreligious affairs in 1980 is but one example of the tempering of ISKCON's distrust of outsiders and desire to have dialogue with persons of other faiths. Nonetheless, it is still common to see in published interviews with ISKCON devotees their long-standing tendency to judge all persons and behavior external to ISKCON by the high standards of its antimaterial theology while making excuses for the very same kind of persons and behavior within ISKCON.

A second assumption that underlies much of Indian spirituality is the notion that one's subsequent births are the product of one's behavior and thought in a previous or current lifetime. In technical terms, one inherits good or bad consequences or fruits (*karma*) of one's actions in relationship to the performance or nonperformance of one's required religious duty (*dharma*). While this could be interpreted as a crass and mechanistic retribution theory based upon social and religious responsibilities, in the theistic context of the *Bhagavad Gita* it simply means that one's duty (*dharma*) must be complete and unequivocal devotion to God (Krishna). Thus Prabhupada quotes the famous *Bhagavad Gita* passage, "All that you do, all that you eat, . . . should be done as an offering to me" (*Gita* 9.27).

The third general understanding of Indian religions is that the religious practitioner is to a great extent responsible for his or her own salvation. In the Krishna context it is understood that Krishna's mercy is finally required for salvation. Nonetheless, regular and concentrated chanting of Krishna's name, studying Krishna scriptures, offering all food eaten to Krishna, and active preaching of Krishna's way to lost souls all constitute the heart of one's spiritual discipline (*sadhana*).

What is important for the Western reader to understand is that these assumptions are simply taken for granted in most Indian theistic texts. Consequently, when Prabhupada came to America to preach his Krishna faith he was really offering an alien yet attractive alternative worldview to many young people who had begun to question the materialist or historicist answers of their own culture.

More than half the devotees I interviewed said, "It was the philosophy," when asked what attracted them to ISKCON initially. When I questioned them further, it became clear that it was not the complete and sophisticated theology of Caitanya's successors or its full translation into modern terms by Prabhupada that these devotees had in mind. Rather, they felt that their lives confirmed the teaching that the material body is not our true or eternal self. One devotee said succinctly, "When I first heard the Krishnas preach 'You are not your body,' I just knew that it was true. My own life proved that it was true." In one way or another, this comment was repeated by one interviewee after another.

Thus, Krishna's lecture to Arjuna in the *Bhagavad Gita* more than two thousand years ago—devotees place this event five thousand years ago—is still relevant today for American and Indian Krishna devotees. The heart of that lecture given on the battlefield is clearly stated: "[The soul] is not born, nor does it ever die. . . . Unborn, eternal, everlasting, this ancient one is not slain when the body is slain" (*Gita* 2.20).

In a packet of three paperback books that ISKCON devotees have been offering to the general public during the past several years is one called *Coming Back: The Science of Reincarnation.* The book begins by quoting Socrates, Emerson, Hesse, and Tolstoy among others as those Western intellectuals who believed in reincarnation. The remainder of the book represents a defense of this premise as the most logical one to explain the human predicament and to offer hope for an escape from that predicament. Since its introduction into America, ISKCON's appeal has been based to a great extent upon the plausibility and appeal of the idea that each of us has within us a divine spark that seeks liberation from its pleasure-seeking and deluded material shell. For young people burned out on drugs, or just for the thoughtful person who seeks a happiness material success cannot buy, such a message has had some predictable existential attraction.

The story of Krishna likewise assumes the explanation of reincarnation as it proposes that the gopis in Vrindavana were all saints or special devotees in a previous lifetime. Also, the two trees that the young Krishna uprooted were simply viewed as the material shells of two souls whose previous lives required such a low rebirth. And the text of the story makes the point repeatedly that the souls of even the demons merged with Krishna when he destroyed their bodies. To the religious mind-set of persons raised in Christian or Jewish homes with an emphasis on the linear nature of history and the finality of each earthly life, reincarnation must surely appear as falsehood, blasphemy, or worse. My point is simply that the idea of reincarnation linked with the notion of the eternality of the soul has been for millions of people around the world (and for the Hare Krishnas in America) a viable alternative view.

The claim of Prabhupada that devotion to Krishna, as described in the *Bhagavad Gita,* is the highest duty of all adherents of all the world's religions moves beyond the general proposition of this Hindu text. The *Gita* does say that worship of the *devas,* or traditional Vedic gods, is worship of Krishna because he is the creator of all of them (*Gita* 9.20–25). However, it is clear that the *Gita* had in mind the myriad gods and goddesses that enjoyed reverence in India over the ages as those whom Krishna created and ruled (*Gita* 10.19–42). Yet Prabhupada, like Gandhi, Tagore, and other Indians before him with a Western education, did assume that the *Gita* 's assessment was truly a universal one. Hence, all the "gods" of the world are considered "demigods" by Prabhupada, and all specific religions (Hinduism, Christianity, Buddhism, etc.) are their culture-bound manifestations.

Prabhupada said, "When a man claims allegiance to some designated faith or sect, such as Hindu, Buddhist, Muslim, or Christian, this is not eternal. Such faiths can be changed. . . . *Sanatan Dharma* means the eternal religion . . . that which cannot be changed. . . . *Sanatan Dharma* lies outside of history, as it belongs to the living beings who have no birth and who never die."[11] Consequently, during his earliest days in America, Prabhupada claimed that he was preaching an eternal path that could not fairly be called a "religion." To this day, most of the devotees who introduce their teaching to potential converts proclaim honestly according to their master, "I am not preaching a new religion. I want you to listen to an eternal teaching about life." Prabhupada concludes, "Now, when we speak of Krishna, we should remember that this is not a sectarian name. Krishna means all pleasure. . . . The purpose of human life is to return to the Abode of the Lord [i.e., Krishna]."[12]

For many young Americans who were suspicious of their family "religions" and the mainline institutions those religions spawned, Prabhupada's message encouraged their spiritual quest without the stigma of calling their faith a religion. In the early days of the ISKCON movement in America when there were few regularized rituals or schedules and when each day, as one devotee told me, "was ours to live at play with Krishna," the Krishna faith *did* appear to be void of the trappings of religious institutions. However, as ISKCON has matured and struggled with the everyday problems of leadership, finances, and legal battles, the temple routines and daily ritual schedules look very much like their counterparts in monasteries and temples throughout the rest of the world. Furthermore, scholars of Hindu *bhakti,* or devotional traditions, would dispute Prabhupada's claim that Krishna is nonsectarian or that his teaching is eternal and culturally nonspecific.[13] Nonetheless, the fact remains that Krishna devotees argue they are presenting a spiritual path that is "transcendental" and "eternal" and not limited by the sectarian flavor of their family traditions. Sometimes these comparisons are more condescending than even the authors intend or realize.[14]

When Prabhupada says in his summary of basic beliefs that the Absolute Truth is contained in all the great scriptures of the world but that the *Bhagavad Gita* "is the literal record of God's actual words," he is really saying that he accepts the *Gita* 's pronouncement on this matter. This too is very Indian.

Every Indian guru or religious teacher throughout the ages claims his teachings to be consonant with the Vedas (literally, "knowledge" or "wisdom") —though which scriptures constitute the Vedas may differ greatly according to time and place.

Originally, the Vedas (four collections of hymns and incantations from the twelfth century B.C.) were constituted by the scriptures that were "heard" *(sruti)* by the ancient seers from the lips of the Divine itself. Throughout the ages in India, however, various theological schools have named their scriptures as the "true Vedas" or "end of the Vedas" (Vedanta). Consequently, the particular practice in ISKCON of chanting the name of Krishna as the primary religious discipline is associated with Caitanya's assertion that the Vedas, or ancient books of spiritual knowledge, are primarily the *Bhagavad Gita* and *Bhagavata Purana*. Not all Indian devotees of Krishna would agree. In short, many of the features of ISKCON's *sadhana,* or spiritual discipline, which we will see in practice in the next chapter, are not only culturally specific Indian ones but specifically sectarian ones not required by all Indian interpretations of what constitutes the Vedas.

On the one hand, then, the story that began this chapter reveals a god who intervenes in history to punish evil and to reward devotion. What the story portrays is the realization that Krishna's life is a divine play *(lila)*. Consequently, to speak of Krishna's *lila* is to recount the descent of the divine into a world that is transitory and yet deludes its citizens into believing their material lives in it are real. Krishna's multiplication of himself to be present with each gopi who adores him is one way of showing the playful seriousness with which he takes the world. But most important, the longing of the gopis after Krishna is finally not sexually motivated at all. Theirs is the desire for the eternal Lord that each devotee of Krishna should feel. On one level, then, the story of Krishna is a story of divine love and its reciprocation.

On the other hand, the story of Krishna is to be taken literally. For devotees, there is a spiritual world such as Vrindavana ruled over by the beautiful Lord Krishna. In one of his earliest publications, called *Easy Journey to Other Planets,* Prabhupada put his Krishna faith and teachings in a context he thought modern nonbelievers would understand. In this book he quoted a 1959 *Times of India* news release that said that two American atomic scientists had just been given a Nobel physics prize for their discovery of antiproton antiparticles. Prabhupada goes on in the next eighty pages to show how the Krishna scriptures confirm the antimaterial world as Krishna's luxurious abode. Throughout this book, as in many of his writings, Prabhupada takes seriously and literally the story of Krishna. The net effect for his students and disciples is that such books by their master prove the existence of a loving and personal god who does have a specific "transcendental" form and does live in his heavenly realm with the gopis.

What should be apparent to even the antagonistic reader is that Prabhupada's message was that one must completely love and serve Krishna—not Prabhupada. Of course, as we saw in chapter 2, the Krishna scriptures affirm the absolute necessity of each devotee having a spiritual guide who stands in the disciplic line of Krishna-Caitanya and serves as the conduit to God. This is an important teaching of ISKCON, namely, that Prabhupada was a direct representative of Krishna through the disciplic line *(parampara)* ordained by Krishna. Nonetheless, Krishna's abode is the ultimate goal, and to be as close to Krishna as the gopis is the heart's final desire.

What should also be obvious to the careful reader is that Prabhupada's message about Krishna is but one of several Indian alternatives. Caitanya's *sampradaya*, or "received tradition," is only one major sectarian strand among other Vaisnava or Krishnite alternatives. Nonetheless, it is but one of several major alternative views of the Vedas in general and the *Bhagavad Gita* in particular that are currently influential in India. Yet even when one recognizes that Prabhupada's faith is a sectarian one, it is clearly the case that he was not simply just another preacher from India. He was, for his disciples, a living example of the faith he taught. And even to many outsiders who met him, he was a pious example of the beliefs he preached.

The Logic of the Dark Lord

The claim of anticultists that the cults require a convert to give up his or her mind includes more than the notion discussed in the previous chapter as a surrender of will. Most anticultists and deprogrammers insist that the process of cult joining requires that one also give up all ability to question or to reason about those teachings which guide one's life in the cult. Andrew Pavlos speaks for many anticult writers when he says, "Religious dogma has often been a barrier to rational thinking and free and open inquiry. At the present time, the dogma of cults is more irrational and absolutist than that of more established religion."[15]

In her 1975 study of the Krishnas, Francine Daner seems to agree with Pavlos when she reports, "A former devotee [blooper] believes that the devotees are rejecting the mind's ability to think. While she was in the movement and was attending *Gita* classes, she would look around at the devotees sitting in the temple chanting japa [Krishna's names] silently and listening to the lecture, and all she could think of was Orwell's novel *1984*."[16] Daner sees this aspect of conversion to be just part of the greater ideological design that strips individuals of their old pre-Krishna identity and substitutes the new identity of the devoted servant.

A recorded conversation between Prabhupada and a graduate student in January 1974 seems to confirm ISKCON's inclusion in those groups which reject reason, or at least unfettered reflecting, as a condition of belief. The following exchange between guru and student is recorded:

STUDENT: But don't we have to experiment with different mental perspectives if we're going to understand the world?
SRILA PRABHUPADA: Actually, mental speculators have been condemned [in the Krishna scriptures] because they are simply carried away by the chariot of the mind. The mind is flickering, always changing. . . . All these mental speculations are doing just that. Somebody's putting forward some theory, and after a few years he will himself reject it. All these mental speculators [i.e., scientists, philosophers, and psychologists] are doing just that.[17]

While it is true that new devotees are encouraged to surrender themselves and their "mundane" thinking to their guru, it is not the case that this means one should stop thinking and reasoning altogether. What Prabhupada advocates in his discussion with the graduate student is the value of spiritual insight over human explanations. Here the old guru is mimicking the age-old Indian mistrust of the mind and its fleeting truths, which will be superseded by newly reasoned conclusions, and is encouraging instead faithful acceptance of the revealed truths of scriptures. He says, "So if you remain on the mental platform, . . . you'll never come to a lasting conclusion. One has to rise to the spiritual platform. That is eternal, everlasting."[18]

Such a preference for spiritual "solutions" to human questions and predicaments over disciplinary ones guided by reason alone (e.g., philosophical or scientific knowledge) is one commonly expressed by some person or sect in each of the world's religions—and one hotly contested as well. Prabhupada's view implies that reason's proper role is to be a handmaiden of faith, not its opponent. We can readily see the conflict that necessarily will arise between such a religious position (whether ISKCON's or fundamentalist Christian's) and the post-Enlightenment Western mind-set which tends to value reason above all else.

Langdon Gilkey, a contemporary Christian theologian, argues that indifference, not antagonism, leads the new religious movements to subordinate the role of reason to that of experience. He says, "My own brief relations to various groups have indicated that theological issues and convictions were important neither to the individual's conversion to the community nor to his or her continued loyalty to it. . . . These are religions of direct experience, and only secondarily of reflection and understanding."[19] In short, Gilkey says that not only do the Krishnas deny the importance of the faculty of reason but they also deny the value of a systematic or reasoned worldview (i.e, a theology). The evidence presented above would appear to offer exactly the contrary view.

Many social scientists and humanists alike recognize that whatever else religion is, it is first an ideological system. What anthropologist Anthony Wallace calls a "mazeway," theologian Michael Novak describes as a "standpoint," and what sociologist Peter Berger identifies as a "nomos" is what Clifford Geertz means when he says that "religion is a symbol system."[20] In their hurried rush to find malevolent psychological or social processes at work in cult conversions, *all* anticultists dismiss the possibility that the systematic religious worldview (i.e., the theology) that a given cult presents may, in fact, be enticing in itself. The same could be said of sympathetic scholars who vary only in their more positive evaluations of the "normal" processes that lead to affiliation.

A startling and unexpected conclusion forced itself upon this author after his four years of research into the Hare Krishna movement. The "philosophy" that Prabhupada taught was one of the critical factors, if not *the* critical factor, in the *majority* of the conversions to ISKCON of the more than one hundred devotees interviewed. Before my first three weeks of living in Krishna temples and interviewing devotees, it had seemed reasonable to me to expect primarily unconscious psychological and sociological processes at work in most devotee conversions. Such was not the case. Yes, it is true that emotional upheaval and distress were attendant—and still are—upon most conversions. This fact should not be surprising to anyone who has read William James's *The Varieties of Religious Experience.*[21] However, as we shall see in chapter 7, the picture of the instantaneous and unpredictable conversion is far less universal than the anticult rhetoric would have us believe.

What the interviews, participant observation, and a broad-based collection of information revealed was that most devotees studied and reflected upon Eastern philosophy for months or years prior to contact with ISKCON. Furthermore, more than 80 percent of the devotees interviewed took longer than six months to join ISKCON after their first contact. Consequently, most converts to ISKCON did consider critically what Prabhupada taught both before and after becoming a Krishna devotee. Simply put, most converts joined ISKCON because they found plausible its "philosophy" regarding the need for a spiritual master who can assist the devotee in the discovery of his or her true self and in finding the way back to God, that is, Krishna.

Clifford Geertz has given us a good way to understand the interrelationship of the conceptual and affective dimensions of a religion like ISKCON. In a seminal article entitled "Religion as a Cultural System," Geertz concludes:

> Religion is: (1) a system of symbols which acts to (2) establish powerful, pervasive, and long-lasting moods and motivations in men by (3) formulating conceptions of a general order of existence and (4) clothing these conceptions with such an aura of factuality that (5) the moods and motivations seem uniquely realistic.[22]

From this point of view, a religious tradition provides an *interpretive conceptual system* that organizes adherents' everyday experiences in a meaningful way. Geertz agrees with Salvador de Madariaga, who says that a minimal definition of religion must assert "the relatively modest dogma that God is not mad"[23] —that is, that every religious worldview, whether Christian, Jewish, or Vaisnava, does make sense and have an inner logic.

For Geertz, religious symbols are those religious acts, objects, events, or statements which "serve as a vehicle for conception."[24] Religious symbols serve both as "models of" (i.e., they reflect) and "models for" (i.e., they shape) the cultures in which they arise. For example, the very name of Krishna reflects his Indo-European cultural roots and yet his "play" *(lila)* in the world calls into question commonsense feelings about the permanence of the material world. Prabhupada's conception of Krishna is thus reflective of (i.e., a model of) the Indian linguistic, cultural, and textual traditions in India pertaining to Hindu "high gods" and yet shapes (i.e., provides a model for) some distinctive conclusions of that heritage (e.g., that the divine and impersonal Brahman is actually the supreme and personal Krishna). In Geertz's formulation, religious symbols "give meaning, i.e., objective conceptual form, to social and psychological reality both by shaping themselves to it and by shaping it to themselves."[25]

Symbols shape an adherent's life by inducing in the devotee a distinct set of dispositions (i.e., "moods") and inclinations toward action (i.e., "motivations") that lend an identifiable and usually coherent character to his or her life. In the Krishna case, an attitude (mood) comprised of submission and awe linked with a fervent intention (motivation) to praise and to serve Krishna determines the way the ideology intends to shape each devotee and his or her actions. In other words, a religion's theology or ideology affects, in a systematic fashion, the way a person experiences and understands himself or herself and interacts with the outside world. In sum, the different assumptions and assertions encapsulated in Prabhupada's rendering of his received Bengali Krishna faith fit into a coherent, interpretive whole.

Consequently, any one conceptual statement taken out of context will often lose its religious import and appear ridiculous or offensive to an outsider. This is exactly what happens when anticult antagonists quote Krishna in the *Gita* as telling Arjuna to kill his friends and relatives *without* bothering to mention that the context for that statement was a long monologue whose intent was to convince Arjuna that his transitory body and eternal soul were two distinct entities. Furthermore, it is clear that the *Gita* is *not* advocating that devotees under any circumstances kill parents or relatives who do not support ISKCON! And it was precisely this kind of caricature of ISKCON's "immoral and irrational" theology that was presented in the celebrated Robin George trial where the prosecution cited the above *Gita* passage as proof that the Krishnas actually taught this young woman to hate her parents and to consider killing her mother![26]

It was not simply one aspect of the Krishnas' teachings, such as "You are not your body" or "You can reach Krishna only through a spiritual master," that appealed to the devotees who were interviewed. It was the whole, seamless web of ideas—though often only partially understood—that seemed reasonable and could stand rational scrutiny. And, as we shall see in the next chapter, it is in the ritual life and in the moral discipline that the moods and motivations explained in the symbol system "seem uniquely realistic."[27] What Prabhupada provided for his young disciples was an alternative and specifically detailed Indian theistic interpretation of the world to satisfy the religious questions they were raising.

And what are those religious questions? Geertz says that it is when interpretive chaos threatens an individual that religious answers are often marshaled. He says:

> There are at least three points where chaos—a tumult of events which lack not just interpretations but *interpretability*—threatens to break in upon man: at the limits of his analytic capacities, at the limits of his powers of endurance, and at the limits of his moral insight. Bafflement, suffering, and a sense of an intractable ethical paradox are all . . . challenges with which any religion which hopes to persist must attempt somehow to cope.[28]

It is when, as one interviewee said, "my life seemed to make no sense" or "I didn't know who to believe" that the religious web of meaning contained in Prabhupada Krishna faith did provide an interpretive framework for the seeking convert.[29] Religion must provide interpretations, if not solutions, for the unexpected death of a child, the seemingly undeserved suffering of a friend, or—as was often the case for Krishna converts—for times when the institutions of one's religion and country both appear hopelessly embroiled in defense of a materialistic life-style or a Vietnam War that seems indefensible.[30] What religious symbol systems do, says Geertz, is not to provide simple answers for every chaotic event, but rather to teach one how to endure and to make bearable war, death, suffering, and other such chaotic events.[31]

In relation to the point that Rothbaum and his associates made in chapter 4, the Krishna story and Prabhupada's theological interpretation of it provide

Krishna devotees with a protective and secondary "interpretive control." Whether this interpretation is only partially understood at a time when chaos threatens to overwhelm the convert, or is fully understood by the mature devotee, ISKCON's Krishna theology does provide a detailed religious world-view. And to put the whole matter in a more positive frame of reference, for those persons who are sincerely seeking a positive frame of reference and meaning (cf. Frankl's *Man's Search for Meaning*), ISKCON's theology provides one religious solution to the perennial religious or spiritual quest. A significant number of Krishna converts who were interviewed seemed really to be seeking a religious faith they could trust, when they found ISKCON.

Contrary to the claims of the anticultists that conversion to the cults is a move from rationality to irrationality, we can assert that faith in Krishna *does* make sense—once one is inside the whole symbol system and sees the relationship of the parts to the whole. Furthermore, in opposition to Gilkey's claim that theological issues and convictions are not important to cult converts, I can only say that the opposite is true for the Krishna devotees I interviewed. Precisely because Krishna devotees were attracted to ISKCON's theology, they were not likely candidates to become Moonies or Jesus Freaks.[32] Whatever else attracted converts to ISKCON, the cogency of the Krishna worldview and story was a major one.

Ideological Totalism?

Marcia and James Rudin link what they perceive to be the antirationalism of cults with a fanatic and total commitment to the cult or its leader as particularly destructive aspects of groups such as the Hare Krishnas. In their list of characteristics of "destructive cults" they include:

> Members swear total allegiance to an all-powerful leader whom they may believe to be a Messiah. . . . Rational thought is discouraged or forbidden. The groups are anti-intellectual, placing all emphasis on intuition or emotional experience. . . . The cult or its leader makes every career or life decision for the follower. The Hare Krishna group regulates every hour of activity for those members who dwell in the temples. The cults determine every aspect of the adherent's personal life, including sexual activities, diet, use of liquor, drugs and tobacco. . . . Career and schooling may be abandoned and all other interests discouraged so that the cult becomes the follower's total world.[33]

The Rudins state clearly here a message repeated time and again by those who warn of not only the irrationalism of the cults but their fanatical totalism as well.

The best-defended of the anticult critiques cites what is viewed by some to be the classical statement on ideological totalism, namely, Robert Jay Lifton's book *Thought Reform and the Psychology of Totalism*. In his study of "brainwashing" in Chinese communist prison camps during the Korean War, Lifton defines *ideological totalism* as "the coming together of immoderate ideology with equally immoderate individual character traits—an extremist meeting ground between people and ideas."[34] Lifton continues:

> Any ideology—that is, any set of emotionally-charged convictions about a man and his relationship to the natural or supernatural world—may be carried by its

adherents in a totalistic direction. But this is most likely to occur with those ideologies which are most sweeping in their content and most ambitious—or messianic—in their claims, whether religious, political, or scientific. And where totalism exists, a religion, a political movement, or even a scientific organization becomes little more than an exclusive cult.[35]

The primary concern of persons who call the cults "totalistic" or "fanatical" is that the cult members have sacrificed not only their reasoning ability but also their self-identity. The image of the robot or the zombie is one of a person whose total personality is altered by the cult, so that *all* that is thought or done is dictated by cult ideology and authorities. One's previous sense of self is destroyed and replaced by a cult-defined self. Francine Daner's interpretation of ISKCON as an institutional and ideological system makes this point.

Daner uses *Asylums,* the work on "total institutions" by Erving Goffman, to describe conversion to ISKCON:

> Entrance into the temple provides a crucial self-degrading ritual whereby many disoriented individuals find new identities as devotees. . . . A Krishna-consciousness temple setting can be considered a total institution as Goffman defines it in *Asylums.* . . . These institutions are "forcing houses for changing persons; each is a natural experiment on what can be done to the self." . . . One's self-concept (identity) is directly attacked by depriving him of the deference which his accustomed demeanor brought him outside the temple.[36]

According to this point of view, the ideology of the Krishnas regarding surrender to the guru and seeing the self as an eternal soul and not the body has the effect of cutting the devotee off from other points of view regarding these matters. Daner says, "One surrenders desires, thoughts, and actions to Krsna so that one's own will becomes completely dovetailed with Krsna's. . . . The devotee faces a constant struggle to maintain his attitude of bhakti [devotion] by subjecting himself to degradations and assaults on his identity which are designed to detach him from his former self-concept."[37]

We have already seen in chapter 4 the problem with assuming that the surrender of a new convert's will is either complete or destructive to self-control. What is even more problematic is the assumption that Krishna theology really *is* determinative of every act, thought, or decision a devotee makes. Yes, that is the ideal, but not the way it works in practice. While living in one ISKCON farm community, I stayed in a farmhouse that also served as the quarters for the male devotees who were dairy workers. I can imagine what a parent would have thought if he or she had visited this place. There were young men all with shaven heads, ocher robes, and Sanskrit names looking very much the same—much as a group of Marines or Catholic schoolchildren in uniforms do. The highly stylized and repetitive speech of these devotees seemed to confirm the existence of the "private language" syndrome common in closed communities.

But as the devotees in the house began to settle down for the night and I lay quietly on my mattress on the floor contemplating the next day's interviews, I heard a counseling session through the thin wall that separated my room from an adjoining one. That discussion went, in part:

DEVOTEE 1: You *must* surrender to your guru. That is the only way to Krishna's abode.

DEVOTEE 2: I have tried, but I can't. I have tried to keep up my chanting, and have tried to keep the four vows, but keep falling down [i.e., failing]. It all seems so futile.

DEVOTEE 1: But you know what the scriptures say [long quote in Sanskrit]. Only those devoted to Krishna will be liberated.

DEVOTEE 2: Yes, I know. I know! But the harder I try, the less progress I seem to make. Furthermore, I look all around me and see devotees who are puffed up and yet fall down all the time. I am sick and tired of working in the barn with ——. He is so arrogant. I just want to leave.

DEVOTEE 1: But where will you go? You know that sex and success will only lead you further into *maya* [the material world]. You have tried that road once and look where it got you, half dead on drugs. You know too much to go back now.

DEVOTEE 2: But what difference does all that make when devotees act like *karmis* [nondevotees] anyway. I'm not sure I can stay.

The next day I learned that both devotees in that adjoining room were older disciples who had been in ISKCON for more than three years. What is important about their discussion (which went on for more than an hour) is not only what it says about the tentativeness of "surrender" or commitment to one's guru and ISKCON's teachings but what it reveals about the ability of devotees privately to doubt and to criticize (i.e., to think rationally) as they compare their ideology to the actions of themselves and others. It is hardly the case *in practice* that all of a devotee's "desires, thoughts and actions" are controlled by Krishna ideology. Rather, the ideology serves as a guiding interpretation of the world, the Divine, and oneself that is imperfectly (not totalistically) lived by devotees.

Because the Krishna faith does challenge all social norms and values built on material success with its "otherworldly" emphasis on self-discipline and devotion to Krishna, ISKCON will appear "immoderate" to critics who value secular education, vocational success, and mainline social institutions. However, *all* religious traditions of the world radically question the values and institutions of the material world as they insist on a higher, spiritual perspective and valuation.[38] Nonetheless, neither the materialistic view nor ISKCON's theology is really "totalistic" in the conceptual sense.

ISKCON's worldview and that of the everyday world overlap at many points—for example, on the nature and function of electricity or a printing press. It is the priority of ISKCON's interpretation of the values and aims of life over that offered by the materialists that is the issue. Consequently, it is not so much *what* the ideology says that makes it totalistic but *how* one holds that worldview that makes totalism an issue. It is from this perspective that fanaticism is a virtual synonym for totalism.

The Fanatic and the Liberal

None of us who have followed the events in Iran in the late 1970s and early 1980s can doubt that religious fanaticism can be a destructive mind-set. The disagreement arises over what constitutes fanaticism. On the one hand, as the Ayatollah Khomeini has aroused the religious fervor of hundreds of thousands of Iranians, many onlookers have attributed the resultant suffering, death, and destruction (from the American hostages to the Iran-Iraq war) to the violent tenets of the Islamic Shi'ite religion.

It can appear from the Iranian hostage crisis that religious fanaticism is a product of the *content* of faith, in this case, the Islamic notion of *jihad*, or "holy war." On the other hand, most analysts of the Jonestown massacre attributed that religious holocaust to the blind faith and obedience of the followers of Jim Jones (excepting those who were apparently killed while trying to escape). In the first instance, fanaticism has to do with *what* a religious ideology says and in the second case, with *how completely* and fervently an ideology—in the Jonestown case, a self-destructive one—is personally held by adherents. Ideological totalism, as defined by Lifton earlier, requires both extremes.

We have seen—contrary to the anticult view—that the content of ISKCON's theology is not inherently extreme or dangerous. On the other hand, many ISKCON devotees are guilty of a closed-minded attitude that borders on fanaticism at times. In making this assessment, we are simply recognizing that ISKCON devotees are not immune to the tendencies toward extremes of commitment apparent in new converts to *any* religion or ideology (or in those of a persecuted religious tradition). In chapter 7, we shall explore James Fowler's notions of stages of faith that explain the differences between new and mature levels of faith. Here we should simply note that one reason why ISKCON devotees—and those of other cults too—are often taken to be lost in ideological totalism is not the radical or extreme claims of their adopted faith but rather the uncompromising way in which they espouse what they believe.

One characteristic of the new converts to ISKCON that became obvious from interviews and observation over four years is their tendency to try to embrace unflinchingly and completely the tenets of their fragile new faith. Quite naturally, such new converts appeared to parents and outsiders as "blind followers." For example, the new devotees who were interviewed gave theological answers "by the book," with literal interpretations of scriptures and beliefs being commonplace. Some interviewees tried to preach to their interviewer out of the fervor of their new commitment but were unable to debate their position effectively when presented with information or arguments they had not yet been instructed to refute.

It seems fair to conclude, then, that what many anticult critics assume to be a new convert's *inability to think* because of the implantation by brainwashing of a totalistic ideology is actually nothing other than the *attempt at total immersion* in a faith one is not fully familiar with or comfortable defending. As Eric Hoffer says, "The true believer is without wonder and hesitation."[39]

In a fascinating study done over two decades ago, Milton Rokeach explored the nature of belief systems and how rigidly people hold the beliefs they espouse. His book, *The Open and Closed Mind*, startled those who believed that persons on the far right or left of the ideological spectrum were necessarily more rigid or closed-minded than those people holding views more toward the center. His book begins:

The relative openness or closedness of a mind cuts across specific content; that is, it is not uniquely restricted to any one particular ideology, religion, or philosophy, or scientific viewpoint. A person may adhere to communism, existentialism, Freudianism, or the "new conservatism," in a relatively open or in a relatively closed manner.[40]

Rokeach saw as fallacious the argument that those persons who rely on an external authority (whether persons or scriptures) are more apt to be closed-minded. He consciously argued with the findings of T. W. Adorno, who felt that far right religious attitudes led to racial or religious intolerance. Rokeach concluded instead that all knowledge relies to greater or lesser extents on external authorities (scientists, doctors, weathercasters, historians, etc.). Consequently, dependence on an external authority is not the issue; it is the character of that dependence that is the key.[41]

In general, Rokeach found that the more flexible and discriminating a person was when encountering an opposing belief system, the more open-mindedly that person held his or her own beliefs. On the other hand, the closed-minded person was rigid and inflexible in dealing with new beliefs and reacted in an "all or nothing" way to ideological challenge.[42] Rokeach concluded that "a basic characteristic that defines the extent to which a person's system is open or closed . . . is the extent to which the person can receive, evaluate, and act on relevant information received from the outside on its own intrinsic merits."[43]

Perhaps the most frustrating aspect of a parent's or any other outsider's attempt to communicate with many Krishna devotees is their constant quotations from Krishna scriptures to validate ISKCON's viewpoint over against that of any other view expressed. Clearly the most annoying aspect of my four years of conversations and living with devotees was to hear many of the leaders brag about "defeating" all their opponents with their newfound faith and its scriptures. I was often reminded of Rokeach's judgment that all belief systems are also disbelief systems. That is, those who have a need for a cognitive framework to provide meaning and understanding also use that system to ward off threatening aspects of other belief systems.[44] Quite often, those who *need* to defeat others' belief systems are the least able to do so to anyone's but their own satisfaction.

Rokeach postulated that one cause of closed-mindedness is the anxiety produced by social upheaval and the consequent personal uncertainty in what to trust and value.[45] In other words, for the person in turmoil about basic questions of meaning and truth, a need arises for the security of a single all-encompassing belief system that one can accept with no compromises or qualifications. It is not surprising, then, that the new convert is closed-minded as he or she struggles to believe completely what he or she so strongly defends.

It also should not be surprising that those persons in positions of authority who are charged with the maintenance of ISKCON's traditions and institutions often remain at a relatively dogmatic and immature stage of faith as they interact with others both inside and outside the movement. There are both new devotees and established gurus who present and defend their Krishna faith in a "take it or leave it" fashion. These are the hardliners when it comes to dealing with criticisms or challenges from the outside. For example, one public relations spokesman in Los Angeles consistently makes announcements that deny ISKCON's affiliation with or responsibility for devotees who come into conflict with the law, while the facts may vary considerably from case to case. In many cases, the denials are accurate, while in others they are little more than self-righteous, defensive rationalizations.[46]

Some Krishna devotees laughed during their interviews at the immaturity of their early faith and at their insensitivity to the way those attitudes and behaviors could be perceived by their parents and critics. One such devotee reported that he tried to convert his parents over the phone on the day he called to inform them of his own conversion! Another devotee said, "I must have looked like a flaming radical to my parents, who did not realize how far I had grown away from their conservative Christian faith." Yet another remarked, "I spoke confidently of Krishna to everyone, but in my heart was not sure at all." In every such description of their early Krishna faith, the devotee remarked how much more congenial or improved relations were with his or her family when the early period of enthusiasm gave way to a more mature and reflective faith.

One sign of a maturing Krishna faith is a devotee's ability to appreciate and enter into dialogue with other religious and nonreligious standpoints. One such devotee, Subhananda dasa, reflects a minority but growing interest in ISKCON with improving relationships with scholars and religious leaders outside ISKCON. Subhananda keeps up an impressive correspondence with many professors and scholars of Asian religions in America, Europe, India, and around the world. One example of the fruits of this effort is *Hare Krishna, Hare Krishna,* a book of interviews on ISKCON with five noted scholars, by Subhananda (Steven Gelberg is his pre-Krishna name). In addition, though Jewish by birth and a Krishna devotee by choice, Subhananda regularly visits a Catholic monastic retreat to experience that form of spirituality as an aid to understanding a religious tradition not his own.

What also puts Subhananda in the minority of the devotees who were interviewed or observed is his mature and nondefensive assessment of ISKCON as an institution and a way of life. Conversations into the late hours of the days and nights of the weeks spent traveling together from one Krishna temple to the next confirmed an early impression that some devotees of ISKCON could not only tolerate the imperfections of other religious institutions but even qualify the usually unbridled praise of their own.

Such maturity of perspective as I found in seasoned Krishna devotees like Subhananda dasa and Satsvarupa dasa Goswami, though hardly universal, stood out in stark contrast to the more dogmatic, inflexible, and self-aggrandizing styles of many of ISKCON's new devotees and some of the new gurus and institutional authorities. It should be clear, however, that length of time and official positions in the movement are not the only significant variables in determining open- and closed-mindedness in devotees. The preconversion attitudes and life-styles of devotees also clearly affected the ways they appropriated their new faith. As Adorno noted more than three decades ago, "It may be that the mere acceptance or rejection of religion is not so important as *how* the individual accepts or rejects it, that is to say, the pattern of his ideas about religion."[47]

To a great extent, preconversion attitudes and personal qualities do carry over into the new "style" of believing. As David Loye points out so well in his study of the ideological personality, it is not the liberal or conservative nature of the *content* of a religious or political ideology that makes a person a fanatic or an ideologue; it is the unreasonable extreme to which the ideology is taken and the extent to which it serves as a model for excessive speech and action. For example, fasting may be an aid to piety in the Christian faith, but fasting that leads to ill health may undermine the effectiveness of the very committed life it was intended to enhance. Thus, as Loye concludes, the ideological personality is a wedding of "ideology—extremism—activism."[48]

Consequently, *any* ideology is capable of being misused and misapplied and of subverting even its own stated aims. It is precisely this phenomenon that Melton and Moore in their book *The Cult Experience* describe when they discuss "the new bigotry." They argue that "those who consider themselves children of the Enlightenment—militant secular humanists, arrogant reductionists, and intellectually and ethically proud liberal religionists—are the most susceptible to the temptations of the new bigotry."[49] Melton and Moore argue convincingly that it is precisely those who claim reason as their "God" and liberality and tolerance as their guides who are the most passionate in denouncing not only the cults but any religion or religious worldview that is expressed with any seriousness or passion.

It is also such "liberal" psychologists and educators who often demand that their extremely optimistic views on reason and pessimistic attitudes regarding religion and/or the cults be accepted and acted upon by parents of Krishna converts to "save" their children. We will see in chapter 8 how such defenders of rationality and free will act to subvert precisely those values they espouse. In sum, it is not the story of Krishna, the Dark Lord, nor the Enlightenment story of the supremacy of reason that makes fanatics or moderates among holders of those traditions; it is how those stories are appropriated and lived that seems to make the difference.

The story of Krishna told at the beginning of this chapter is a myth. But unlike the popular view that says that myths are fictitious stories or tales, in all religious traditions the story of one's sacred reality is the most true story one can tell and live.[50] For example, for Christians the story of Jesus' baptism and of the final meal with his disciples are two episodes of God's contact with his children that are remembered as critical encounters with God that are to be reenacted in the communities' worship life. Likewise, the story ("myth") of the Buddha's search for and acquisition of enlightenment has served as a model for literally millions of Buddhist monks and nuns over the past twenty-five hundred years. In like fashion, the answer to this chapter's basic question, Why worship a blue god? is a simple one: because it *makes sense* to live within the symbolic and meaningful universe circumscribed by Krishna's *lila*, or play.

6

New Identities: Secure in the Arms of Krishna

Of all the anticult stereotypes, none is so powerful and pervasive as the image of an intelligent young person being turned into a manipulated, unthinking, undernourished "zombie" or "robot" by the cults. Even when other charges against the cults seem not to fit a certain group, the claim that the cults change the actual identity *and* behavior of their converts appears plausible. For example, are not new converts of the Krishnas cut off from their families and old "material lives" and swept into a secretive community that bestows on them a new, foreign name, Indian dress, vegetarian diet, and mind-numbing chant? Is not this new life oriented around totally different values that entice young persons into begging on the streets, pestering travelers in the airports, and working endless hours each day for no pay?

Not only does the new devotee exhibit observable physical changes different from previous ones but the devotee's behavior and demeanor change as well. For example, anticultists who describe the Hare Krishnas speak of the vacuous look or "the thousand mile stare" associated with devotees dancing on the street or in the temple with the Krishna mantra on their lips. Ted Patrick puts this view of the Krishnas most bluntly: "They're simply into self-hypnosis. They are programmed to chanting and their beads and once you prevent them from doing that, it's a snap to make them see how they've been deceived."[1]

Even if one does not agree with Patrick's analysis, it is true that the Hare Krishnas' public chanting and dancing *(sankirtan)*, bookselling in the airports, and public festival displays all call attention to a real change in behavior that a new convert must undergo to be faithful to the new worldview. That is, there is necessarily a change in both personal appearance and behavior that is associated with accepting the new world of Krishna as outlined in chapter 5. The logic necessitating this change is the subject of this chapter as we look behind the devotee's gaze. Here is Lakshmi's story.

I was truly a child of the counterculture. Born in 1950 as the youngest of three daughters to a Jewish family in upstate New York, I was raised in a cultural-ethnic background. My father was an atheist and my mother was a

typical Jewish mother—anxious for her children to become educated and suc-
ceed in the material world. I was an A student from the time I entered elemen-
tary school until I graduated from high school. I was also an adventuresome
spirit who was never satisfied with my peers' social status quo. I guess I hung
around with the wrong crowd early in my high school years and had a dark side
of my life which, from the outside, nobody could see.

I was into drugs by my junior year in high school, and advanced from the mild
stuff to LSD by my senior year. The night of my graduation, my parents arrived
at the school only to discover that I had not come to my own graduation. I was
out with some friends blowing my mind with drugs. I also was active sexually
in high school and often felt guys took advantage of me in that way. I didn't go
steady, so I got to know lots of boys well during my high school years.

My parents moved to California about this time and I went with them. I
entered Los Angeles Junior College and remained in the drug and rock concert
scene. My mother had a nervous breakdown from all the grief we children were
causing her but had been weak emotionally ever since I was born. Even though
I was into the counterculture scene, I still was an A student when I shifted from
the junior college to UCLA.

At UCLA, I lived in off-campus housing which gave me even more opportunity
to live the life-style of a hippie. I became a vegetarian mostly because my friends
were but also because I had begun to read Asian philosophies which encouraged it. I still enjoyed sex and continued to take drugs to attempt to expand
my consciousness. I joined in anti-Vietnam War groups and protests and began
to question the traditions I had been taught. I got into a variety of alternative
psychology groups that had nothing to do with religion but promised to teach
us how to "find ourselves." I also was introduced by one of my professors to
Hatha Yoga [physical postures and disciplines based on Indian religious teach-
ings].

I ran into the Hare Krishnas—this would be 1970—dancing and singing on
campus and occasionally even went to one of their feasts. I listened to them
preach about chanting the name of Krishna and even tried the chant a time or
two myself. But I never dreamed of becoming a devotee. I was reading this
philosophy and trying that yoga, trying to find out what the truth was.

Then I decided to drop out of school for a while and look for meaning beyond
school and books. I went with a male friend to Colorado, where he said we
could find fellow seekers. Instead, we spent six months in the Rockies making
love and doing drugs. After a stint at school again, I went back to California—
commune hopping along the way. I was introduced to peyote on my California
trip and traveled with a self-proclaimed guru and his wife for a while. However,
wherever I went, all the men tried to exploit me. I was seeking truth and all they
wanted was a sex life.

Upon my return to UCLA the fall of 1972, I stopped drugs and did more yoga.
I did very well in school that year and finally graduated the spring of 1973.
During the year, I had met an American artist who had lived in South America.
He called himself Soma, which was a name some guru had given him. We
started living together and I agreed to go back to South America with him. He
got me back on hard drugs and I had such an adverse reaction that I could
hardly stand the noise of a car starting or door slamming. He convinced me that
we were just like husband and wife. So I moved to a hacienda in Colombia with
him when I graduated.

My year and a half in Colombia was fraught with problems as I searched for
some lasting satisfaction. I moved from place to place with Soma and tried all
kinds of drugs, native roots, and other intoxicants. This whole time, I was trying
to find out who God was and who I was and what the purpose of life was. I knew

that I didn't want to live in this materialistic society. I didn't want to live like my parents and friends lived nor like my friends had lived. But what I was doing wasn't real either, like taking these intoxicants and having always to come down.

After I followed Soma to an island off the coast of Colombia, he abandoned me for another woman. I returned to the hacienda where I had begun my South American sojourn and buried myself deeper into drugs. My body began to protest and I became very ill. A girlfriend of mine came from America to visit me and convinced me to come back home to California. Since my visa was running out anyway, I returned home.

I lived with my parents for a short time before I returned to school. While at my parents' house, I went on a yoga retreat and gave up all intoxicants. Then I moved into Muktananda's retreat center located in an old house off campus. The first time Muktananda came to the center, I saw a divine light and became convinced that yogic practice centered upon Shiva [an Indian deity] would lead me to my long-awaited goal. I began a very disciplined yogic practice of praying to Shiva and practicing Siddhi Yoga. I was very attracted to the Shiva mantra, om nama sivaya ["Oh, praise the name of Shiva"], which formed the basic practice of those living in the center.

The Hare Krishnas would come to Muktananda's house from time to time to preach against the impersonalism of Muktananda's teachings. They said that Siddhi Yoga was just a higher form of materialistic philosophy. I would become very angry with them and came to dislike them very much. Nonetheless, I once went with a friend to the Krishnas' Sunday feast and saw a film of Prabhupada crossing the Ganges River in India with his devotees. I just cried. I thought he looked so pure. Then I said to myself, Why am I crying? These are the Hare Krishnas!

A short time after my experience in the Krishna temple, Soma returned from Colombia and convinced me that Muktananda's trip was not the true path. So I traveled with Soma to the mountains of California to continue my search on my own. While in California, I met this boy named Rudra [another name for Shiva]. Muktananda had earlier predicted that I would meet a young man named Rudra, and I thought his prophecy was coming true. So, although I had been burned by one man after another, I began to travel with this young man five years my junior. As I was soon to discover, Rudra was not a Shiva devotee but was a Krishna "fringie."

Rudra would chant the Hare Krishna mantra while I chanted the Shiva mantra. He had been involved with other Krishna devotees but had never joined ISKCON. Nonetheless, he preached Krishna philosophy to me—especially the notion that God is a person and not an impersonal absolute. He gave me beads to use in chanting and taught me Krishna philosophy from the Krishna books. We lived for a time on a commune where the leader finally pronounced us husband and wife.

In 1976 I went with Rudra to the L.A. temple to meet Prabhupada. We stayed for one week and I became convinced that ISKCON was authentic because its guru was pure. One moment's association with a pure devotee is enough to free one. And though I didn't think I wanted to join the L.A. temple, I was impressed with Prabhupada's obvious devotion. Rudra and I lived in California as fringe devotees for several months after meeting Prabhupada. We lived from hand to mouth. Then we decided to go to Hawaii, where we heard a new Krishna community was being built.

When we arrived in Hawaii, we stayed with a fallen devotee named Gaurasundar. Before long we decided that the Hawaii community was not serious at all about religious seeking. So Rudra and I decided to get married legally and return to New York City, where my parents had offered to help support us while Rudra learned the piano-tuning trade. Shortly after arriving in New York, I heard Satsvarupa speak, and when you hear a pure devotee speak, all doubts are removed. It was at that time that my husband and I decided that we both would formally commit ourselves to Krishna and join an ISKCON temple.

Rudra and I went to the Los Angeles temple to join because he knew Ramesvara, the initiating guru of that region. It was in October of 1978 that I first met Ramesvara. We had arrived in Miami only two days earlier, and when we met this young guru, my husband asked him if he would accept him as a disciple. Since Ramesvara knew my husband from an earlier time, he accepted him immediately. He then turned to me and said, "And what about you?" I said I wanted to join and he accepted me even though I had not been living in the temple. . . . For me it was a dream come true that I had had from my high school days, that is to find a spiritual master.

The Los Angeles temple did not have additional space for a married couple, so my husband and I lived in separate quarters with the young *brahmacaris* [unmarried male devotees] and *brahmacarinis* [unmarried female devotees]. My husband moved out after a short time and began to tune pianos and fall into old material habits. He got an outside apartment and began to get involved with drugs and illicit sex all over again. He took off for Hawaii again and tried to get me to go with him. I talked with Ramesvara and he discouraged me from going.

Since I was so upset from my husband's behavior, I got to talk to my spiritual master a lot, and he encouraged me to focus my attention on my spiritual life and not on my material relationship with my husband. I talked with my husband from time to time and finally decided to divorce him. Though he was fallen, living with another woman, and had a child by her, he said he still wanted me. He threatened to kill himself if I didn't come to him.

I talked to the temple president and he said that if my husband wanted spiritual advice, he would have called a *sannyasi* or his spiritual master; but to have called his former wife, it was clear that he was just trying to play on my emotions. . . . I concluded that I would never take him again as my husband. He has so much material success and yet is so miserable. I have found something that is permanent, my faith and devotion to Krishna. I don't want to turn back now.

Now that I'm in the Hare Krishna temple I'm protected by my spiritual master, the temple president, and by Krishna. [The] temple president is very advanced spiritually. All he cares about is my spiritual life. He has no real need for sense gratification, like "What can I get from her?" There is no illicit connection there. . . . Krishna is clearly protecting me through my spiritual master and his representatives.

In Krishna consciousness, I am actually happy. I get up, chant my rounds, serve the deities, and assist other devotees. . . . And if I have any problems, I call my spiritual master. Someone always wanted to exploit me at the other centers, supposedly spiritual centers. But I don't have that anxiety anymore. This is the first place that has been interested only in my spiritual life. I don't have the anxiety anymore that I will be used sexually. There is a special taste in the Krishna temple and its chanting.

Listening to the tapes of my spiritual master is also an aid to my spirituality. It helps quiet the chattering of my mind. Listening to a spiritual master is like waking up and learning how to purify one's heart, how to engage in Krishna consciousness, how to help other people. And Srila Prabhupada's books are likewise a help to spiritual progress. I see Ramesvara as my spiritual father and Prabhupada as my spiritual grandfather. Everything is contained in Prabhupada's books and tapes. Before, I was going here and there for answers to my spiritual questions. Now I go only to Prabhupada's books. His philosophy is so deep, so deep. It just explains everything. . . . Given my past experience, I am happy to just have Krishna as my husband and his protection through his bona fide representatives.

The Inauguration of a New Life

While Lakshmi actually learned various facets of ISKCON life and ritual prior to her joining the Los Angeles temple, the formal introduction into the Krishna faith is done with two formal stages of initiation. The first is called the *Hare Nama Diksa* (literally, "Sacred Name Initiation") and usually occurs after a period of six months to a year of trial living in a temple. The second, or *Brahminical Diksha* (literally, "Priestly Initiation"), is performed for those sincere devotees who are ready to commit themselves to full-time spiritual and institutional responsibilities as a Krishna devotee.

Thus, in the eyes of ISKCON, Lakshmi began her spiritual odyssey formally only when she took her first initiation from Ramesvara in Los Angeles and submitted herself to the four vows and to a guru in the disciplic line and received her new spiritual name, her own set of rosary beads upon which the guru had already chanted one round, and a ritual necklace. During the second initiation, the sacred *gayatri mantra* (ancient Vedic prayer) is given to the devotee (men also receive a sacred thread they wear over the shoulder and across the chest), who thereby completes his or her commitment to journey back to Krishna that is already assumed in the first initiation.

The Hare Krishnas follow the classical Caitanya traditions in terms of their understanding of initiation into the spiritual life and worship of Krishna. The primary purpose of initiation is to begin a process of spiritual awakening that will free one from past sinful acts.[2] It is also the point at which one's link with the spiritual master is effected and thus the connection with Krishna established.[3] It is the duty of each initiated ISKCON devotee to chant sixteen rounds each day on the 108-bead rosary that he or she is given in initiation. There is, in ISKCON, no religious practice that supersedes the chanting of the Krishna mantra, or prayer formula. The logic of the Krishna theology is clear: (1) The human soul lies slumbering in a material body and is overshadowed by an everyday material consciousness that is enamored with the sensual world of *maya*, (2) and thus, to awaken the soul and to supplant the material consciousness with God consciousness (i.e., Krishna consciousness), (3) one need only prayerfully and frequently chant the names of Krishna in which he substantively resides.

Traditional Krishna explanations of the saving effect of the Hare Krishna chant are not easily squared with anticultists' claims that the Krishnas' chanting is primarily a brainwashing technique initiated by the charlatan guru Prabhupada.[4] For the Hare Krishnas, the necessity and efficacy of chanting Krishna's name stems from the sixteenth century in India with the incarnation of Krishna in Caitanya, who said, "After searching all the Vedic literature one cannot find a method of religion more sublime for this age than the chanting of Hare Krishna."[5]

When Prabhupada came to America in 1965 he was convinced that the salvation of America lay with the conversion of the masses of people to chanting the Hare Krishna mantra. Just as Caitanya had spread his Krishna faith throughout all of Bengal and much of India by public and private chanting, Prabhupada resolved to pursue the same course in America by promoting the transforming quality of the age-old Krishna chant.

Whatever else the Krishna mantra is or is not, it is not a *contemporary* technique of mind control or manipulation developed by a money-hungry Indian guru. Mantras have been used as powerful prayer formulas as far back as the earliest written texts known in India, the Vedas of the twelfth century B.C. Furthermore, unless we would claim that all Christian monks and nuns who repeatedly recite the Jesus prayer are brainwashed, we should take the Krishna's mantra *first* at face value as a religious aid to spiritual concentration and development. Unless we would ignore all the scientific evidence on the temporary and salutary effects of *all* kinds of meditational devices, we should recognize in the Krishnas' mantra a religious disciplinary device that is no more effective than the sincerity, dedication, and persistence of the chanter allows it to be.[6]

The tenth-century Krishna scripture called the *Bhagavata Purana* makes clear the implications of initiation: "Human beings must be twice-born. A child is first born of a good mother and father, and then he is born again of the spiritual master and the *Vedas.*"[7] The parallel here with the Christian view of the spiritual life is obvious. For example, in John 3 the story is told of Jesus' conversation with Nicodemus during which Jesus says a true disciple must be "born again" in the spirit through the baptism ritual. What is not present in John's account is the emphasis on the need for a spiritual master —though in chapter 2 we saw that the Catholic tradition did include the need for a spiritual guide as authentically Christian. So too does virtually every Buddhist and Hindu monastic tradition in the world require a master or spiritual leader for the religious novice.

Following ancient Indian ascetic traditions, Prabhupada required four vows from his followers from the very beginning of his preaching in America: (1) no meat, (2) no illicit sex, (3) no intoxicants, and (4) no gambling. Requiring specific vows to be taken is common in all ascetic or monastic religious traditions around the world. For example, ascetic Hindu, Buddhist, and Jain traditions of classical India required of their initiates a fivefold vow of no killing, no stealing, no lying, no sexual activity, and no attachment to material possessions (or no intoxicants, in the Buddhist's case). To these universal or Sadharana Dharmas, most groups added special restrictions required by their theologies. For example, the Buddhists added the five additional prohibitions of no eating at forbidden times, no dancing or singing, no personal beauty adornments (e.g., perfumes or jewels), no use of a bed or a seat, and no use of gold or silver (i.e., material currency).[8]

Prabhupada initiated his first disciples in March 1966 in New York City. While all the basic elements of the Sacred Name Initiation were present at Prabhupada's first American performance of this Indian rite, it is clear that his early disciples did not understand the full significance or import of the rite they experienced.[9] The ritual took place in a small storefront apartment on New York City's Lower East Side. These earliest disciples were not obligated to shave their heads, did not wear the saffron robe, and were not even sure what initiation into the Krishna faith entailed in all of its theological and ethical details.

The devotees in this first group of initiates included a musician who was as interested in his music as in his new faith, a serious student of Indian literature who was quite aware of the solemn and weighty consequences of being initiated, and a young man who was an occasional visitor to Prabhupada's apartment who decided to give initiation a try even though he recognized his own lack of seriousness. All the initiates had to be instructed by Prabhupada how properly to construct a necklace of prayer beads with double knots between each bead. He had to tell them about the seriousness of the four vows that each must take, even though several of the initiates had little intention of giving up the sex life and drugs to which they were accustomed. Most of all, these first disciples of Prabhupada were shocked to learn that they would "have to worship him as God," until he clarified for them the relationship of the spiritual master to Krishna. That is, the spiritual master is to be treated as God's representative. "Only God is God," Prabhupada told them.[10]

When the day for the first initiation came, Prabhupada performed the whole ceremony himself, explaining to his disciples what each action and Sanskrit phrase meant. There were no senior disciples who could assist. There were no texts in English to explain what the prayers said or intended. The initiates had to be told when to respond and with what words. While Prabhupada brought his entire cultural understanding and religious piety to this ritual occasion, it is clear that his disciples did not fully understand the life into which they had been initiated. No longer is this the case in ISKCON.

Because of Prabhupada's extensive translations into English of the Krishna religious texts and because of the Indianization of the movement that took place in its early years, all new converts in ISKCON today are instructed thoroughly in the life, dress, ethics, and ritual life incumbent upon an initiate. For example, in February 1981, in the Krishna farm community called Gita Nagari (in central Pennsylvania), a formal Hare Nama initiation of both men and women was performed. All the initiates were instructed how to purify themselves physically and spiritually. The priest of the ceremony was Satsvarupa dasa Goswami, one of the new gurus. Through Prabhupada's books, all the initiates had the opportunity prior to the service of reading and studying his translations of and commentaries on the major Krishna scriptures and had available to them a pretty clear picture of the nature and extent of the religious life to which they were committing themselves.

Furthermore, the new devotees had access to the sixteenth-century songs and prayers of Caitanya's Bengali Krishna faith through the instructions of senior devotees and texts translated into English and published by ISKCON.[11] Finally, each devotee had available to him or her rather full descriptions, in English, of the religious rites central to Krishna worship and of the daily ritualistic activities associated with Vaisnava etiquette (e.g., proper dress and toilet habits) and worship (e.g., waking the Lord Krishna properly each day and retiring the image appropriately each night).[12]

As the initiation commenced at Gita Nagari, no one needed to instruct the initiates when or how to participate. They all knew when to respond and what words to use—unlike Prabhupada's first disciples, who had to be led through the ceremony word by word. Satsvarupa began the ceremony with a purification mantra (prayer), sipped the holy water *(acamana)* three times with the initiates, and then gave a short lecture.

In his sermon, Satsvarupa talked about the importance of chanting the holy name of Krishna in order for the initiates to advance in their spiritual life. He then spoke briefly about the ten offenses one should avoid when chanting the Hare Krishna mantra. Each initiate then approached Satsvarupa and received his or her new spiritual name and a necklace of very small beads. Then Satsvarupa instructed older devotees to tie the neck beads—which signify surrender to Krishna—around each new member's neck.[13]

Satsvarupa then kindled the ancient Vedic fire (used in Indian rituals for more than three thousand years) that symbolically reconstructs the very creation of the world. The fire was laid out on a bed of sand that was decorated with the proper symbolic colors and designs of Krishna's domain replete with the plants and fruits that have special religious import to Krishna. After building the sacred fire while muttering appropriate mantras, Satsvarupa kindled the twigs and poured a libation—a mixture of clarified butter *(ghee)*, barley, and sesame—on the fire as an offering to Krishna. The initiates responded to each libation offering by repeating the ancient Sanskrit response, *"Svaha,"* three times.

The whole ceremony ended with a lively and lengthy *sankirtana,* or dance and songfest to Krishna. Those who had entered the initiation ceremony as novices whose lives had been diverse and, from their point of view, unfocused left their initiation as new children of Krishna whose life had been dedicated to perfecting a spiritual path by which their soul could find its way back to Krishna. Just as the Bar Mitzvah in Judaism and the baptism ritual in Christianity mark a person as a spiritually responsible disciple whose feet have been set on the proper religious path, so too does the Krishna initiation mark the second or spiritual birth of the initiate (one now "twice-born").

A Krishna initiation can therefore be seen as a ritual surrender to God and an incorporation into the world of Krishna as described in the previous chapter. In Clifford Geertz's terms, the Krishna initiation ceremony clothes the conceptions of Krishna (i.e., the Krishna story) with such a symbolic aura of factuality (through the ritual performance) that the moods and motivations generated by the symbols and acts of the ritual appear uniquely realistic. Geertz says, "For it is in ritual—i.e., consecrated behavior—that this conviction that religious conceptions are veridical and that religious directives are sound is somehow generated."[14]

Likewise, the Krishna initiation ceremony moves the novice through the three critical stages—separation, liminality, and reincorporation—of all initiation rituals as described by Victor Turner.[15] First, the initiate is physically and spiritually separated from the everyday world by the fasting, prayer, and dress that precede the initiation ceremony. Then the ritual officiant (the guru) provides an especially sacred period of time and space with the preparatory prayers and actions that allow the initiates to "exit" from the mundane world and the lives they usually experience.

The central part of the ritual then occurs "betwixt and between" the old social and religious "self" that has been left behind and the newly committed religious "self" that has not yet emerged. Turner calls this the "liminal" period of the ritual during which all initiates share a common sense of community *(communitas)* and form religious and social bonds that will endure beyond the ceremony itself. The ritual then ends by introducing to the world a "new" or "reborn" person whose social status has changed and whose life has been marked in a special way. The last responsibility of an initiation ritual, then, is to "reincorporate" or reintroduce the transformed initiate to the everyday world once again.

The Krishna initiation ritual clearly moves the initiates through all three stages of traditional initiation rites as they are found throughout the world's religions. The novice is transformed socially and spiritually into a new religious status when the ritual is effective.[16] But as Geertz points out so well, perhaps the greatest benefit of such rituals is their ability to make the symbolic world of belief come alive for the individual. When the Krishna initiation is successful, the new devotee both feels and knows what it means to be a servant of God with a new spiritual name and life marked off toward that end.

In a very real sense, a person like Lakshmi who is initiated into the Krishna faith adopts not only the religious but also the social trappings of Prabhupada's Bengali Hindu faith. For example, the *varnasrama-dharmas,* or "duties of the stages of life," are modified only slightly in ISKCON from their Indian formulation. According to the *asrama* theory, there are identifiable stages of life through which devotees ideally move. First, there is the "student" phase *(brahmacarin)* which commences immediately after initiation and has as its central purposes the studying of the sacred Krishna texts and rituals, the chanting of sixteen rounds of the Hare Krishna mantra each day to enhance the devotee's faith, and faithful engagement in the duties assigned by one's guru or senior godbrothers.

When Prabhupada first came to America, he initiated *brahmacharis* to become the priestly class—both men and women—that would spread the Krishna faith worldwide. While initiating women into the monastic life-style is not ubiquitous in India, it did occur in the Caitanya tradition from which Prabhupada came and thus his initiation of women *(brahmacarinis)* was not his innovation—though male and female roles were much less delineated in the early days of the ISKCON movement than in traditional India or the current ISKCON institution.

The second stage of life is that of the "householder" *(grihasta)* and commences with marriage. While there were some married couples initiated into ISKCON from its very inception, it was only in the late 1970s and early 1980s that this mode of life was given a higher status than it enjoyed initially. In fact, married couples were encouraged to separate temporarily and live like *brahmachari* and *brahmacharini* students for a lengthy period of time during the early years of the movement. Representing the earlier, predominant view, one devotee interviewed in 1980 said, "Marriage and the householder's life is only there for those who cannot control their sexual passions. The *brahmacari* is free to devote all of his time to Krishna." However, this sentiment is fast fading in most ISKCON quarters as more and more farm communities such as Gita Nagari and New Vrindaban are expanding to provide a home base for the children and families of ISKCON.

The Devotional Cycle in ISKCON

In the early days of the Krishna movement in America, devotees could experience quite different devotional life-styles and levels of commitment as they moved from temple to temple. Depending upon the orientation of the temple leadership, the devotional and ritual demands could be loosely or rigidly conceived. Consequently, in some temples devotees rose early for devotional activities that lasted for several hours, while in other temples devotees would rise later, have brief devotional services, and then depart for lengthy book distribution sessions in the airports. Consequently, some new converts were on the streets selling Prabhupada's books and magazines only days after moving into the temple and before they even minimally understood the theological content of the books they were offering to the public.

In the early 1970s, Prabhupada realized that his disciples' zeal to spread their newfound faith through book distribution and public chanting could lead to serious deviations from his original missionary intentions unless his disciples' behavior was well grounded in a disciplined devotional life. Thus Prabhupada instructed all his temples and farms to follow a regular devotional regimen regardless of the adjustments that were needed to accommodate the particular work of the community. Consequently, for the past fifteen years in ISKCON, the following schedule which Lakshmi follows is commonly observed, with only slight alterations in all Krishna communities:

A.M.	3:30	Rise and shower
	4:15–	Morning deity worship ,
	4:30	*(Mangala-aratrika)*
	5:00	Chant *japa* (Krishna mantra)
	7:30	Scripture reading and lecture
		(Also time for chanting of additional rounds)
	8:30	Breakfast—End of morning devotions
	9:00–	
	12:00	Various work schedules
P.M.	12:00	Noon meal *(Prasadam)*
	1:00–	
	5:00	Various work and rest schedules
	4:15	Afternoon deity worship
	5:30	Shower, dinner, and free time
	7:00	Evening class at temple
	8:30	Retire for sleep

Obviously devotees who live on farms such as Gita Nagari or New Vrindaban must schedule their work around their barn chores or building projects, while urban temple devotees are often tied to office schedules and the rhythms of the city. Furthermore, the attendance rate at the morning devotional activities varies considerably from temple to temple, depending upon the character of the community.

As should be clear from the schedule outlined above, the American Krishnas follow their Indian counterparts in emphasizing the early-morning hours as especially auspicious, and therefore the morning deity worship *(Mangala-aratrika)* and the mandatory chanting of Krishna's names *(japa)* are the pivotal points in the daily life of devotees. To persons not familiar with Indian devotional *(bhakti)* practices, deity worship and chanting can appear foreign and strikingly different. Anticult critics only know of the private devotional life and practices of the Krishnas mostly from secondhand and pejorative sources and usually conclude that deity worship and chanting are techniques of manipulation (see chapter 7). Millions of Indians would be surprised to learn this about their daily devotional practices!

The theological underpinning for image worship, or *deva-puja* (literally, "to honor or to venerate God"), in Hindu devotional traditions is the notion that the unmanifested divinity (whether Krishna or another Indian divinity) can assume human, animal, or material forms for the benefit of the world and committed devotees. The *arca,* or "deity image" made of wood, metal, or stone, therefore does represent the intensified presence of the divinity, although one should not imagine that the physical image perceived by the human senses represents the sum and substance of God. Just as devotees learn from the Krishna story that the earthly Krishna "descended" from his spiritual domain to assume a human form, so too they are taught that the material images of Krishna in temples and homes are to be treated as "nondifferent" from Krishna himself.

What makes image worship among the Krishnas even more perplexing to noninitiates is that the images themselves have a bewildering array of forms, colors, and features. The materials used in Krishna images may be wood, marble, stone, or metal alloys. The color of the Krishna image may be white, blue, black, or green. The form may be of a young cowherd boy playing a flute, of Krishna dancing on the hoods of a many-headed serpent, or of a nondescript, squatty, round-eyed black form. Each region of India has its own locally adapted image of Krishna as well as those of an all-India character (e.g., Krishna with flute).

In his article "Encounters with the Lord of the Universe," Ravindra Svarupa gives one intimate portrayal of the personalistic theology that lies behind all Krishna deity worship and chanting. Explaining that he too was shocked to learn that devotees treated Krishna images as real persons (e.g., bathing, dressing, and feeding them), Ravindra said he finally recognized that he was influenced by the "impersonalist" Hindu view of God that considers anthropomorphic theologies inferior to theirs.

He then asked himself, "If God has no name, form, or qualities, how can we talk about Him? If He is not an individual person, how can we serve Him?"[17] Ravindra had assumed that Krishna devotees were speaking to him figuratively and symbolically when they described Krishna as having a "luminous blue complexion" and standing with a "silver flute raised to his lips." When Ravindra overheard one devotee explaining to someone else that the transcendental form of Krishna is embodied in every concrete deity image and thus it takes a spiritually keen eye to see the same Krishna in all of his disparate material forms, "all the different pieces of the Krsna conscious philosophy I had heard came together."[18] Ravindra concludes his spiritual, autobiographical account of his meeting of the Jagannatha images by saying that "the deity worship of the Krsna devotees . . . is based on a cogent and powerful philosophy of personalism."[19]

In an essay describing how "the transcendence comes into view" in Krishna images, Jayadvaita Swami says simply, "The Lord has not only a form but also a name, an abode, personal qualities, an eternal entourage, and spiritual activities."[20] Jayadvaita goes on to say that when Krishna descended to earth five thousand years ago, he thereby made himself briefly visible to all to see. But since then, only "those whose eyes have been anointed with the ointment of pure devotion can see Lord Krsna in their hearts perpetually."[21] How does one acquire "pure devotion" and learn to see the transcendental Krishna in the midst of his earthly images? The answer comes across the ages from Caitanya himself: "It is that simply by chanting the Hare Krsna mahamantra, one can become free from material bondage and be promoted to the transcendental kingdom [of Krishna]."[22]

Given the understanding provided by the above theological framework, it is not surprising that Lakshmi and other devotees rise in the early hours of each morning for deity worship (which Krishnas call *aratrika* after the oil "lamp" that is used in the ceremony). What to uninitiated persons might appear as an uncoordinated ceremony of individualistic dancing and singing before idols is to all Krishna devotees—whether in America or India—an opportunity to be in God's presence, to receive his favorable benefaction *(darshan),* and to express their love and devotion.

The Krishna altar contains the freshly bathed and dressed images as the curtains open each morning to songs and dance attended by cymbals and drums. Therefore, the day begins for most devotees with a joyous dance, accompanied by prayerful songs, that is called a *kirtana.* For some, the *kirtana* may be simply a sensually pleasing release of emotions—and for some of the devotees interviewed, this apparently was the extent of the ritual. However, for others, the morning *aratrika* ceremony set a mood of service to Krishna that extended throughout the day.

Japa, or chanting the Hare Krishna prayer sixteen times on the 108-bead rosary, is an even more important part of the morning devotional period for Krishna devotees. As one interviewed devotee said, "Chanting Hare Krishna is the biggest connection we have to Krishna. All other things are based on it." Unlike the communal chanting and dancing of the *kirtana,* the japa is done by each individual in his or her own way and place. One young woman devotee interviewed in Philadelphia said, "The nice *kirtanas* are the ones where the mantra can be heard; noisy ones are bad and I just walk out. I prefer to chant japa because I feel so peaceful. . . . So many times I just walk and chant." Another woman devotee from Gita Nagari said of her chanting, "You do transcend the material world [while chanting japa]. It's a whole new consciousness that makes our everyday lives seem like a dream."

No one feature of ISKCON is more misunderstood than its injunctions to chant: "Hare Krishna, Hare Krishna, Krishna, Krishna, Hare, Hare / Hare Rama, Hare Rama, Rama, Rama, Hare, Hare." According to Caitanya, and subsequent gurus in his tradition such as Prabhupada, the whole purpose of human existence is to assist the soul in its journey back to Krishna. Since human beings have lost the self-awareness of their souls, it is the chanting of

God's holy name that awakens the soul to its intended purpose. And since the name of God is "non-different" from (i.e., "identical" to) Krishna himself, chanting the Hare Krishna mantra is the best way to approach God directly. It is in this context that we should understand the ubiquitous practice of japa in ISKCON. From their rising in the morning until their retiring in the evening, most devotees will chant Hare Krishna whenever the time and circumstances will allow. Many devotees have to chant while riding in a public bus or while walking on the street in order to complete the sixteen rounds required by the vow they took when they were initiated, a number established by Prabhupada as a concession to his American disciples—most Krishna traditions in India require sixty-four rounds a day. However, it is not uncommon to hear devotees chanting whenever they have to pass time or find themselves in distress. In fact, Lakshmi referred several times to the solace that chanting provided for her when she had doubts or was upset with the behavior of other devotees living in her temple.

It is not surprising that the Krishnas' chanting raises suspicions among worried parents or persons who are unaware of the Indian context out of which this practice comes. Chanting is one way of focusing the mind's attention as Christian monks and nuns who practice the "Jesus prayer" know. Also, chanting in most theistic traditions does have as its goal a lessening of material and worldly attachments so that one becomes more attached to God than to oneself, one's friends, or one's family. However, only in the monastic traditions of Christianity is the admonition of Jesus to love God more than family really taken seriously (see Matt. 10:37–39).

Since ISKCON began primarily as a monastic tradition in America, and one that demanded complete surrender to the religious path, it is a mistake to compare ISKCON's life and practices with those of Protestant Christianity or Reform Judaism which do not require—except in lip service—a full twenty-four-hour, seven-days-a-week religious life-style. Congregational Christianity and Judaism are quite distant from their own monastic traditions that require the undivided attention to the religious life that ISKCON does in its devotional practices. Nonetheless, anticult critics continually insist on viewing the deity worship and chanting of Krishna devotees as fanatical devotion caused by malevolent manipulation.

A more reasonable interpretation of such devotional life as expressed in Krishna rituals is that of Geertz and Turner. They see such practices as attempts to bring theology (i.e., "symbol systems") to life and, at the same time, to validate the moods and motivations engendered by the theology. In ISKCON this means that the deity worship and chanting practices that stand at the center of each devotee's religious faith and practice create and sustain the feelings of devotion and attachment to Krishna that the Krishna story says is the ideal mode of life.

Preaching and Selling on the Streets

No public activity of ISKCON has drawn more vociferous or continual criticism than its bookselling in airports and on the streets. Anticult antagonists link the stereotype of the greedy guru with that of the cult as "big business," not religion, in their descriptions of ISKCON's economic activities.[23] Most critics would be surprised to learn that the same theological premises that undergird ISKCON's deity worship and private chanting have also given rise to its practice of book distribution.

While thus far in this chapter we have examined the private life of devotion into which a new member is initiated, street preaching and bookselling are public extensions of the devotee's private religious life. The first time Lakshmi was interviewed, she had just finished her temple's "morning program" (i.e., deity worship and japa chanting). Her interview had to be cut short and continued later because she was obligated to join her temple's daily *sankirtana* book distribution team that distributed Krishna books in the local airport from 10 A.M. to 4 P.M.

Lakshmi—like all Krishna devotees—was initiated into an energetic preaching tradition when she accepted her Krishna vows, and though her method of proselytizing (i.e., distributing books) is different from that of her Indian counterparts (i.e., street preaching and singing), the ideological justification is the same. Therefore, to become a devotee is to become a preacher of Krishna's story. Not surprisingly, the roots of this aspect of the Krishna devotee's commitment reach back to the days of the reformer Caitanya in the sixteenth century in India.

Not only did Caitanya revitalize an emotional devotionalism in India that expressed itself in congregational chanting in homes and temples *(kirtana)* but he also inaugurated a public form of preaching that consisted of his dancing and singing through the streets of Bengal to the accompaniment of cymbals and drums *(nagara sankirtana;* literally, "city praising") in order to attract new devotees to Krishna or to reinvigorate lax ones. Caitanya was noted for his ecstatic and emotional displays of devotion that drew thousands of disciples closer to Krishna. Much as John and Charles Wesley sang their proletarian Methodism into England utilizing their devotional hymns, so did Caitanya revitalize Vaisnavism in Bengal and much of India by means of his congregational dancing and singing, or Sankirtan.

Prabhupada grounded his missionary emphasis for ISKCON in Caitanya's words: "Spreading Krishna consciousness is Sri Caitanya Mahaprabhu's mission; therefore his sincere devotees must carry out his desire."[24] Just as deity worship and private chanting are viewed as indispensable ingredients to a stronger bond to Krishna, preaching has been viewed by ISKCON throughout its history as the "best service to the Lord" and the fulfillment of one's whole devotional life.[25]

To a great extent then, ISKCON exists to spread Krishna consciousness. Every devotee is a preaching missionary and assumes that identity immediately upon initiation (though not all devotees persist in their street preaching). While in the earliest days in America Sankirtan meant to preach by dancing and singing in the streets, devotees often handed out pamphlets or copies of the *Back to Godhead* magazine and accepted small donations. However, books and magazines were always viewed by Prabhupada as the supreme vehicles of preaching. For example, two decades before Prabhupada came to America he saw his special task as bringing the Krishna faith to the English-speaking world primarily through the printed word. While the sixteenth-century reformer Caitanya used drums and cymbals as he danced and sang the praises of Krishna *(sankirtan)* throughout the streets of Bengal and

India, Prabhupada's guru called the printing press the "big drum" that could reach the whole world with its sound. Thus Prabhupada stressed book publication and distribution as the best contemporary form of Sankirtan or preaching from the time he made his first disciples.

By 1972–73, Prabhupada began to urge his young American disciples to support his ambitious and expensive book ministry by seeking donations for the literature that was distributed (again emulating his own pattern of preaching and solicitation in India). One devotee interviewed said, "No one had the slightest idea of how you took a book out on the street to sell it or distribute it. . . . But we had complete confidence that this scripture was the absolute truth, and so we managed to get by."

Prabhupada taught his disciples that the spiritual transaction of preaching to another person benefits the person even when he or she remains a non-devotee *if* the person has given money that will benefit the spread of Krishna consciousness. This view is not new to Prabhupada but is as old as the Indian institutions of monasticism and mendicancy themselves. Traditionally, both Hindus and Buddhists have asserted that a symbiotic relationship exists between the monk and the worldly layperson. The layperson gives tangible gifts to the ascetic in return for spiritual benefits and a better rebirth. Prabhupada states this view bluntly: "Money given in charity to a suitable person is guaranteed bank balance in the next life."[26] And Prabhupada viewed his world-renounced disciples as such "suitable persons"—even when he recognized that they too were neophytes who often fell short of their professed faith and ethics.

Passages such as those above have led to conflicting interpretations in ISKCON over the years of what Sankirtan can mean and include. Some devotees have argued that the stress on book distribution as the best form of preaching *and* financing that ministry means that *no* other fund-raising activities are needed to support ISKCON. Others have argued that selling paintings, records, buttons, or other "secular paraphernalia" can also be considered "sankirtan" *if* the money collected is used for the central preaching mission of ISKCON (i.e., publishing more books). Consequently, battles have raged over the years inside ISKCON on what constitutes the limits of legitimate economic enterprise and techniques of selling and their relationship to the spiritual development of devotees and the evangelical mission of ISKCON.

One of the new gurus who was interviewed offered a minority opinion, saying, "Our maintenance should not come from Sankirtan. Sankirtan should simply be for preaching."[27] Another new guru said, "Prabhupada made it very clear that book distribution was intended to be our only economic activity."[28] Prabhupada did make it clear in several of his commentaries on the Krishna scriptures that preaching in the form of book distribution was more important than deity worship or building temples.[29] However, such admonitions by Prabhupada seemed to leave little room open for the current ISKCON practice in some zones that treats Sankirtan as a money-making activity (e.g., "selling" paintings) that underwrites free book distribution.

Two very different consequences have arisen from ISKCON's linking of evangelism and economic survival in the same "preaching" activity. In the first place, the emphasis on book distribution has had deleterious effects on some devotees who have found street selling to be an onerous task and a hindrance to—not aid of—their spiritual development. One devotee said, "It can be hard sometimes to keep one's mind on Krishna when there is a quota to meet or an angry person to deal with." In the second place, there are negative implications for economic stability in ISKCON arising out of its ideology which makes a restrictive connection between book distribution as the primary evangelistic or preaching medium and as the preferred economic activity. For example, one effect of this linkage has been to discourage creative economic problem-solving by insisting on book distribution long after that activity was no longer viable or profitable in certain temples or regions of the country. In short, the conservative effect of ISKCON's theology (i.e., the stress on "preaching") is sometimes an economic liability.

In spite of increased economic support from the Indian community for some city temples in America and the emergence of new "businesses" such as the selling of artworks, many temples in America are still struggling economically. Most important, book distribution seems not to be the long-term answer economically even though that is what the ideology encourages. The economic support for temples and communities in America is as diverse as they are. Some rely almost entirely on book distribution. Others support themselves with separately incorporated businesses that sell Asian art reproductions. Still other communities exist to a great extent on what can be raised on their farms. Yet nearly all call their money-making activities Sankirtan (and their money *lasksmi* after the Krishna goddess of wealth), whether those activities are connected with preaching or not. One could compare the Krishnas' view with some Catholic monasteries' understanding of their vineyards and wineries.

The continuing threat of economic instability to ISKCON's future in America is well known in the inner circles of ISKCON's leadership. One temple president said recently in an interview, "We know our painting businesses are not a permanent source of income. It is only a matter of time until that source dries up. But Krishna will show us the way when we come to that bridge to cross." Complicating the economic problem is ISKCON's need to make itself a more visible and accepted alternative religious community in America (i.e., accommodate itself more fully to conventional religious laws and practices). But that too takes money. For example, in the summer of 1983 the Denver temple held its first Ratha Yatra festival (made famous in Puri, India) but could not afford the traditional carts to carry the Krishna deities and held a truncated version in a local park. One primary goal of that venture was to increase public awareness and acceptance of ISKCON and its mission. The major impediment in Denver and elsewhere to this task is often the lack of financial resources.

An additional facet of ISKCON's monetary problems is the fact that the selling techniques used in ISKCON's book distribution and temple businesses have raised protests from many quarters—including outside sympathizers. Besides the well-known "change-up" and other forms of "transcendental trickery" that have been employed in the past in book distribution, many temples have ignored or been ignorant of the law in the ways they have conducted their painting businesses. For instance, one traveling Sankirtan party in Maine was found guilty of fraud in its sales of art reproductions. One devotee interviewed by this author described in detail the false claims he had been urged to use in selling similar oriental art reproductions. He was told to identify himself as a representative of a painters' studio in Maryland that was breaking up and moving to California. The customer was then led to believe that the paintings being offered were original paintings from that fictitious studio that were marked down for sale. The paintings were actually cheap oriental oil reproductions. The devotee telling this story had left ISKCON on several occasions because of his discomfort with the tactics he was asked to use to sell paintings. It is in such illicit economic activities that the Krishnas have often given their opponents the most leverage.[30] Furthermore, such activities seem a pale reflection of the evangelistic theology that originally spawned them.

Anticult antagonists have warned that the Krishnas have "gone underground" as they have donned wigs and secular clothes to do their bookselling and other businesses. Even though there is nothing necessarily illegal, immoral, or subversive about the Krishnas' abandonment of clerical clothes (compare the move toward secular dress among Catholic nuns in America), heightened suspicion of their intentions has resulted from this practice. In short, both deservedly and undeservedly, the Krishnas are finding it more and more difficult to do business when their identity is known. This fact worsens not only the picture of their economic future but also their prospects for preaching as well.

The distortions and aberrations of Sankirtan brought about by some temples' devotees selling secular paraphernalia and using questionable, if not illegal, selling tactics can only stand as barriers to genuine religious growth instead of assisting that growth as Caitanya and Prabhupada intended. Sankirtan is as much a challenge to ISKCON's future and integrity as a religious faith as it is to its economic health and well-being. Likewise, for better or worse, the role of preacher (in the form of book distribution) is another dimension of the new identity that devotees in ISKCON are asked to assume even when this religious role is clouded with economic overtones. Of course, not all devotees remain street preachers for their whole life in ISKCON, but *ideally* they begin that way.

The Place of Women and Children in ISKCON

Just as ISKCON's visibility and improprieties in book distribution and selling have engendered strong negative public reactions, so too have its views regarding the roles of women and the education of the children born to devotees. Ted Patrick says bluntly, "I have yet to discover a cult in which women are not employed as a servant class."[31] Andrew Pavlos agrees when he says, "It can be concluded that cults enhance an atmosphere of female inferiority."[32] The Hare Krishnas are especially vulnerable to such criticisms because they do admit that Prabhupada assigned a subordinate position to women materially and socially, while he recognized absolute equality spiritually for both men and women.

When Lakshmi was initiated into ISKCON, she not only assumed the private and public roles of a devotee described thus far, she also acquired the stereotypic status accorded to women in ISKCON. Just as Christian missionaries of the nineteenth century imported Western cultural values along with their religious proselytizing, so too Prabhupada brought with him a faith that incorporated pan-Indian social roles and values that transcended any particular Indian religious tradition. Consequently, it is instructive to see how the same symbolic net that encompasses practices as varied as ritual devotion, chanting, and book distribution also extends to include very specific social roles for women that come out of India's traditional past.

First of all, building upon the *Bhagavad Gita,* Prabhupada points out that *all* material (i.e., bodily) distinctions are transitory and differentiated; only the hidden soul is real and eternal. Consequently, Prabhupada reasons: A man's bodily structure and a woman's bodily structure are different. How can you say that they are equal? If a man and a woman are equal materially, then why doesn't the man also become pregnant? . . . But despite this distinction, when the man and the woman think in connection with Krsna—I am a spirit soul; my function is to serve God—then they are equal. Our proposition is that artificially we should not try to make equality.[33] Prabhupada accuses feminists of seeking masculine roles and values that are just as temporal as the bodies their souls inhabit. Therefore he chides feminists to become truly liberated by seeking God (Krishna) and thereby liberating their eternal soul.[34]

In the second place, Prabhupada adopts wholeheartedly the ancient Indian dictum of "male protection" for women who are viewed to be emotionally sensual creatures and who therefore need to be guarded from abuse from opportunistic males. A strong statement of this position comes from a Hindu religious ethical treatise compiled in the second century B.C. called the *Laws of Manu* which says:

> Day and night women must be kept in dependence by the males of their families. . . . Her father protects her in her childhood, her husband protects her in her youth, and her sons protect her in her old age; a woman is never fit for independence.[35]

Prabhupada reflects this traditional Indian sentiment when he says, "Unless you protect women, low-class men will seduce them, and society will be burdened with the children."[36] Whatever the positive spiritual role and equality assigned to women, it is clear that a considerable amount of cultural baggage attended Prabhupada's theological analysis of the role of women in ISKCON.

In a thoughtful essay written in 1982 and called "What's the Role of Women in Krsna Consciousness?" a woman devotee named Sitarani repeats many of the theological justifications given by Prabhupada for the protection of women in ISKCON and then adds her own perspective: "This protection of women by men is not a matter of egoistic domination or exploitation, but of genuine care by loving relatives."[37] Sitarani informs the reader that in ISKCON it is standard practice for male devotees—regardless of rank or age —to call women devotees *mataji,* or "mother." Why? Because a man doesn't view his mother "as an object of sexual enjoyment" and therefore he should view all women as his mother.[38]

Sitarani's conclusion that "it's natural for a woman to want a man to protect her and provide for her" should not be ignored. While many feminists find ISKCON's view of women repulsive and offensive, most women devotees feel that the Krishna position makes sense for them. Again and again, women devotees made it clear during their interviews that they believed their previous counterculture and/or feminist views led them to sexually active lives where they were abused by men. Several, like Lakshmi, could be said to have fled from failed attempts at primary control of their lives—to use Rothbaum's logic—by seeking the secondary control provided by the "male protection" theology of ISKCON. Other Krishna women simply feel comfortable with the clearly defined male and female roles that ISKCON offers. While radical feminists might view such responses as products of "false consciousness," seeking common ground for such a normative debate is not easy, given the radically different points of departure of the Krishnas and most feminists.

What ISKCON does provide for women and men is a consistent theology of male and female relationships that strictly limits sexual activity and discourages abuse, while at the same time providing a context for a full-time religious life whether the devotee remains single or marries. The comparison here with the role of convents and monasteries in most religious traditions should be obvious.

As with most missionaries—regardless of time, place, or tradition—Prabhupada's faith was historically and culturally contingent, based, in his case, upon his native Bengal. It is not surprising then that his pronouncements on the role of women starkly imported to America not only a religious viewpoint based on Krishna theology but also a traditional Indian stereotype of women. Nonetheless, Prabhupada also expanded the role of women beyond that usually allowed in Bengal (e.g., allowing women to be priests, *pujaris*) and was sometimes criticized in India for the equality he gave to his American women devotees.

As the recipients of ancient Hindu traditions and their modifications by Prabhupada in America, women devotees in ISKCON seem to understand their primary social role—that of wives and mothers—as being religious or spiritual as well. With the gopis, or cowherder women, who adored Krishna as their devotional models, women devotees who were interviewed did indicate that their social roles make sense and provide meaning only to the extent that they are included in the larger religious picture where it is Krishna and not human males who are the primary object of respect and adoration. Thus the role and the behavior of women in ISKCON are yet additional threads of the whole cloth of the Krishna religious worldview that reflects a symbiotic relationship between faith and action.

Leaving aside the considerable normative questions raised above, the most worrisome practical aspect of the Indianization of American Krishna female roles is what has evolved as the education for young girls in ISKCON schools. Unlike the women devotees who joined ISKCON as young adults and *chose* to accept a social position inferior to that of men, the female children now being raised in ISKCON are generally given no choice about the matter. Leaders of ISKCON's schools *(gurukulas)* differ on the education they feel should be granted to young girls. One schoolteacher said bluntly, "Girls and boys are not emotionally suited to study the same subjects and have the same vocations. We let girls and boys have the same education until they are eleven or twelve and then the girls learn to cook and sew, while the boys learn manual skills or continue to study the Krishna texts and become teachers and preachers." It was this type of attitude which prompted one parent to say in his interview, "As long as the *gurukula* insists on treating young girls as second-class citizens, my daughter will continue to attend the public school."

The Krishna *gurukulas* have been the target of much external criticism not only for their views of education for young girls but also because they have been quite uneven in quality and are shrouded in mystery for most outsiders. The explosive media (television and newspaper) attention given to the first Krishna school founded in 1971 in Dallas, Texas, raised doubts in the public's mind that have never been fully assuaged. For example, one newspaper article in 1974, entitled "Krishna School Seems Another World," characterized the Dallas *gurukula* this way:

> The boys and girls are sent here from across the United States to be raised in a monkish existence of Eastern mysticism cut off from the outside world and amid clouds of incense, drumbeats and recitations from the Bhagavad-gita. . . . "These people," said Dr. Emileo Alonzo, a physician who treats the commune adults and children, "are regressing into the 13th and 14th centuries."[39]

The newspaper article went on to say that the school primarily taught Sanskrit, English, and the *Bhagavad Gita* and only touched lightly on such important subjects as mathematics, history, spelling, and the physical sciences. The picture painted of the Dallas *gurukula* was one of a harsh, bleak, and intellectually deficient educational environment.

It has been tough for ISKCON to shed the image of its schools spawned by the Dallas *gurukula*. In their short section on the oddities of ISKCON compared to its Indian parent tradition, Carroll Stoner and Jo Anne Parke use the Dallas school as one illustration: "The idea of children within a temple is also outrageous to the Indian believers. . . . The children at the [Dallas] gurukula led severe lives with no toys, storybooks, or even the great American 'pacifier,' television."[40] Francine Daner deepens the general criticisms when she reports that the lax rearing practices of many ISKCON parents result in unruly children who receive little attention or affection and who are then shipped off at the age of five or six to be raised by others in a *gurukula*.[41]

For anyone visiting a temple or farm that has a *gurukula* at the present time, the above descriptions appear ludicrous. First of all, upon entering most classrooms one is immediately struck by the disciplined but open learning environment in which students bubble with excitement that is irrepressible. Whether the class involved rote recitation of Sanskrit or a discussion of one of the exploits of the ornery child Krishna, the children in the *gurukulas* in Los Angeles, Gita Nagari, and Vrindavan, India, all were eager to show what they had learned and yet were respectful of their classmates and teachers. With only a few exceptions, the teachers obviously cared for their students and conveyed that concern effectively. It was common to see teachers getting impressive results by working one-on-one with those students who were encountering the greatest difficulties. In all the *gurukulas* visited, the students were performing well above their grade level in English and mathematics according to standardized tests.[42]

In the second place, the current ISKCON *gurukulas* remind one of a typical parochial education in America where all learning is put in a value-laden context. Prabhupada's evangelical legacy is everywhere apparent: "This is our mission: whatever we have, teach others. The whole world is filled with distress. Therefore, our Gurukula school is meant for this purpose: to teach the student, and then let them go all over the world to teach others."[43] The secular subjects such as English are often taught with the use of translations of the Krishna story so that two objectives are accomplished at the same time. Likewise, the extracurricular activity outside the classroom often includes dramatizations of episodes of the Krishna story, so that it is common to find children play-acting the characters from the Krishna scriptures rather than the detectives from *Miami Vice* or *The A-Team*.

The boys and girls in a *gurukula* usually live with a married couple (not their parents) who act as "houseparents" (*asrama* parents) for six to eight children. When the children are not in school, it is the responsibility of the houseparents to engage the children in their daily household chores (e.g., washing their own clothes) or in periods of play (e.g., swimming or hiking are common activities). One houseparent named Jaya Gauracandra put his responsibility in the context of Prabhupada's teachings: "Srila Prabhupada wanted us to be strict with them [children] to make sure they don't become lazy. But he also taught us that the basis of strictness must be love. The children can benefit from our strictness and instruction only when they know we love them."[44]

A lasting impression one receives from living in Krishna temples and farms is that the children appreciate the childhood Krishna stories most of all. Since Indian devotees have tended to revere Krishna as an infant and young child in their poetry and songs, Krishna images and stories have always provided for children an immediately identifiable playmate and friend. Nonetheless, it should be pointed out that ISKCON children's faith is often just that, the faith of children. Children often love to dance and sing at *kirtans* in front of the deities, but it is not uncommon to see them get carried away in their playful exuberance while forgetting the worshipful atmosphere that is intended. In one temple, such childish excess was observed when two young boys tried to outdance each other and were separated by their houseparent. In another temple, one young boy kept trying to throw his flowers high in the air into a ceiling fan rotating overhead. Likewise, one can often see children rubbing their eyes and not focusing their attention on the deities at the early-morning deity worship. Children are children in ISKCON too.

By their own admission, the Hare Krishnas are building their *gurukula* educational system mostly by trial and error. Significantly, one constant in their educational philosophy is that Krishna must be at the center of whatever the *gurukula* finally becomes. Perhaps it is more than a bit ironic that two guiding principles of the Krishna schools to date have been the censorship of school reading materials "to remove the godless stain of most commercial textbooks," as one devotee teacher put it, and the control of "associations" by cloistering students together apart from the *karmis*, or outsiders, they tend to mistrust (except to proselytize). The irony, of course, is that many devotees owe their discovery of ISKCON precisely to experimentation in their reading of Asian (i.e., "foreign") religious texts and to associations with persons quite different from themselves. Hence, in one sense, the Krishnas are imposing on their children a Vaisnava view of the world they gained for themselves through freedom of inquiry and thought which they now refuse their own children.

The wisdom of the Krishnas' educational philosophy that distinguishes between the education of girls and the education of boys will, of course, be tested most thoroughly in the next generations of ISKCON children. For those are the ones who will live out the hierarchical roles of the Indian *varnasrama-dharma* system in an American culture where there are competing egalitarian understandings of the social, vocational, and religious roles of men and women. At its best, the *gurukula* is a parochial school that indoctrinates children born to ISKCON parents into the Krishna faith and practice. At its worst, the *gurukula* is a conveyor of an idealized Vedic culture that never has existed in India and could lead to disillusionment and even defection as devotees fail to have their expectations realized in the living laboratories of the Krishna temple and farm.

An Image of Faith and Action

From the point of view of outsiders who are critical of the cults—and, by extension, of ISKCON—Lakshmi could appear to be a counterculture youth who lacked direction and purpose in her life and who therefore was vulnerable to the beguilement of any cult. According to this logic, it just happened to be the Krishnas who discovered Lakshmi first, immersed her in a totally foreign way of life, and thereby stripped her of her previous identity. Lakshmi has become another Krishna "robot."

In talking about the changes that occur in a new devotee's name, dress, and economic status, Francine Daner says, "This stripping of personal possessions together with the mandatory appearance alterations divest a person of what Goffman calls his 'identity kit.' "[45] Not only does this personal transformation alter how a devotee thinks about himself or herself but it also dramatically alters the way the devotee presents himself or herself and his or her former self to others. Thus a mother, a father, or a previously close friend will often experience not only a "new person" but also one who rejects his or her past—including family allegiances.

Obviously there is another way of understanding the transformation that took place in Lakshmi and other devotees like her. After a series of severe disappointments in her attempt to find mutually satisfying relationships and a meaningful framework out of which she could live her life, Lakshmi sought the personal protection that the Krishnas' life and practice afford. On the one hand, Lakshmi sought refuge from a world in which she was abused sexually and emotionally. On the other hand, she discovered in ISKCON a religious context and a worldview out of which she could live meaningfully.

From this more positive point of view, Lakshmi's initiation and that of other devotees provide a comprehensive and meaningful identity where a coherent one was previously lacking. Her adopted role as a devotee of Krishna provides a "model for" living, in Geertz's terms. A devotee's initiation, then, can be construed as the *rebuilding* of a shattered, confused, or unsatisfactory identity for an individual as well as a positive choice of a new self (a "rebirth" in religious terms). Daner also recognizes this possibility when she says, "The ISKCON temple provides an institutional setting which allows its members a well-defined ideological and structural situation as well as formal rites and positive identifications and models."[46] What from one point of view is an imposed and restrictive change is usually viewed from the initiated devotee's standpoint as the choice of a liberating and meaningful new life.

If the Krishna story (i.e., theology) provides a conceptually complete worldview (see chapter 5), so too does it provide a new religious identity and life. The initiation into ISKCON sets parameters of the new life that govern what the devotee should and should not do. For example, the four vows set an austere framework of a vegetarian diet, restricted sexual behavior, and an absence of intoxicants and frivolous habits. Most important, the initiated devotee is introduced into a devotional life-style that includes opportunities for corporate worship (deity worship and scripture classes) and private spiritual advancement (prayerful chanting of japa and requirements of personal hygiene). In effect, the daily ritual cycle of prayer, study, and work puts flesh and blood on the conceptual skeleton of Krishna theology.

Caitanya's admonition to "preach Krishna consciousness into every town and village" has provided for ISKCON devotees perhaps their greatest mixed blessing. On the one hand, the public preaching of Krishna faith in song and dance was the way Caitanya revitalized one form of the Krishna tradition in Bengal. At the encouragement of his guru, Prabhupada utilized the printed word in magazines and books as the modern extension of Caitanya's proselytizing techniques. Book distribution can be, and for some devotees is, a devotional act that brings the cool waters of salvation to a temporal world on fire with passion and greed.

On the other hand, when Prabhupada linked the mission of preaching the Krishna faith to its economic support and survival, the seeds of conflict with an uninformed, wary, and finally hostile American public had been sown. It was easy from an unsympathetic, secular view of religion's equation with the passing of a collection plate to resent the Krishnas' "begging" and panhandling in the airports and in the streets. Furthermore, some devotees have believed that any selling tactic—whether legal and moral or not—was justified by the supposed benefits that accrued to the duped purchaser of a Krishna tract. Of course, some critics within ISKCON itself have pointed out that immoral behavior for whatever purpose undercuts the very spiritual raison d'être of Sankirtan. Furthermore, the hostility that slick selling tactics have evoked in the general public have only made it more difficult for ISKCON to get its message across to the public.

Two additional legacies of the controversial Sankirtan practices of ISKCON are the stereotypic images that such practices have encouraged for both devotees and anticult antagonists. For many devotees, the rejection, hostility, and religious indifference of the general public to their religious pleadings vindicate and confirm the Krishnas' view of the "fallenness" of the *karmi,* or outside world. Not perceiving their offenses and presumptions as causes of the public's behavior, many interviewed devotees described at length the abuse they had endured for Krishna. Likewise, the Krishnas' linking of economic support and the sporadic permission of questionable selling tactics by some temples and ISKCON leaders gave room for anticult exaggerations and stereotypes of Sankirtan as a giant public ripoff. Such criticisms of book distribution never mention the religious intent of this practice by the founder of ISKCON and by the actual practice of many Sankirtan devotees.

The traditional Indian life-style that ISKCON initiation introduces has controversial consequences for women and children, as we have seen. Not only are both women and children sheltered and protected from the secular world's abusive and godless ideas and habits but boundaries are erected that "protect" women and children from the *karmi* world and that raise charges of sexism and manipulation by cult antagonists. Likewise, it is not clear even to sympathetic observers of ISKCON what the full consequences of the Indianization of women and children's roles will be.

Will young women in ISKCON who are socialized with gender-specific educations into domestic vocations remain satisfied when they see the disparity between themselves and other women in ISKCON who have been "liberated women" with a secular education and who have more vocational choices inside ISKCON? Will children educated entirely within an ISKCON *gurukula* system that lacks certain contemporary technical subjects find themselves unable to function in a society (or in a world) that demands such skills for economic survival in the twenty-first century? Will ISKCON survive economically unless it finds permanent and traditional bases of financial support, and can it do so with the next generation of devotees trained primarily to become citizens of a reborn Vedic village culture?

ISKCON has accommodated itself to American culture as it developed from a charismatic, monastic movement that primarily trained missionary preachers into a complex institution that now includes a variety of social and religious options for devotees that may span a continuum from full-time preachers to family members of temple "congregations." As a result of ISKCON's transition from a volatile and somewhat unregulated missionary movement to a modified institutionalized replication of traditional Caitanyite Krishna faith, ISKCON's devotees are farthest from the robot and zombie stereotypes at the very time when those images have gained perhaps their widest acceptance in America.

ISKCON will not be immune from the biting criticisms that feminists have leveled at patriarchal religious traditions.[47] Likewise, secular enthusiasts will always decry parochial education as stultifying and limiting. Nonetheless, whatever the legitimate or exaggerated criticisms of ISKCON's faith and practice, it should be obvious to the informed observer that ISKCON offers to its initiates not only a cogent and complex worldview but also a religious and social life-style that animates the Krishna story. Perhaps better than any outsider could, Ravindra Svarupa describes the meaning a Krishna life-style has for a devotee:

> Gita-nagari has become a place of pilgrimage for me, a source of spiritual restoration. Coming out of the hard-surfaced city, . . . where devotion to God hangs in as a tenuous and frail anomaly, I enter a complete community where the devotional spirit sustains and pervades every part of it. This, a peaceful rural village, is the natural setting for Krsna consciousness. . . . Here I see people living as people are meant to live. Gita-nagari is the homeland of the soul.[48]

Whether the devoted life is that of Mother Teresa serving the destitute and dying in India or that of the contemplative monk in a Trappist Christian monastery, religion at its best seldom offers more than a vision that is lived. It is such a complete and thoroughly Indian vision, modified over the centuries and carried to America by Prabhupada, that ISKCON devotees aspire to live and into which they are bound with their initiation. Whatever else one may think of ISKCON, it cannot be denied that it has become in America and other countries of the world an implanted Hindu religious institution with all the attendant ritual and social trappings that are easy targets of secular criticism or praise.

7

Pathways to Krishna: Conversion or Brainwashing?

So far in this book the usual progression of the anticult argument has been rehearsed and tested against the realities found in ISKCON. The stereotypes explicitly derived from this generalized anticult scenario were found to be seriously wanting or simply false when placed against the variegated and complex American Krishna tradition.

What all the stereotypic building blocks of the typical anticult scenario have in common is the implicit or explicit cement of "brainwashing" or "mind control" that holds together the whole rhetorical edifice. Consequently, it is clear to any careful listener that the anticult critiques of ISKCON —or of any cult, for that matter—ultimately revolve around the claim that unwilling or duped youths are brainwashed or programmed by the Krishnas as one would a mechanical robot (and hence, the robot stereotype).

Given most cult critics' facile painting of all cults with the same brush of suspicion, it is not surprising that ISKCON has been a leading target of the brainwashing charge throughout the past decade. In 1976 Michael Schwed, a New York assistant district attorney, said, in bringing charges against the New York Krishna temple, that, based upon psychiatric and parental testimony, two of the temple's devotees were "definitely brainwashed and under the mind control of the Hare Krishna sect."[1] In this celebrated landmark case that involved charges brought by the parents of Ed Shapiro and Marylee Kreshower, the court was asked to determine whether ISKCON was a bona fide religion that engaged in proselytizing or a cult that brainwashed its "victims." After acrimonious pretrial debate between the prosecutor and the accused, State Supreme Court Justice John J. Leahy dismissed the suit against ISKCON with these words:

> The Hare Krishna religion is a bona fide religion with roots in India that go back thousands of years. . . . The said two individuals [Shapiro and Kreshower] entered the Hare Krishna movement voluntarily and submitted themselves voluntarily to the regimen, rules and regulations of said so-called Hare Krishna religion, and it is also conceded that the alleged victims were not in any way physically restrained from leaving the defendant organization.[2]

While Judge Leahy's ruling was the first judgment on a brainwashing charge brought against one of the contemporary cult groups and appeared to be definitive in its legal opinion of ISKCON as a legitimate religion devoid of coercive persuasion, the Shapiro case was only the first of several major legal suits involving the Krishnas. For instance, in 1979 in Denver, Colorado, a former member of ISKCON, Frances Agliata, had been deprogrammed, only to return to the Krishnas. Fran found herself in court defending her sanity and trying to thwart court-sanctioned parental control over her life. A district court turned Fran Agliata over to a court-appointed attorney and subjected her to examinations by two psychiatrists because her parents argued that Fran was "currently under the control of a group which has used . . . highly refined and concentrated thought-reform techniques for the purpose of obtaining control over [Fran's] thoughts, beliefs, and actions."[3] Fran's parents sought *permanent* guardianship over their twenty-year-old daughter under state conservatorship laws. (Such laws have been—and continue to be—used by cult members' parents in many states to gain custody of their adult children.)

In a case that will be discussed more fully in the next chapter, Robin George and her mother were awarded $32.5 million dollars (later reduced to $9.6 million) by a superior court jury in Orange County, California. One newspaper headline announced, "Landmark case awards cult victim $32.5 million: Jury says Krishnas brainwashed teen."[4] Three complicating factors in this case were the age of Robin (fifteen), the acrimonious family situation that resulted in Robin running away from home to join the Krishnas, and the fact that some Krishna devotees assisted in hiding her from her parents. The prosecuting attorney, Milton Silverman, perhaps summed up the feeling of many on both sides of the aisle in the courtroom when he said, "The decision sends a message to all cults in this country."[5] That is, regardless of the specific issues and information involved in the George case, the members of the jury clearly considered the George evidence in the context of their general stereotypes regarding all cults. While the Krishnas' appeal is still pending, it is clear that the issue of brainwashing is still a live issue and that some jurors are willing to generalize the mind control charge to all groups they consider cults.

Brainwashing has become such a commonplace—and popularized—way of casting blame on one's detractors or opponents that it is used in a variety of noncult contexts too. For example, Joe Charboneau, a former Rookie of the Year in the American Baseball League, explained why he had returned from an injury to play baseball, only later to claim that his injured back was not fit for play: "They [the Cleveland Indians] more or less brain-washed me into playing."[6] Such use of mind control terminology by a disgruntled baseball player appears relatively harmless compared to the widening application of the generalized brainwashing explanation to any conflict situation ranging from mainline religious conversions to recalcitrant partners in a marital dispute. One sobering example of the widespread acceptance of brainwashing as an accepted fact—and something to be feared more than kidnapping or sexual imposition—is the celebrated 1982 case of Stephanie Reithmiller in Cincinnati, Ohio.

Stephanie's parents thought their daughter was a mental captive of her reportedly lesbian roommate and bought the services of associates of the famed cult deprogrammer Ted Patrick in order to have Stephanie kidnapped and deprogrammed. Most facts of Stephanie's case were not disputed. She was physically abducted from the street in front of her apartment and transported to Alabama. She was forcibly imprisoned against her will. It is also clear that one of Stephanie's captors had sexual relations with her to effect a heterosexual cure (Stephanie's claim of rape was not upheld by the jury). Yet in the face of such horrific evidence of personal abuse, the jury acquitted the defendants of all but the charge of abduction, a charge that produced a hung jury.

Why was such obviously offensive behavior exonerated in the Reithmiller case? The jury believed that the real issue was brainwashing/mind control, not kidnapping, false imprisonment, and rape! One woman jury member said simply, "They [the prosecution] made it seem that Stephanie's parents wanted her deprogrammed from homosexuality, but it was the mind-control situation that had them concerned."[7]

What the juries of the Robin George and Stephanie Reithmiller trials shared in common was the conviction that brainwashing or mind control is a fact and can be practiced in a variety of cult and noncult contexts. Chapter 4 on the nature of devotees' "surrender" to ISKCON makes it very clear that many Krishna disciples can appear to have relinquished total ("primary") control of their lives only to have resorted to "secondary" forms of control in which the decision to stay or leave ISKCON remains theirs. Nonetheless, we must take brainwashing charges seriously in great part because they have become so ingrained in the popular American lore surrounding the cults— including the Krishnas. Let us turn then to the conversion story of a young Krishna woman, Sita Dasi, that could appear *from the outside* to be a radical case of mind control.

Sita Dasi

The night I finally decided to commit suicide I considered the events in my life which had brought me to this point. I was an army brat who was born in Oklahoma but lived in seven or eight places throughout the United States. My family was Jewish, but seldom lived in places with heavy concentrations of other Jews. Consequently, I was often the only Jew in my school's classes and received a great deal of teasing and criticism because of that fact.

My family was middle-class Jewish, and religion was not an important thing to them. The only time I ever attended synagogue was for the high holy days. We would drive about sixty miles to attend the synagogue on those days. On Hanukkah [Jewish New Year] my parents would always light candles, but we kids got our presents on Christmas because my parents didn't want us to feel left out. None of us went through Bar Mitzvah or Bat Mitzvah.

When I was in eighth grade, my parents moved to Rhode Island and immediately put me in a Jewish Sunday school. I felt very intimidated by this experience, because I didn't know any of the Bible stories nor most of the Jewish religious traditions. I was also put off by the "Jewish-American Princess" role I was expected to adopt for my friends. They were preoccupied with heavy makeup, stylish clothes, and common social stereotypes. I really didn't fit into that whole mode of living, and I tended to reject my Judaism, because I really didn't feel a part of it.

My family life was pretty typical of most American homes. My two brothers and I fought a lot but didn't really hate each other. My mother was a moody person who couldn't be approached easily and I remember my family life as not being very warm. My mother had a strong temper and would sometimes simply put on her coat and leave the house. I remember one night when I was going to bed I told my mom I loved her. She became very angry and said, "You don't do anything around the house, so how can you say you love me?" For several years after that, I didn't tell my mother I loved her. My family never did things together, and I remember longing for such activities.

I was pretty lazy in school for the first several grades. Then I had a teacher who had taught my brother. I wanted to do well for this teacher and felt myself in competition with my brother, who had been a straight A student. I got a lot of positive feedback from my family and other teachers which led me to do really well for the remainder of my high school career. My two best subjects were math and science.

I went to high school in Boston, Massachusetts, and my social life was very full during those years. I was a cheerleader, and class officer, and was heavily into the social scene. I was into having my name appear on every page of the yearbook, but feeling less and less satisfied with the accolades. I had two really close friends with whom I did a lot of drugs and dating. I also had older friends who lived in a commune in Boston and would stay with them a lot of weekends telling my parents I was staying with a school girlfriend. I was really into drugs and sex . . .

The Vietnam War was raging during my high school years, but I could never really get into all the protests. I did do a couple of rallies because it was the fashionable thing to do. However, I could see both sides of the issue, why we should be there and why we should be getting out. Finally, I took a stance against the war because my friends did.

Basically, my high school years were times of sense gratification. The more highs I had, the more I wanted. Still, like our *Bhagavad Gita* says, these things taste like nectar in the beginning, but turn sour later. That's the way it was as I entered college. I was still excited by any thrill that could turn me on, but was getting less and less satisfaction from them.

I went on to Boston University, where I continued my sensual ways. My relationship with my parents had improved because I was now dating Jewish men almost exclusively. As long as I associated with other Jews, my parents were happy with me, and a lot of Jewish kids went to Boston University. I was active in socializing and was popular on campus. I was a psychology major and graduated with a 3.5 cumulative average.

Even though these years looked pleasurable and successful to those on the outside, I couldn't really grasp the real pleasures, the essence of life. . . . I could see that the world was very much empty. I contemplated suicide frequently even though my friends thought I was happy and carefree. I read poets that talked about the darker side of life and I wrote that kind of poetry myself—though I never showed it to anybody.

My brother tried to commit suicide several times by drinking shoe polish, closing himself in his car while the engine was running, and so on. One day I got a call from one of his friends in the Buddhist house who said, "Your brother has just hung himself in the basement." I was really sad but felt I had lost him as a brother long before, when he was no longer like himself.

As far as my feelings toward God at this time, I externally had a bitter attitude. . . . I would ask, "If there's a God, why is there so much suffering in the world?"

I would laugh at people being religious and yet every night I would pray to God, saying, "Please help me to find the truth." Ever since I was a little kid I would always say a prayer at night. No matter what kind of intoxicated condition I was in, I would make a prayer every night. But no one would have known that. I put on a real atheistic show.

At this same time, I tried to get in contact with a friend who had joined the Hare Krishnas when I was a junior in college. When he became a devotee, I more or less wrote him off my list of friends. My first contact with the Krishnas was through a cooking course they taught at the university. And while I saw them as being sort of "exotic," I couldn't see myself having any kind of conversation with these people. Well, the summer before I was supposed to run the university's freshmen orientation program, my anxiety was running so high that I tried to contact this Krishna friend. I was overwhelmed by all the responsibility I had been given and was taking a graduate summer course to boot. As I grasped at friends of whom I could ask my "big question," I thought more and more of this devotee friend and tried to find him through mutual friends.

I was playing tennis daily to relieve some of my stress. By September I was eating strictly a vegetarian health-food diet. I felt even more strongly than before that there was this great oneness that one had to merge back into and that I simply had to find someone who could help me get there. I also felt like a charlatan who had tried to create a whole facade that was unreal. I realized as I talked to a black janitor one day that I really was prejudiced. And I said to myself, "I don't have any really good qualities. I don't really have any understanding of life. But I just put on a good show for people." I felt real liberation. I felt that liberation that comes, really, with death.

So that is how I came to the realization one night that suicide was the only way out of life's suffering. I told my boyfriend, "I have the answer—the answer is suicide!" It was such a positive realization to me, but to him it was kind of a depressing thing. My boyfriend decided that I had become crazy and got all of my friends around me that night to give me support. My graduate counselor came over to my room and tried to convince me that I was overworked. My whole apartment was filled with people who were telling me to "hang on" until the next day when I could see the school psychiatrist. But I didn't feel there was any problem. I felt that they didn't understand I had really found the solution. I had never felt better about anything in my life.

I went to the psychiatrist the next morning and he appeared to understand my problem. I was outraged when he then suggested that I go to a mental institution for the weekend. And then I realized that there is no way they're going to understand what's wrong with me. No one does. They think I'm crazy and I think they are crazy! I had insisted that they call my friend in the Krishna temple and learned that he no longer lived in that temple. I thought of him because I felt that perhaps he could understand why I felt the need to either commit myself to a spiritual master or commit suicide. They tried hard to reach him, thinking that he might be able to calm my ravings, but they could not find him. Even the Baltimore Krishna temple did not know where he was. He was on the road between temples, they thought.

Just as I got down to the street, after leaving the psychiatrist's office, I ran into the Krishna friend I had been looking for. I just ran up to him and hugged him! He had not been alerted that I had been looking for him. I realized that this must be Krishna's arrangement. He had just come back to Boston that day. Even the Boston temple did not know he was back.

Even while hugging him I said, "I don't know what you're doing, I don't know what it is, but I want to surrender to it!" I was crying I was so happy. I just knew it was what I had to do. I knew that I had to become a Hare Krishna devotee.

I had read the *Bhagavad Gita* briefly once. I had tried chanting the Krishna mantra for about five minutes once. But I knew very little about what the Krishna faith or life-style entailed. I just knew I had to try it.

When my friend took me to the temple I said, "This is home." I had really committed suicide that day to my material life. . . . In my own mind I had really given up. I had decided to commit suicide, so my material life was simply over. Hence, I wasn't concerned about giving up anything in the material world. I had already made that decision. But I didn't understand what it was all leading to. I just had faith in this devotee.

The counseling service actually felt relieved that I was heading off to the Krishna temple with the devotees. They knew the devotees from this temple because of the vegetarian meal program they had on campus. The next morning I called my parents and told them I was living in the Hare Krishna temple. My mother just broke down and cried. My parents came to visit me the next day, which happened to be a Sunday feast day. They were a bit overwhelmed with the program and Indian meal and could not understand my joining. I did not tell them I had been contemplating suicide, since I did not want them to think I was joining out of mental illness. I was convinced that I had joined out of divine providence. But I knew that nobody else would understand that—except the devotees.

To make my decision sound plausible, I told my parents that I had been studying the Krishna philosophy for several years and that these people in the temple had been friends of mine for a long time. I knew that they would not really understand, and to this day, they still do not understand how I became a devotee. Yet I think I am now closer to them than I have ever been. And they like all of the devotees a lot.

My parents come often to the temple to see me and my friends. They have done a lot of service for the temple. They have donated a couple of cars, they have given me money and bought me a lot of things. They have done a lot of things and have been purified. . . . Their ideal for me now would be for me to be a Hare Krishna, to marry a nice Jewish boy, and to live on the outside.

What appealed to me that day, and still does, is the Hare Krishnas' explanation of our true spiritual position before God. The true love, the truly personal plane of spiritual existence with Krishna was what attracted me then and made my decision to commit suicide seem silly.

Popular Brainwashing Theories

Virtually all current brainwashing theories hark back to the 1961 seminal study by Robert Jay Lifton of coercive persuasion of American soldiers in Chinese communist prison camps. Lifton's book on the study of brainwashing in China[8] has served as a canonized handbook for anticult critics as they have sought explanations for the conversion of American youth to the cults. Some cult critics who have utilized Lifton's work do so superficially,[9] but other authors have extended Lifton's analysis by offering a physiological explanation of the psychological process he describes.[10] While an American journalist, Edward Hunter, was the first American to translate the Chinese phrase *hsi nao* (literally, "wash the mind") into English as "brainwashing," it is Lifton's study based on interviews with forty persons who had undergone this process in Chinese prisons that has remained the primary source on this issue.

Lifton describes an eleven-step process of Chinese thought reform that seemed to emerge consistently from his interviews of former prisoners.[11] Brainwashing in this context includes:

1. An *assault upon one's identity* through physical and emotional assaults on the prisoner. For example, sleep deprivation and abusive interrogations were common.

2. The *establishment of guilt* by tapping deep feelings of confusion over real identity and right and wrong.

3. The *self-betrayal* brought about by forced confessions of sins and denunciation of friends.

4. The *breaking point* of mental and physical integration resulting in a deep and basic fear and anxiety.

5. A period of *leniency and opportunity* during which unexpected acts of kindness and some relief from the intense physical and emotional pressure occurs.

6. The emergence of *a compulsion to confess* all the sins of one's past life.

7. The *channeling of guilt* through the categories and worldview provided by one's captors.

8. A period of *reeducation* through group study that systematically dishonors one's former self and provides communist categories for new personhood.

9. *Progress and harmony* are the by-products of the emotional support and gradual adaptation to the communist environment by the transformed prisoner.

10. A *final confession* is usually brief and now fully believed (unlike earlier confessions) by the political convert.

11. *Rebirth* of the prisoner by uniting his new ideological selfhood with the skills of his former (e.g., doctor or priest) and vocational self. This is a period of reintegration of ego identity and a sense of relief from fear and retribution.

Lifton says that all the above stages of the Chinese brainwashing can be encapsulated in the notion of the "death and rebirth" of the self. The old self must die and a new self must be put in its place. (With only a slightly different meaning of "self" and an alternate view of the reborn self, this *process* virtually duplicates the Christian view of "rebirth"; see John 3:3–15). The engine that drives the Chinese process of change is fear caused by the threat of death, the controlled environment, and the sheer psychological force of imprisonment. Lifton concludes, "This penetration by the psychological forces of the environment into the inner emotions of the individual person is perhaps the outstanding psychiatric fact of thought reform."[12] In other words, physical captivity can help to create a feeling of psychological captivity as well.

Lifton adds a twelfth stage to the brainwashing process that actually stands outside the indoctrination sequence as the beginning of a new round of identity formation. He calls this stage "release: transition and limbo" and it occurs when the prisoner is released back into his previous society. Lifton says of this situation, "Release and expulsion . . . do not put an end to one's troubles. Instead they thrust the Westerner into an environment which immediately questions all that has been so painstakingly built up during the years of imprisonment."[13] Having internalized a great deal of his prison environment, the liberated prisoner experiences the "limbo" which Turner describes as being "betwixt and between" the world of the former self and of the socially and religiously new self. All released prisoners found that they had "profound struggles with their integrity, their ability to trust, and their search for wholeness."[14] Freedom was experienced as a frightening experience, not the pure bliss the prisoners had anticipated.

Lifton's description is essentially a psychoanalytic one that attempts to discern the *unconscious* elements of the brainwashing process. Most anticult critics who adopt Lifton's description as the appropriate model to explain cult conversions also stress the unconscious factors at work in cult proselytizing. For example, two prominent psychologists who build on Lifton's analysis are John Clark, a Weston, Massachusetts, psychiatrist, and Margaret Singer, a California-based psychologist.[15] Both these psychologists have been very active in professional anticult activities that include counseling deprogrammed youths, serving as expert witnesses at cult trials, supporting conservatorship cases brought by parents, advising anticult organizations, and promoting exaggerated claims of brainwashing in professional and popular journals and in public speeches.

Although both Clark and Singer have developed rather popularized versions of what they both call "the mind control process," their basic assumptions and conclusions are only slight modifications of Lifton's brainwashing analysis adapted for cult conversions. However, both these mental health professionals have turned Lifton's descriptive analysis into prescriptive and indiscriminate attacks on all groups they lump together as "destructive cults."

Earlier portrayals of cult proselytizing pale by comparison to that of Flo Conway and Jim Siegelman.[16] Conway and Siegelman dismiss previous brainwashing theories as well as the terms "brainwashing," "ego destruction," "coercive persuasion," and "hypnosis" as useful categories to explain contemporary cult conversions. They simply assert, "Studies of brainwashing . . . fall far short of explaining the phenomenon we call snapping."[17] Unlike the Chinese's brainwashing which represented a program to change people's beliefs and behavior, cult conversions can be described as a process of "shutting off the mind, of not-thinking."[18]

According to Conway and Siegelman, the initial stage of cult affiliation is, in contrast to previous brainwashing practices, voluntary. Like Christian evangelists who use rhetoric skillfully, the cult messiahs use persuasive techniques that require normal functioning of the human brain. Then physical and emotional stress are increased through sleep and food deprivation to "weaken the individual to suggestion." It is then that a process Conway and Siegelman call "communications overload" radically alters the convert in a sudden break that has both physiological and psychological consequences. While previous brainwashing theories assume that cult conversion techniques operate unconsciously, Conway and Siegelman assert that such proselytizing is a direct attack on the conscious and conceptual dimensions of the mind—although the convert is unaware of the process that is occurring.

In substituting a physiological explanation of conscious thought processes for a religious or theological one, Conway and Siegelman assume that religious experiences are "natural products of the organic workings of the human brain."[19] Therefore, any change in a belief system or personality orientation must be discernible in terms of a scientific theory of the mind's workings. Otherwise, Conway and Siegelman ask, "How could an individual whose mind had been shut off, who had been robbed of his freedom of thought, display such cunning and initiative?"[20] The answer lies in information theory, according to Conway and Siegelman.

Conway and Siegelman assert, "Information, not matter or energy, is the stuff of human consciousness. It is the soul of communication and the key to the phenomenon of snapping."[21] Cybernetics is "the study of communication and control in the animal and machine" and holds the answer to the mystery of how the cults psychologically manipulate converts through effective physiologically deterministic information techniques. And the cybernetic model that best describes the way the brain functions is the hologram. A hologram is a three-dimensional image produced by the "interference patterns" created by two intersecting beams of light that are then stored on photographic film. Billions of bits of information can be stored holographically in a single cubic centimeter of space and, amazingly, each bit of film contains the whole image.

If we assume, with Conway and Siegelman, that the human brain stores bits of information like a hologram, then we can explain why the brain can retrieve information in either a linear (over time) or spatial (simultaneous) fashion.[22] Since information that the brain stores comes from accumulated experiences, "each individual can be viewed as a kind of complex hologram of his culture and his time."[23] The logic follows: (1) Billions of sensations bombard the brain in the form of minute electrical impulses; (2) the brain spreads out and stores these innumerable bits of information throughout the brain and nervous system; (3) therefore, psychological and physiological symptoms can occur from a single feeling (e.g., shocking news can give one a stab of pain in the chest), and all levels of consciousness (from the everyday to the mystical) are "alternative slices of each individual's holographic reach and flexibility. . . . Experience literally *creates* the workings of the human brain."[24]

Cult conversion techniques consist primarily of "barrages of new information." Cults engage in an assault on the novice's sensory system, and the flood of new information simply overwhelms the capacity of the brain to sort and to store the new information. Such an assault leads to dramatic changes in the physiology of the brain. Conway and Siegelman conclude:

> In many religious cults and mass therapies, the sudden injection of experience may destroy some specific pattern of thought, feeling, or belief, but it may also alter the entire focus of consciousness. . . . These intense experiences effect physical changes in the organization of the brain. . . . [In some cases,] they actually destroy the fundamental pathways of thought and feeling that make up an individual's personality.[25]

Conway and Siegelman identify the Hare Krishna *kirtana* and *aratrika* rituals of dancing and singing as "perhaps the most practiced at inducing the snapping moment that brings about sudden changes in personality."[26]

For Conway and Siegelman, snapping is an "information disease" that occurs when the mind is shut off and "individuality is surrendered to some religion, psychology, or other recipe for living."[27] Whether the surrender is voluntary or not does not matter, according to these observers. Snapping is an escapist legacy from the experience-laden 1960s, and "it is an act of betrayal both of one's individuality and of one's society."[28]

From the more generalized claims of mind control found in various anticult books,[29] to the specific and detailed speculations of Conway and Siegelman, certain general themes recur again and again. First of all, with almost no exceptions, the witnesses who testify about their being manipulated by the cults are ex-members who were deprogrammed. With such varied proselytizing techniques and ritual life-styles in the cults, should not one be suspicious that deprogrammed ex-cultists' stories sound so nearly identical?

One wonders how many persons would believe a marriage counselor or a book author who used only divorced and alienated spouses as his or her sampling and research pool? The acute feeling that something is very wrong about such skewed research will arise in anyone who has lived with the Krishnas, has scrutinized them carefully, has seen their warts with their beauty marks and then reads the above accounts of brainwashing and the cult life. Not a single one of the studies mentioned above tried to ascertain what the conversion experiences were of those who remain in the cults or to interview those thousands of young people who have left the cults voluntarily.

Some of the case studies we have surveyed in this volume are themselves examples that do not neatly fit the anticultists' explanatory theories. From the lengthy and suspicious search for a guru by Govinda Dasa, how can one seriously maintain the "snapping" scenario? From Mahema's clear admission that her surrender was slow in coming and still is not complete, how can one so quickly believe that chanting the Hare Krishna mantra will make a devotee completely susceptible to the guru's control and suggestions? More important, what to Sita's parents and friends could only appear as a radical conversion to a Hindu theistic faith by a young psychology graduate student who was an atheist was viewed by Sita as a move amidst crisis, undertaken to find a faith and life that was continuous with her private thoughts and prayers. Finally, Lakshmi's conversion clearly has as much a sociological overtone— that is, "protection" from abuse—as it does a psychological one.

Months of living with the Krishna devotees from West Coast to East, as well as in India, strongly suggest to this author that there were nearly as many different conversion stories and timetables as there were devotees. To be sure, several common threads can be discerned that mark dominant pathways to Krishna; for example, social networks, quests for meaning, spiritual searching, and escape from responsibility—or to a disciplined way of life. In any case, it is simply ludicrous to assert that the woeful tales and warnings of deprogrammed ex-cultists yield an adequate sampling and that "brainwashing" is a useful guide to understanding why some young people are attracted to the Krishnas and choose to stay.

Second, without exception, the anticult books lump all the cult proselytizing techniques together. Can one take seriously the claims of those who indict *all* serious religious practice, from singing, dancing, and rejoicing ("overexciting the nervous system") to prayer, meditation, and fasting ("understimulation of the nervous system")? Are such claims not only "anticult" but "antireligious" ones? It is clear that the Moonies' very systematic proselytizing techniques as practiced on their famous weekends are much more sophisticated and regularized than the more low-key, "philosophical" approach of the Krishnas. Likewise, while the Moonies can hide their identities if they choose, it is impossible to bring a potential convert to the Krishna temple and not lay bare virtually the whole Krishna symbol system replete with Indian dress, food, deities, and rituals. Nonetheless, Conway and Siegelman's book continually gives examples of one conversion tactic in one cult (e.g., deceit involved in *some* Moonie weekends) and extends by inference that practice to *all* cults. Such an argumentative and literary device is distorting, if not deceitful in itself.

What is important for the reader to know is that not only are the roads into the various cults predicated on quite different conversion experiences but so too the pathways to Krishna are extremely varied. Some devotees are convinced by the philosophy, while other devotees continue to shy away from the philosophy after ten years in the movement. Some devotees come back to the temple the first several times because they genuinely like the Indian cuisine and the warm friendliness they experienced. Other devotees still prefer pizza to *puris* (a puffed-up Indian wheat bread). Still other devotees (often abused women) need the security and protection that ISKCON offers, while other ISKCON women assert their rights and clearly have not escaped into ISKCON for protection but for opportunity. In short, not only is it impossible to lump together the recruiting techniques of all the cults, it is not even possible to give a single characterization of the most familiar proselytizing techniques of ISKCON, since these techniques are effective selectively for those who finally join ISKCON.

Third, the mistaken notion that is promoted by all the anticult and brainwashing books is that the cult convert is a *passive victim.* John Lofland, a professor of sociology, warns that even in the case of the sophisticated proselytizing weekends of the Moonies, one's attention should not rest solely on what the Moonies are doing. What gives Lofland's observation special bite is that it comes from a reassessment of his and Rodney Stark's study of the Moonies' recruiting weekends a decade earlier.[30] In his essay " 'Becoming a World Savior' Revisited," Lofland reaffirms the notion that the Moonies "have elaborated some incredible nuances" in conversion techniques in their fivefold process of "picking-up, hooking, encapsulating, loving, and committing."[31]

However, Lofland ends his essay by offering several important qualifications to his theory: (1) The world-savior model is as much a descriptive as it is a causal theory; (2) it is wrong to generalize from this model to all cult practices, and thus there is a need to develop other descriptive models and state their limitations; (3) and finally, the world-savior model assumes a "thoroughly 'passive' actor—a conception of humans as a 'neutral medium through which social forces operate.' "[32] Lofland ends by saying that what is needed is for students of conversion to invert the questioning and ask how it is that "people go about converting themselves." Most of the above studies of brainwashing have assumed that the cult convert is either an unwilling or an unwitting "passive victim" of cult recruitment techniques. This is a mistaken notion, as we will see later in this chapter.

Fourth and finally, the notion that a cult guru can—by any psychological or physiological means—wipe the mind of the convert clean and implant new beliefs or ideas simply does not fit the overwhelming evidence that secondary control *is* maintained by cult converts who may act as fully devoted believers up until the day they voluntarily defect from the Krishnas (or other cults). J. A. C. Brown, a British social psychologist, carefully distinguished between the variety of types of persuasion from propaganda to brainwashing. He warns, "We are going to be seriously led astray if we are induced to believe that the mind under stress can be wiped clean like a slate and new patterns imposed upon it which have no bearing upon what has gone on before—in other words, that a personality can be wholly changed . . . from the original one."[33] Brown insists that there is a clear continuity between the preconvert's "self" and the convert's "self." This observation certainly coincides with the experience of Sita, who knew very well how her previous life and new life fit together once she descended from her momentary crisis.

Brown qualifies Lifton's analysis by pointing out that those whose beliefs were permanently or "near-permanently" altered by their Chinese prison experiences were already inclined toward the "totalist authoritarian" end of the personality spectrum and were seeking a "self-sealing system" of belief.[34] Furthermore, four years out of prison, most of the prisoners had neutralized the ideological effects—if not all of the emotional trauma—of their brainwashing experience. Brown concludes by saying, "The whole fallacy about brainwashing . . . is the peculiar notion implied in Sargant's book *Battle for the Mind* that an idea is a thing located in the brain which can be planted there or dug up at will."[35] The same can be said of Conway and Siegelman's quasi-scientific explanations.

Perhaps the most convincing evidence of the fallacy of the fears of brainwashing engendered by studies like the ones above is the recognition of the *actual ineffectiveness* of so-called mind control techniques. For example, Eileen Barker in her carefully controlled and quantitative study of more than six hundred British and American Moonies found that less than 12 percent actually join the Unification Church after a weekend retreat and follow-up retreats, and in less than a year one third of those who had joined dropped out.[36] In a similar fashion, of the more than nine thousand devotees that Prabhupada initiated, fewer than two thousand remain in ISKCON. And of importance to the topic of our next chapter is the fact that all but a handful of the defectors left ISKCON voluntarily and without any need of deprogramming. Such ineffectiveness of "brainwashing" by the cults is paralleled in psychologists' failures in the reform of recalcitrant violent prisoners or long-term mental patients. If those clinical psychologists who purport to know the precise physiological operation of mind control can't duplicate it in their own practice, how much of a "fact" can brainwashing be?

While anticult writers ignore the persons who remain in the cults, the systematic psychological studies that *are* done of cult adherents render less plausible the brainwashing/mind control hypothesis. For example, the recent study by Michael Ross of all forty-two members of the Krishna temple in Melbourne, Australia, is striking in its thoroughness and results. All members of the temple were administered the MMPI, the General Health Questionnaire, and the Eysenck Personality Questionnaire. Six devotees were selected at random for in-depth interviews and were given the Present State Examination. Dr. Ross presented each of the forty-two profiles to two outside assessors who were unaware of who it was that was being examined. None of the examiners found any evidence of pathology.[37]

From his study, Ross reached several significant conclusions. First, the profiles of all the Krishna devotees were in the normal range. Second, "the argument that joining the Hare Krishna movement is an attempt to stabilize an unstable personality does not appear to have a strong basis." Third, there is "no evidence for claiming that membership in the movement leads to psychopathology" (in fact, members in the movement more than three years "appeared happier and less anxious"). Fourth, by all the evidence, the devotees are both sane and rational in their mental functioning. Finally, "these findings cannot be generalized to members of other so-called cults, which cover a vast range of operations, individuals, and beliefs."[38]

To Ross's study the only rebuttal is the tortured and tautological arguments of anticultists like Conway and Siegelman or John Clark who say that the brainwashing is so new and different that current psychological tests can't detect it. (This double bind is similar to that used by Salem witch-hunters who demanded that witches testify at their trials and then called them bewitched liars when they denied they were witches.) Nonetheless, Ross's findings provide independent confirmation of a study that was done of West Coast Krishna devotees a decade earlier.[39] Furthermore, the studies by Marc Galanter of the Moonies and other groups show that while there are marked differences between the Krishnas and the Moonies, conversion has a relatively *positive* effect on new disciples—including those of the Rev. Moon. Galanter concludes, "The average convert apparently experienced emotional distress before joining. . . . [Yet] affiliation with the Unification Church apparently provided considerable and sustained relief from neurotic distress."[40] It appears that joining ISKCON or the Moonies can alleviate rather than increase stress and that these two groups clearly serve quite different groups of young seekers.

One important lesson to take from current psychological studies is that the *evidence gleaned from one cult may not be applicable to another.* While ISKCON is essentially a Hindu missionary movement from India and not a "new" religion founded by a self-proclaimed messiah, the Children of God movement more clearly fits the common notion of a cult and has engaged in practices that are abusive of some of its members in a way that ISKCON in general has not. Also, practices can vary significantly within a single group, especially in the early, unformed days of a movement. For example, the intense, deceptive recruiting process used by the West Coast Moonies in the Berkeley family simply were anathema to some East Coast families whose techniques were more open and low key.

Likewise, some new gurus in ISKCON treat their subordinates harshly and their disciples in an authoritarian manner, while other ISKCON gurus serve as a spiritual model for their disciples and appear to be loved as well as obeyed. Obviously, then, the "stress" experienced by devotees in some temples and zones is higher than in others. But what is absolutely obvious to any perceptive and relatively neutral observer of ISKCON recruiting practices is the realization that brainwashing in any of the above forms does not exist in ISKCON. Brainwashing is more of an anticult rhetorical device than a useful description of the conversion process. When proponents (e.g., Margaret Singer) of the mind control model modify their analysis in response to criticisms, they usually retreat to positions that characterize brainwashing as "social control" or "psychological manipulation." Understood in less-exaggerated terms, "mind control" is finally reduced to social or psychological processes that are better described in social-scientific literature. Such literature has much to teach us about conversion, and it will be helpful at this point to examine some of these approaches in detail.

Psychological Perspectives on Conversion

Experiences like Sita's, which William James calls "sudden conversions," are chronicled throughout religious history. In the Hebrew scriptures we are reminded of the life-altering and sudden experience of Moses' encounter with a burning bush or the direct vision and call of the reluctant prophet Jeremiah. In Christian history, the radical conversion of Paul on the road to Damascus or the mass conversions on Pentecost have been duplicated by later Christians such as Augustine and John Wesley.

Likewise, Muslims believe that Muhammad had a direct vision of Allah which sparked his sudden transition from businessman to prophet, and many Sufi saints seek such a life-transforming experience for themselves. In the Buddhist monastic traditions, the very path to salvation is essentially one of duplicating Siddhartha's immediate experience of Nirvana that transformed him into the Buddha or Enlightened One. So too, many elite Indian schools of yoga and asceticism focus all their religious disciplines upon achieving the life-altering and liberating experience of *moksa*.

Nonetheless, it has been not only the sudden conversion that has caught the eye of students of religion but also the radical conversion that appears to be discontinuous with observable life experiences leading up to it. A classic case of the unexpected conversion is that of Paul, who, while on the road to Damascus to persecute members of the new Jewish sect called Christians, had an experience that made him a Christian. All of us are likewise familiar with stories of foxhole or deathbed conversions by persons who have spent their whole lives denouncing religion. Such "crisis conversions" are simply an extended form of the radical variety of conversion and clearly serve as an initial or preliminary description of Sita's experience.

As we now turn to some of the prominent psychological theories of conversion that have been used to describe the adoption of the Krishna faith, we should be alert to the limitations inherent in these theories as well. In any case, the primary question to be addressed is, What current psychological explanations or interpretations of religious conversion can help us understand the specific case of Sita Dasi?

We will begin with this single case because Sita's dramatic transformation represents what is usually considered to be the paradigmatic type of sudden change upon which laypeople and scholars alike often focus. In like fashion, the field of conversion studies is so broad and the perspectives are so many that to recount the history of psychological, sociological, and religious studies of conversion would require at least a book-length study, if not half a library shelf. Consequently, the interpreters have been selected—in this section and the next—in order to present several basically different approaches to religious conversion that will allow us to view Sita's conversion from varied angles.

One of the most obvious explanations of Sita's conversion comes out of the Freudian psychological tradition. Leaving aside Freud's discredited primal horde theory, many persons would still agree with him that dramatic religious conversions are best understood as an unconscious infantile regression. Freud understood religious conversion as a pathology analogous to a childhood neurosis. That is, a religious crisis resulting in conversion is actually an outbreak of previously repressed, unconscious feelings or wishes that erupt into consciousness and disrupt normal psychological functioning.

Freud's only specific study of religious conversion was published in 1928.[41] In it Freud reports that a young doctor was converted to Christianity as the result of seeing an old female cadaver on a dissection table. Freud said that this startling experience reawakened in the young doctor oedipal feelings of jealousy and rage directed toward God (the father figure) for the sadistic and degrading treatment of the mother (represented by the old woman). Freud submits that the initial impulse of the young physician to rebel against his father was finally resolved in capitulation to that same father in the disguised form of the God of his childhood faith.

Because Freud found the oedipal conflict at the root of religious conversion, he concluded that all religion was at its core an infantile regression into childhood fantasies and conflicts that led to a childish dependence. These childhood fantasies were simply disguised projections of deep-seated and unconscious wishes that finally *should* be overcome.[42]

Freud's negative assessment of religious conversions as a pathological condition has become commonplace for subsequent psychological interpreters. Leon Salzman in 1953 and Carl Christensen in 1963 report from their studies of sudden religious conversions that they are regressive and usually stem from guilt, anger, and other such destructive preconversion attitudes.[43] Salzman recognizes gradual conversions as "progressive" because they *can* contribute to emotional maturity and development. However, he focuses his study on sudden conversions which he calls "psychopathological conversions." In other words, a sudden religious conversion represents a pathological state of mind.

Though Erik Erikson allows more room for social and environmental factors to be considered, this renowned Harvard psychologist follows primarily in Freud's footsteps. In his book *Young Man Luther*, Erikson applies his eight-stage psychological developmental model to Martin Luther's religious experiences. He concludes that Luther's conversion and subsequent faith were projections of his oedipal conflict with his father. That is, Luther's repressed resentment over his father's heavy-handed thwarting of his childhood initiatives resulted in a guilt that Luther projected onto a stern and authoritarian Father-God. Erikson concludes:

> I have implied that the original faith which Luther tried to restore goes back to the basic trust of early infancy. In doing so I have not . . . diminished the wonder

of what Luther calls God's disguise. I assume that it is the smiling face and the guiding voice of infantile parent images which religion projects onto the benevolent sky.[44]

It is precisely Erikson's psychological model of identity crisis that Francine Daner applies in her attempt to explain why American youths would turn to such a foreign faith as the Hare Krishna. In her book *The American Children of Krsna,* Daner concludes a six-page Eriksonian analysis of Krishna converts with the statement:

> The search for identity, for a definition of self, is one of the main concerns of youth today. Young people appear preoccupied with personal consciousness and experimentation. . . . The ISKCON temple provides a total-institutional setting which allows its members a well-defined structural and ideological situation into which they can fit themselves. It creates a social situation in which they can realize their identities, thereby eliminating much of the ambiguity which is generated by modern society.[45]

Applying the Freudian/Eriksonian psychological explanations used by Daner to the case of Sita's conversion yields some valuable insights. First of all, it is clear that the severe anxiety and guilt that Sita experienced prior to her conversion to ISKCON might be explained, in part, by her family relationships. According to Sita, her mother was an impulsive, unstable authority figure. She was given to periods of strong depression spiced by fits of outrage. Sita remembers her mother getting so angry with her and her brothers that she would strike out at them just prior to stomping out of the house for a cooling-off period. Sita's father was gone much of the time, making her mother the primary parent for the family. Her recollection of her family life was that "it was not a very warm environment."

It may well have been that unresolved and unconscious conflicts with her authoritarian mother did play some role in Sita's preconversion state of mind, but she does report that during her first years of graduate school she and her parents had begun to understand each other and that their relationship had never been better.

Gordon Melton and Robert Moore in their book *The Cult Experience* caution us to consider the roles played by *all* members of the family of a cult convert.[46] Using family systems theory, Melton and Moore submit that "problem children" are often encouraged either to submit to familial discipline or to abandon the family in search of freedom and an accepting environment. Consequently, the decision to enter a deviant religious group may well reflect problems resident in the whole family environment and not just of one individual family member.

As we will see later, Sita's psychological crisis does not necessarily require one to assume either an unconscious conflict with her parents or specific role conflicts originating in the family. Still, the particular focus provided by the psychoanalytic interpretation of religious conversion or by family systems therapy brings into view the motivational factors that could *unconsciously* intensify the feelings of worthlessness and despair that Sita was feeling when she decided to end her life. Furthermore, it can hardly be doubted that, according to Erikson's descriptive terms, Sita was experiencing a crisis of "ego identity."[47] Clearly Sita *did* question whether or not any continuity existed between her image of herself and that of significant others (e.g., parents, classmates, teachers, and close friends).

Sociological Perspectives on Conversion

One sociological theory that takes the role of significant others in conversion very seriously is that proposed by Rodney Stark and William Bainbridge.[48] In their essay entitled "Networks of Faith," Stark and Bainbridge argue that older sociological models of deprivation that focused on the ideological appeal of so-called cults must be supplemented by theories that place more emphasis on interpersonal relations and contacts to explain the conversion process. They say of their social network model, "It argues that faith constitutes conformity to the religious outlook of one's intimates—that membership spreads through social networks."[49] Not confining their theory to cult conversions alone, they argue that both recruitment and commitment to conventional faiths are supported by social networks.

Stark and Bainbridge provide quantitative evidence of the critical importance of social and kinship bonds in spreading religious faith. They cite Jane Hardyck and Marcia Braden's 1962 data on a doomsday group, Ted Nordquist's 1978 study of Ananda Marg, and their own statistical survey of Mormon conversion patterns. In the case of their Mormon cohort, Stark and Bainbridge describe the Mormons' missionary strategy which directs missionaries to develop personal relationships *first* before preaching to potential converts. Specifically, only in step five of a thirteen-step guide for missionaries to follow does religion enter the picture at all. Stark and Bainbridge then demonstrate statistically the recent burgeoning of Mormon converts through the conversion of whole families and their friends.

Stark and Bainbridge support their study by recalling Kevin Welch's research that points to the same network process at the center of recruitment and commitment successes in mainline American churches. They conclude their essay with the claim that final conversion is primarily a process of coming to accept the opinions of one's friends.[50]

The Stark and Bainbridge network theory has been applied to Krishna converts in an essay published elsewhere, and the reader should be aware that there is much of value in their perspective.[51] Whether or not Sita's friendship with a Krishna devotee actually saved her life, at least it did affect her decision to join ISKCON. Sita had kept up communications with her Krishna devotee friend throughout her college and graduate school years. And when she needed to find religious answers to her anxiety-producing questions, she trusted that what was good enough for her friend was good enough for her. Therefore, even though Sita had never been to a Krishna temple before, she joined her friend's temple.

One can criticize the network theory as being obvious, since no one is likely to join a group made up only of strangers, yet the real challenge of this theory is much the same as that of sociology of knowledge made popular by Thomas Luckmann and Berger. That is, such theories push us to accept or reject the notion that conversion to a new religious standpoint is primarily a social process, not a psychological one. It should be clear that Sita's extreme psychological distress and sudden conversion to the Krishna faith cannot be explained by the network theory alone. Nonetheless, new light is thrown upon her specific choice of the Krishnas by applying Stark and Bainbridge's insights.

A role theory approach to conversion is a second type of sociological theory that has been used to explain cult conversions. David Bromley and Anson Shupe are two sociologists who have written several books on the Moonies and the general topic of cult conversions.[52] They adopt the role theory model of conversion as they attempt to combat motivational theories that focus on the predispositions of cult converts.

According to Bromley and Shupe's analysis, motivational theories argue, first, that the cult convert has certain social or psychological predispositions; second, that a cult offers a worldview that satisfies the convert's predisposed yearnings; and, third, that the cult convert will exhibit proper behavior after having been convinced of the truth of the cult's ideology. Whether or not the predispositions are primarily social or psychological in nature, converts choose a cult that will promise that which they seek.

Accusing motivational theorists of putting the cart before the horse, Bromley and Shupe view conversion to any new religion "Not in terms of individual experience and personal feelings, but rather as socially structured events arising out of role relationships." Instead of answering the question of why people convert, they ask how they convert. In answering the "how" question, Bromley and Shupe insist that stages two and three of the motivational model are reversed. That is, the new cult behavior *precedes* belief conversion. According to the role theory model of conversion, "an individual begins performing a role as the result of the initial interactive process between the individual and the group which may or may not involve attitudinal change."[53]

The role theory approach does describe well what actually happened to Sita at the point of her conversion decision. She joined the Hare Krishna movement *and then* asked her new friends what they believed. In other words, Sita acted and looked like a Krishna devotee long before she adopted fully the beliefs upon which her behavior and dress were predicated. What is important about the role theory approach is that it directs our attention away from considering conversion as a single event and insists that it involves a complex and lengthy process, at least for many new converts.

Some devotees *act* as though they are completely committed even while doubts may be raging inside that finally erupt in a decision to leave the group that catches everyone by surprise. One woman devotee who was interviewed was introduced as one of the first members in ISKCON and a model of Krishna devotion. In her interview, however, she revealed some strong doubts about the way ISKCON was "demoting" many older women devotees who had enjoyed more freedom and responsibility in the early days of the movement. Within a year—and to the surprise of many of her friends—she had left ISKCON.

Shadows of Truth

What Govinda's conversion story does—and Mahema's in a less dramatic way—is to underline a basic *conscious* dimension of all conversions that should not be ignored as we seek to understand and to explain such religious events. The conceptual questioning and content of Govinda's quest and final faith choice are perhaps more obvious in Govinda's than in Sita's case. Nonetheless, in Sita's case a considerable amount of conscious searching took place of which only she and a few intimates were aware. While we must avoid insisting that the theological content alone is the only necessary and sufficient factor in either Govinda's or Sita's conversions, we must acknowledge that the theological element certainly appears to have been a central factor.

When applied to the devotee conversions portrayed in this book, these several social-scientific explanations of conversion clearly suggest the inadequacy of any single approach by itself. But more important, the fact that each model has been taken by some scholars to be an explanation sufficient in itself gives a clearer picture of the dilemma that faces anyone who wishes to enter the debate. All theories of conversion are, to some extent, like the shadows on the wall of Plato's cave: they are human constructs that project images of what it means to become religious and that often distort as much as they reveal.[54]

In the course of the author's five years of research and interviews among Hare Krishna devotees, several challenges to the above conversion theories have arisen. First of all, sudden conversions like Sita's are rare among persons who join ISKCON. Fewer than a dozen of the 120 devotees interviewed claimed any dramatic experience or quick decision to enter a Krishna temple.

The far more common pattern was for a convert to experience at least a year of occasional and unpressured contact with ISKCON, coupled with some significant study of ISKCON's teachings prior to his or her decision to become a devotee and move into a temple. Govinda's conversion certainly represents this pattern well (though his insistent seeking of a guru in India is not typical of most devotees). Consequently, even when psychological theories do appear to account for a sudden conversion like Sita's, they have explained the atypical—as the theories of Freud, Salzman, and Christensen also do, given their biased samplings of only "pathological" cases of religiosity.

In the second place, it would appear that there are many and varied basic patterns of conversion or affiliation instead of the two most commonly named patterns: sudden and gradual. The various conversion patterns include a variety of motives, differences in lengths of time before any decision to join, and idiosyncratic factors such as Sita's incessant preoccupation with human suffering or Govinda's single-minded seeking of a spiritual master. In short, no one model, however complex and sophisticated, can do more than cast *one* shadow on our cave's wall.

The third observation is really anticipated in William James's old but still relevant study, *The Varieties of Religious Experience*. In that book, James defines conversion this way:

> To be converted, to be regenerated, to receive grace, to experience religion, to gain assurance, are so many phrases which denote the process, gradual or sudden, by which a self hither divided, and consciously wrong, inferior and unhappy, becomes unified and consciously right, superior and happy . . . whether or not we believe that a direct divine operation is needed to bring such a moral change about.[55]

James implies in this quote that conversion includes not only a *decision* to convert but also a *conversion process* that culminates in altered moral behavior and a new religious life. He spells out clearly in his chapters on saintliness that religious experiences, no matter how dramatic, do not constitute conversion. Instead, only when the convert fully internalizes the new worldview and demonstrates this change in his behavior can the conversion be said to be complete. Consequently, a seldom noticed insight offered by James is that there is a distinction to be made between a *conversion decision* and the *conversion process* which may or may not follow such a decision.

On the one hand, Sita *decided* to join the Krishna temple in a moment of emotional distress, but she also clearly underwent a *conversion process* during the years following that provided answers to the questions that had contributed consciously to her initial distress. On the other hand, Govinda experimented with various religious life-styles and philosophies and did so with ISKCON before finally making a conscious choice to be initiated. Mahema's conversion was somewhat a combination of the previous two. In the case of Sita, there is a clear separation between the conversion decision and the subsequent faith-rendering process. Alternatively, in the case of Govinda, the two are virtually reversed.

The distinction between decision and process in conversion is assumed, though not discussed, in the recent work done on stages of religious development by James Fowler. In his book *Stages of Faith,* Fowler describes six different and progressively mature types of religiosity.[56] In so doing, Fowler talks primarily about the conversion process for persons born into a religious faith. Consequently, to some extent the issue of decision is skirted.

Fowler says the young child raised in a religious home usually exhibits what he calls an "Intuitive-Projective" faith that is a fantasy-filled imitation of what he or she sees in trusted adults. Subsequent to the naive faith of the infant, five stages of religious realization follow, culminating in what Fowler describes as the fully actualized person of stage six. The fully mature believer has what Fowler calls a "Universalizing Faith" and becomes "a disciplined, activist *incarnation* . . . of the imperatives of absolute love and justice."[57]

In other words, a fully mature person of any faith becomes a living example of his or her particular faith. At the same time, such a person embraces—or takes account of—the world outside the religious community with all its forms of belief and unbelief without feeling any threat to his or her own beliefs. However, between the infant's naive but trusting faith and the compassionate, mature faith lie other more or less literal, dogmatic or liberated forms of believing that tend to be exclusivistic. There are Krishna devotees spread along the whole spectrum Fowler describes. Ironically it is the new convert in the "imitative" stage who so often appears to be the "robot" programmed by the cult when, in fact, the interviews revealed the most doubts to be present at this stage. In the more mature devotees, however, considerably more freedom of action and thought are supported by a more firm—and sometimes totalistic—faith.

What is important in Fowler's analysis for our consideration of Sita's conversion is the realization that psychoanalytic or social explanations that focus upon her *conversion decision* alone neglect the maturing *conversion process* she underwent. Likewise, Fowler's work encourages us to look at Govinda's religious quest as a period of maturation prior to an actual commitment or leap of faith into ISKCON. It is clear from Govinda's story that religious maturation can occur even prior to a conversion decision; also note that the choices that Govinda considered were radically different ones that included atheistic and theistic solutions.

Most theories of conversion will cast the shadows of the experiences and worldviews of the interpreters who propose them as much as they will that of a convert like Sita or Govinda. However, the distinction between decision and process is an important consideration regardless of the theoretical perspective. It is simply the case that Sita's conversion *decision* to enter the temple was quite different *in character* from the *conversion process* that had led to her maturing faith. Though a psychological crisis may have helped to precipitate her joining ISKCON, Sita's study of the Krishna scriptures in the light of her previous existential questions resulted in her becoming a mature Krishna disciple who not only knew who Krishna was but worshiped him knowledgeably. Interviews with other devotees at Sita's temple confirmed the impression that Sita was among the more religiously mature of the devotees interviewed and observed. She was respected as a counselor for new women devotees, as a knowledgeable student of the Krishna scriptures, and as a good representative of ISKCON to the outside world.

What Fowler's theory of six stages of faith represents is one more shadow on our cave's wall, but its shape is dramatically different from that of most conversion theories. It requires that we take seriously the *conscious content* of Sita's distress, Govinda Dasa's search, and Mahema's surrender and see in them a desire to build a future that is ultimately meaningful.

The final, and perhaps most important, lesson to be learned from the conversions of Krishna devotees is that conscious, cognitive factors weighed heavily in most devotees' conversion decisions and were paramount in subsequent conversion processes. Consequently, it is clear that we will miss entirely the significance and origin of Sita's conversion and its similarity to Govinda's if we do not discover why it was the theology of Krishna that finally satisfied Sita. Many have joined ISKCON in a moment of distress only to leave at a later date unsatisfied. Only if one takes account of the process of theological or spiritual maturation in devotees will additional headway be made in explaining why some devotees stay and others leave, even though external factors appear to be similar.

Being attentive to the theological questioning that is so obvious in Govinda's quest sensitizes us to the fact that Sita's conversion decision and process are linked by her conscious religious questioning and despair that finally found satisfactory answers in the Hindu teachings of Krishna. Such a perspective also explains why Sita—and most Krishna devotees—could become a Krishna disciple but not likely a follower of the Rev. Moon.[58]

To understand Sita's conversion as motivated in great part by factors fully known to her (i.e., conscious factors) places a very different agenda before the inquiring scholar than the one allowed by most of the above theories based upon unconscious factors. Such an agenda requires that we focus upon the consciously derived decisions, motivations, and ideological processes of the religious convert even when the intellectual component is not as obvious as it is in the case of Govinda's religious seeking. Such an agenda will usually include more talk about the conversion process[59] than about any single decision to join a new faith and, inevitably, turn the researcher's attention away from social and psychological explanations alone and toward theological and philosophical considerations.

To her family and friends, Sita's decision to commit suicide was a radical departure from her everyday demeanor and attitude. Likewise, her decision to enter the Krishna temple appeared to have no continuity with her former life or thought. However, surprising as it may seem from external appearances, Sita's decision to join ISKCON and her process of spiritual maturation were both continuous with her private life of thought and prayer. While certainly fraught with overtones of psychological crisis, Sita's conversion to ISKCON is not accurately described if it is reduced to a stereotypic instance of mind control. Sita was not a passive victim of the Hare Krishnas. Likewise, brainwashing as an exaggerated and simplistic explanation of coercive control fails to appreciate the active roles taken by Govinda, Mahema, or Lakshmi in their conversions. If there is a common denominator in these devotee conversions, it is that each convert's quest for meaning was finally satisfied in the specific teaching and stories of the Indian cowherd Krishna.

Essentially, the brainwashing metaphor is "a weapon against *deviance.*"[60] The fear this specious concept engenders is pervasive and powerful in the hands of those who would lump all cults together as "destructive." While most anticult antagonists use Lifton's description of coercive persuasion in Chinese prison camps as a validation for their understanding of "brainwashing," none heed his qualifications and warning:

> Behind [the] web of semantic . . . confusion lies an image of "brainwashing" as an all-powerful, irresistible, unfathomable, and magical method of achieving total control over the human mind. It is of course, none of these things, and this loose usage makes the word a rallying point for fear, resentment, urges toward submission, justification for failure, irresponsible accusation, and for a wide gamut of emotional extremism.[61]

While written more than twenty years ago and before the current anticult craze, Lifton's warnings were prophetic. There has emerged in America (and elsewhere) a whole set of movements of hate and suspicion. These are the "new vigilantes" who as self-appointed guardians of youth forcibly rescue and "deprogram" cult "programmed" "victims." Sadly, they are also the products of misinformation, exaggerated tales, and quasi-scientific speculations that surround the term "brainwashing."

8

Deprogramming:
Fear and Its Legacies

Throughout religious history, tales of atrocities have been used to engender fear of new religious movements and to justify violent repression of such movements. The early Christians were accused of cannibalism by some Roman antagonists who misunderstood their secret rite of ingesting wine and bread as blood and body. The fear engendered by such tales of barbarism —linked with their refusal to honor Caesar as God—led many Christians to martyrdom in the arena or at the hands of angry mobs. Such suspicion and hate of "new" religions have been common in American history as well. The Shakers, the Mormons, and the Jehovah's Witnesses all have histories of oppression, violence, and persecution at the hands of those who feared them.[1]

Throughout history, one of the most effective ways of engendering fear of new religions has been to call upon ex-members to tell their horror stories. These defectors could be relied upon "to tell all" about the dangers of the deviant group that required stern and swift reprisals from the concerned citizenry. As David Bromley and Anson Shupe conclude, "American religious history has a rich literature of 'exposés,' [and such] individuals have been able to sway audiences and actually incite mobs with their inflammatory accusations and lurid claims of 'I was there, I saw it happen!' "[2] Whether by ex-Mormons or ex-Catholics, reputed eyewitness accounts have seldom been questioned for reliability. Yet there have been many cases of blatant exaggerations and even fictions that ex-members have used out of spite or malice.

Two celebrated cases of atrocity stories involved Maria Monk and Rebecca Reed, two reputed Catholic nuns. In their books *Awful Disclosures of the Hotel Dieu Nunnery* and *Six Months in a Convent,* Maria and Rebecca claimed to be escaped nuns who had witnessed terrible atrocities during their convent imprisonments.[3] In actual fact, neither woman was a nun and both used ghostwriters in fabricating their stories of the brutality occurring behind Catholic monastery walls.

A centerpiece of the contemporary Crusader Comicbook series of Chick Publications in Chino, California, is the trilogy of magazines telling the story of Alberto Rivera, an ex-Jesuit Spanish monk. In the original issue, called

Alberto, Rivera tells an incredible story of the homosexuality, death, and political intrigue that he claims to have witnessed behind closed monastery doors. Mixing medieval incidents of torture and the burning of heretics at the stake with reputedly contemporary tales of a worldwide Catholic conspiracy to destroy all Protestant opponents, Rivera ends his story with supposed torture at the hands of his Jesuit brothers. In the second magazine, called *Double-Cross,* Rivera ends by exposing Jim Jones and the Jonestown massacre as a Jesuit plot to discredit fundamentalist Christians.

The fires of fear and hate fanned by the anticult movement in contemporary America have been fueled by the testimony of cult defectors, especially those forcibly removed. The vast majority of the published atrocity stories regarding cults in America have been related by deprogrammed Moonies, such as the story told by Christopher Edwards in his book *Crazy for God: The Nightmare of Cult Life.* Edwards tells a tale of deception, physical abuse (sleep and food deprivation), fear of Satan, and rejection of parents that marked his seven months in the Unification Church. He was "saved" by a Ted Patrick deprogramming. In a similar but even more dramatic vein, Allen Tate Wood's *Moonstruck: A Memoir of My Life in a Cult* and Barbara and Betty Underwood's *Hostage to Heaven: Four Years in the Unification Church, by an Ex-Moonie and the Mother Who Fought to Free Her* represent classic examples of the antagonism often felt by those who reject beliefs they formerly held.

It is reasonable to argue that the often intense and sometimes deceptive proselytizing practices and life-style of the Unification Church lend themselves rather well to anticult critiques. (One could say the same thing for many Protestant evangelical traditions as well.) Consequently, it is not surprising that ex-Moonies who have been forcibly removed and deprogrammed often feel they have been particularly embarrassed and misused. The less-pressured, undisguised indoctrination approach of the Krishnas may be less effective in recruiting new members than the Moonies' approach, but one of the advantages has been that no major books relating atrocities within ISKCON have been written by an ex-Krishna even though many devotees have been deprogrammed. Nonetheless, there are occasional newspaper accounts of disgruntled ex-Krishna devotees who sound very similar to the Moonies in their charges of physical deprivation, hate of parents, and sexual abuses.[4]

The one charge that the deprogrammer Ted Patrick made of the Krishnas that surely was designed to engender fear of ISKCON was his claim that "the Hare Krishna cult is kidnapping fourteen people *per day* in this country. Every day. And nobody says a word."[5] The celebrated lawsuit of Robin George that charged that she was brainwashed at the age of fifteen by Hare Krishnas and then hidden from her parents could appear to give some credence to Patrick's assertion. Likewise, in a recent book entitled *Where Is Joey? Lost Among the Hare Krishnas,* Morris Yanoff seems to give more weight to Patrick's claims. On closer examination, however, both these cases reveal complicated stories that demonstrate the Krishnas' bad judgment in entering domestic disputes (i.e., by allowing Robin to run away from home and then hiding her from her parents and by siding with Joey's mother, who was a devotee, and hiding Joey from his father and grandfather); but in neither case did the Krishnas kidnap or hold a young person against her or his will.

What such atrocity stories have accomplished is the creation of a strong fear of the cults in American society at large and therefore parents' willingness to do virtually anything to extricate their child from any cult. Furthermore, the horror stories of ex-members of one cult are collapsed into generalizations that by implication or direct statement are applied to all cults. At the center of all these stories is the ubiquitous specter of brainwashing, the belief in mind control as a fact, which has led to the radical remedy of deprogramming. Many tormented and frightened parents have viewed the kidnapping and deprogramming of their son or daughter as a final resort but as warranted in the light of the dangers posed by cults such as the Hare Krishnas.

Before we turn to an examination of deprogramming as one product of anticult fear, the reader is asked to assess the story of Laksmana in the light of the two conflicting descriptions of cult conversions presented in this book. On the one hand, consider Laksmana's story from the point of view of the anticult scenario of coercive persuasion and robotlike programming. On the other hand, evaluate Laksmana's conversion and deprogramming experience by taking seriously Laksmana's role in his conversion process and by considering the role that reason and a search for meaning played.

I was born in a small town in Mississippi on April 24, 1958. My mother and father were not very educated people; my mother had only finished twelfth grade, my father only the eighth grade in school, and yet both of them were fairly intelligent. They were not particularly religious, though they did go to church once a week. They were a country family who lived on a farm and had a very simple life-style. They also had a very high set of morals and very high standards for us children. Though they were not particularly pious people, they were very strict with my sister and me.

I never had very high respect for my parents, because I could see that they were very confused and didn't know the answers to many of life's really important problems. So many of the questions I would bring up, they couldn't answer and so I would lose more respect for them. I could see that their whole life was centered around providing food, shelter, meeting the bills and things like that. They weren't actually trying to find out the higher questions of life. But my sister was different. She was always interested in art and was more inquiring and philosophical than were my parents. I respected her for that, and for many years she was my role model.

My family was protective, and they wanted to keep me home all the time; they never wanted me to venture out to learn about the world. They were very careful about the people I associated with. Living in a small town of only forty-five hundred people also was very inhibiting. Yet as I look back on my family, I realize my home environment provided a great deal of security. Still, my family did not provide a particularly loving environment.

There was a lot of attachment. My parents were attached to the idea of family life because that's all they had. I've heard them admit on many occasions, "If we ever lose our family, that's all we've got." They talked a lot about God and Jesus and how much you have to love God, but they clearly had no attachment to God. They made a lot of pretenses about love, but my sister and I knew it was false. The actual feeling of love was never there. Therefore, our family had a very strained relationship, especially about the time that I became a teenager.

From the time I was fifteen, I became interested in religious ideas, spiritual ideas. But I couldn't see anyone who was actually practicing; anyone who was actually becoming pure. Although I joined several different Christian camps and all that, I could see the people I was with were not really perfecting their lives —it was just a bunch of words. But I was still interested in that concept and so I spent a lot of time reading. One of the persons I read was Edgar Cayce, who, until I finished college, fascinated me.

I hated school because I could see that the things I learned weren't really leading me anyplace. I could see that no matter how much I learned, no matter what combinations I made of different subjects, I still was not going to be satisfied. I would read different philosophers, British writers, and all the rest, but I could just see they all were guessing. They actually didn't have the answers. . . . I could tell that none of them actually had a personal relationship with God, a reciprocal relationship.

I had my nose stuck in a book most of the time. I didn't care much for sports —such things looked pretty futile to me. As a student, I was an A student in grade school and junior high. By the time I got to high school I had become very lax in my studies and was not studying at all. I just couldn't find anything I was really interested in, anything that was being offered to me in school. I wanted to be a writer and I wrote a lot of poems and stories. When I finally got to college, I started associating with philosophy majors and such people. That's what really opened me up.

I went to a small, religiously affiliated college in Mississippi which imposed very, very strict rules upon its students. There was a pretense that this was a Christian school, but it wasn't really that at all. I went to college for three years and left at the end of my junior year because I was just convinced that a small college like mine was a very small political machine with its own bureaucracy. It was just like the whole United States, condensed a little bit.

While I was taking a course in world religions, at the end of my sophomore year, our professor took us to the Hare Krishna temple in New Orleans. The first time I remember seeing a devotee was at a fair in a small town in Mississippi, when I was about fifteen years old. There were two devotees distributing books outside the fairgrounds. And I laughed as hard as I could; I thought it was the funniest thing I had ever seen—this guy with the shaved head, praying on his knees, on his beads, you know, . . . five minutes, and I forgot all about it.

In any case, when we arrived at the Hare Krishna temple with our college professor, I remember walking into the temple stoned. My friend and I had smoked a joint right before getting on the bus. So when I walked through this temple and saw a huge painting of this big man-lion [one of the avatara forms of Krishna] ripping open the stomach of a demon, I thought this was a really wild place, but I was open for just about anything. Most of the students in the class were pretty mild Christians, but were still offended with much of what they saw and heard in the temple. But I was pretty interested in what little bit of philosophy the guy told us. And it was in line with everything I had been reading and had accepted.

A lot of the things I'd read I would just reject. But the belief in God and a notion of the blisses of the spiritual world that I had accepted I found right here in what this guy was saying. Some additional principles of the Krishnas that agreed with my own included a belief in reincarnation and an understanding that God is absolutely personal in his transcendent form. We listened to a cultural talk on India with slides that one of the devotees presented. And then we had *prasadam* [blessed food].

We then saw a dancing and singing ritual performance [*aratrika* and *kirtana*]. During this dancing and singing, the curtains at the end of the big room where we stood opened up and the deities on the altar were brightly clothed in many colored garments. The devotees all stood on one side of the room as we stood on the other, and they chanted and sang, dancing up and down. Wow, look at this, I thought. Are they on acid or am I on acid? What's going on? This can't be real. I had never seen anything like it, because these people were so fervent. I was attracted to the chanting and wanted to join in, but I couldn't do so because I felt reserved on account of my classmates who were all around me. As we left, the devotees asked us to come back and invited us to a Sunday feast. Even though the temple was a considerable distance from my college, I knew I would come back.

During the next year and a half, while I was in college, I did go back four times to the Hare Krishna temple. When I went, I took part in the dancing and the singing. I would jump up and down and dance and twirl and sing. It was the best thing I had ever been in. I couldn't believe it! I felt so satisfied when I got through. The disciples would preach to me and give me copies of their scriptures. I already had a *Bhagavad Gita*. And though I read those books some, I couldn't make very much sense of them because I was still so intoxicated. I used marijuana regularly and took acid maybe four times in my whole life. I also would drink beer, and though I didn't like it, there wasn't much else to do in college.

The longer I stayed in college, the more I could see that vocational opportunities for me were almost unlimited, but none of them appeared to be satisfying. I really couldn't find the best thing that I should do. So I decided that I would put my life in God's hands. I prayed a lot during my junior year, and the prayers sounded like: God-Krishna, 'cause that's your name, you certainly know more than I do. Whatever you want me to do then that's what I should do.

When the summer came, I went off to a summer camp to teach karate. And though I took my *Bhagavad Gita* with me, I didn't read it much. I was still more into Edgar Cayce and therefore was reading his books all the time. Actually my goal was to go to Virginia Beach at the end of the summer and join up with the Edgar Cayce Institute. I wanted to learn and do whatever Edgar Cayce did and be like him by putting myself into a trance and tuning into God, because that's what I felt he did. So at the end of the summer, I took my sister's car and headed off to Virginia Beach. In the pocket in my sister's car was an ISKCON book. It was the *Perfection of Yoga* and *Beyond Birth and Death* combined. I read the Krishna books a couple of times and they made a big impression on me.

When I arrived at the Edgar Cayce Center, I was very disappointed. All my dreams, my idealistic bubble, was busted. The whole place was nothing but a materialistic organization. They were just after money and it made Cayce's teachings appear hypocritical. I became totally disgusted and asked myself what I was going to do now. When I walked to the parking lot, a young man asked me to give him a lift. I discovered that he was going to a Hare Krishna temple down the street.

The moment I walked in the door of this small temple in Virginia Beach, I was overwhelmed with the energy, the spiritual energy, of this place. Actually, I guess if you can feel purity, that's what it was. As soon as I walked in, it felt so pure. I never felt anything just like it, even in the New Orleans temple. I made a deal to come to the morning program each day if they would allow me to sleep in the yard outside the temple house. But I was still living essentially like a beach bum. I had about $300 left of my own money and would spend the early-morning hours at the devotional program before heading off to the beach to look at women for the day. I would always make it back to the temple in time for three delicious meals.

I parked my car on the beach and would either sit in the car or on the beach trying to decide what to do. I had been through so much in the last week; the changes that I had gone through and the decisions I'd been making were overwhelming. I just remember in my mind I could hear one of the mothers [women devotees] chanting and it was so pure. She was calling on God, but the thing was, I knew God was responding too, just in the inflection of her voice, the way she was acting. . . . There was a relationship there—a very personal thing and something I had never experienced before. I knew it was true; I knew right then that yes, Krishna is non-different from his name. I felt the disciples who were chanting the name of Krishna were linked up with him. I believed that and I knew they were chanting that name many times each day. And so I made my decision right then to move in. I felt that these people were performing God's service twenty-four hours a day and had dedicated their whole life to God.

I could understand and agree with everything—the forms of God, the names, the practices, serving the devotees, and so on—that the devotees were teaching. I couldn't find a flaw in their philosophy and I was looking. I just felt, this is what I've been looking for—I'm sure of it. . . . I'll try it for a little while, but I knew I'd already made the decision right there, that this was going to be my life.

Having made the decision to join the Hare Krishna temple, I called up my parents to tell them. I heard my mother scream six hundred miles, over the phone. No she didn't scream actually, she just went a little hysterical. She said, "The only thing in the world I didn't want you to do—the one thing I was praying to God that you wouldn't do—and that's what you've done." And then my father gets on the phone: "That ain't God, son, that ain't God. I know what God is and that ain't God." I think they would have been happier if I was on drugs in New York City. My decision was a big shock to them.

I tried to explain a little bit, but finally I just quit explaining. I just let them get everything out of their system. I said, "We're going to have a long time to develop this, you know, to work things out." So I just let them get over their anxiety a little bit. So we talked for about a half an hour and I called them again a couple of days later and things seemed a lot nicer. I'd been praying a lot to have Krishna help them understand. And while they seemed to feel that I'd made a bad decision, they did seem to accept the fact that it was my decision. I began to feel that they would work things out. I called them every week and tried to cultivate them a little bit by teaching them about the philosophy—just trying to let them know that I was happy, that I had found what I wanted to do.

My mother was more open-minded from the start. She was willing at least to listen when I talked about Krishna philosophy. And while at home, she began to check out the movement herself. She would buy books about the cults and try to make some sense of this movement I had just joined. I sent her lots of books from the Krishnas themselves. She read a little bit of them, but not much. I went home to visit my parents at Christmas of 1979. It was clear from the start that my father was closed-minded. His philosophy dictated that anything not Christian is from the devil. He would allow me to speak my piece, whatever I was going to say, and would act like he was sort of accepting it. But then as soon as I would get through, he would come back with this Christian stuff. "No, that's not God, this is God. I know what God is."

I knew I was not making very much headway with my father, so I kept working on my mother because she seemed to be more supportive of what I had decided to do. And while I knew my father could not really accept what I had decided to do in becoming a Krishna devotee, I thought he was at least reaching neutral ground—until July, that is.

After I'd been in the movement a short time and had visited my parents during Christmas, I went to a university where the Hare Krishnas had a vegetarian meal program. I was working with a senior devotee in this outreach program at the university. However, I was having a lot of trouble staying with the movement because I was not very strictly following the regulative principles (no intoxicants, no illicit sex, etc.). I was becoming dissatisfied with what life in the movement was really like, and so, about noon one day, I had a talk with the senior devotee who was the head of the food program. He said, "O.K. So make your decision. Sure you can walk out the door; nobody's holding you here. You can pack your things and walk out the door right now if you want to." He then concluded, "But you know what's out there. You've been there before; you know it. I think you should go outside and chant a little bit and think about it. Make your decision because you have to make a decision."

I said, "O.K." So I went outside and leaned up against a car and began to pray [chant]. While leaning against this car, I was glancing around to see what was going on. I saw two guys walking up the street towards me and said to myself, "Ah, you know, just college people, because we're right here in the middle of all the fraternities, and these are college guys walking around." And then I glanced out of the corner of my eye, and there was only one man. "Wait a minute, there were two guys." And right when I thought that—blam, just like that—one guy got me around the ankles, the other got me by the shoulders and they had me literally in the air.

I said, "Oh, my God, what's going on? What are you doing?" I said, "I always thought I wanted to leave, but I didn't really want to leave under these circumstances." And so they had a car. It zoomed up, the door flew open, and they held me and we all three got in at the same time. They had me horizontally in the air. And I cried out for the senior devotee as loud as I could. People came running to the windows everywhere. And the leader of the center saw what was going on.

I said to the men in the car, "What is this? What's going on?" Then I said, "I know what it is. It's some college boys. They're going to beat the hell out of me. They don't want any Hare Krishnas here. They're always yelling at the windows, you know, and they chant mockingly, 'Hare Krishna, Hare Krishna,' and making fun and everything like that. That's what it is. They're going to take me to a back alley and beat the hell out of me." And then one of them, the driver, yelled, "Aha, we got him." I said, "Uh-oh. He's pissed at the disciples." The first thing I said after they got me in the car was, "It looks like Krishna has made another arrangement for me. I wanted to leave and now he's going to put me through a little test to see if I really want to leave or not. Whatever's going to come, I just have to accept it and try to make the right decisions."

So I was pretty calm actually, even though I didn't know what was in store for me. About four blocks away, the car drove up to this weird-looking guy standing on the corner with a sport shirt and a baseball cap and dark glasses. It was my father and he said agitatedly to me, "Now just calm down. Now just calm down. Don't be so anxious." And I responded by saying, "I'm not in any anxiety—you're the one who's flying off the handle. So do you want to tell me what this is all about?" "I knew I would get you back," said the father. "I've been praying and praying. I knew I would get you back." And I responded, "This is a hell of a way to do it, you know. You could have just . . . we could have just talked this thing out or something." And he said, "Well, we're gonna talk now. We're going to have plenty of time to talk."

So anyway, we drove on to a place about a mile and a half from the university —two miles maybe. It was a motel; it was made up of cabins. So, of course, they already had the cabin set up with the windows nailed shut and everything. So they took me there and then they brought in my sister and my mother and my father. It was a whole sentimental thing. I was pretty disgusted with the whole thing, because I just didn't like the situation I was in—forcibly dragged there. I was pretty mad. It was an understatement—I was mad as hell, but I was curious also. I was really curious. I thought, What's this going to be like. Maybe I can learn something that'll be of value.

When we got inside the room, I could see that the deprogrammers believed in what they were doing. They thought they were doing a great service to humanity, you know, reuniting families and so on. First thing is, they cut off my shika, took off my devotee clothes, and put some other clothes on me. Then they began to say to me that the whole trip I had been on was one in which I couldn't make any decisions. Everything was done for me and thought for me and so the purpose of our conversation was to get me to think again. When they determine that I can make my own decisions again, I'll be rehabilitated, you know—I'll have snapped back again.

There were six guys in all—four bodyguards and two deprogrammers. They were very careful to ask me, "Are you all right? Are you hurt?" when I got out of the car and into the room. I guess they didn't want to be sued. I was a little surprised at that, but I figured these guys had been dragged to court so many times. I guess they have to be pretty careful these days. I hope they're a lot more careful than they used to be! Mostly, they wanted to see what my reaction was going to be. There were no bright lights or anything. They just wanted to see what my reaction was going to be.

Well, I was mad as hell. I was talking—I just couldn't stop. Everything was bubbling up. "Why are you doing this?" I asked. "You took away my freedom. You talk about my freedom being taken away, but you just took it away. Sure I'll talk to you. I'll talk to you for hours on end, but not in this circumstance, you know. Not like a caged animal." Anyway, it was a whole scene and went on for a whole day like that, with us arguing back and forth, back and forth. One of the deprogrammers was an ex-devotee and he too had been deprogrammed. He really believed in what he was doing. Yeah, just like I said before—he believed in what he was doing. But that belief was a justification for what he thought was humanitarian activities, but it was just the justification for his envy. He was so envious of true devotees and of Prabhupada. He seemed to feel that Prabhupada was just on a big ego trip—accepting obeisances from devotees. I could tell he didn't have an understanding of the philosophy. But, in any case, he told me his story and after a while, I quieted down. In any case, the first day was pretty tumultuous. We all were tired; we were exhausted. And finally the deprogrammers left and two guards stayed with me.

My parents and the rest of my family were gone. I mean, after ten minutes, they were gone. I only saw them once every day, and one day I didn't see them at all. So most of the time I found myself scheming about how in the hell I was going to get out of here. I was thinking, How can I? It's on the second floor and I certainly don't want to jump. I was so mad I began to think, Is there some way I could kill these guys? I'll take a lamp and hit them over the head—just so I can get out of here. You know, the whole James Bond thing. But, of course, I couldn't do that. These guys were trained professionals. My parents had stuck a lot of money into this and these guys were good.

During that whole first night, I couldn't sleep at all. I was just trying to decide how I could get out. I was praying a lot—the whole night long. I was really going through a fit and clearly this was a very big test from Krishna. From the moment we had arrived, they had said to me, "We're going to be here a while, you know, a couple of months maybe." And so I thought to myself, If I don't give in to them, this is going to go on forever. But if I play their game and if I can convince them, then I could be out of here in a couple of days. So that's what I did.

The next day I started coming around—it was a hell of a hard thing to do—playing their game. It was like a movie, you know. It was like a play, because I was having to act a certain way; I was having to be very careful about what

I said and I had to gradually surrender to them . . . and yet I had to remain Krishna conscious. Now this was a very tricky process, because I had to keep my mind on what I was doing since I was already wanting to leave the movement for other reasons. I really couldn't trust myself. I felt that the best thing I could do was to get back to the devotees and talk this over with them and try to work out my problems. The main thing I wanted to do was just get out.

The deprogrammers kept talking about all the bad things about the movement—the improper sexual activities of some of the gurus, drug-running, and the violence in Berkeley. Most of it was not true, or was, at best, a distortion of the truth. They would then play tapes by Krishna preachers, by ex-Moonies, by ex-devotees, by this person and that person. Then they would talk about their own experiences. I began more and more to play along with the things they were saying, and after about four days, I had them convinced that I had been deprogrammed.

I thought I would be let go or sent back home with my parents and would be able to escape. But then they said, "I think we're about ready to take you to our rehabilitation center," and my heart sank. I felt damned if I'm going to Tucson, though there wasn't a thing I could do about it. They took me from the motel, along with the bodyguard, to a small airport, where we got on a little six-seater Cessna and flew to Tucson.

When we got to Tucson I was taken by car to a pretty ritzy neighborhood. As we drove up to a nice house I thought, Well, this isn't going to be bad. Maybe the doors will be unlocked and I'll be able to split. But, then, as they took me inside the house, it became clear that I was in a place more like a prison, with rolls of concertina barbed wire and all that. I thought, It's not going to be as easy as I thought.

There was a seven-foot-high wood-slotted fence with guard dogs that were constantly patroling on the inside and the outside of it. I tried to fake a toothache, hoping I would be able to escape on the way to the dentist's office. But instead, when the dentist found nothing wrong with my mouth, my guards became more suspicious. By the time we got back to the house, we were all just exhausted and we took a nap. My parents had come out to Tucson as well, and I had to continue with all of my show of hugging and kissing to show them how grateful I was. I had to continue my play-acting.

When everyone else was asleep, I got up and went out into the backyard, where there was a swimming pool, along with one of the guards and a guard dog. The guard had to go to the pool to shut off the water and even though the Doberman was standing near him, I thought the dog was fairly friendly as long as he wasn't instructed to attack. As the bodyguard went over to the pool to shut off the water, I ran to the fence and, in one jump, grabbed the top and pulled myself up, flipped over the wire and landed on the other side. Just as I landed on the other side, I realized I had nearly landed on a German shepherd. The dog was so startled, he didn't know what to do. Since no one told him to attack, he just left me alone and just stared at me. So I started running.

It was 110 degrees and my lungs felt parched after I took only ten steps and I felt as though I could hardly even walk, but my mind kept saying, "I just gotta get out of here, no matter what. Even if they pick me up in the middle of the road, I've gotta do as much as I can." But I didn't hear a sound and I just kept running—mostly jogging because it was so hot—as I made my way to somebody's yard and down strange street after strange street.

I felt such relief and I thought even if it's going to last just a few minutes, I'm going to relish it. I wound my way through neighborhood after neighborhood, down ravines, under bridges, through a mobile home park, and worked my way back into the middle of the city. I was just as afraid of being picked up by the police as I was of being picked up by the deprogrammers because I knew the police would just take me back to them. As I was making my way down one alley in the middle of Tucson, a pickup truck came screeching to a halt at the end of the alley and there were the deprogrammers and two guards. I don't know why I did it, but I waved to them as I took off running again. I flipped myself over some hedges and lay there panting behind some bushes in someone's backyard as the truck roared by.

I stayed in the backyard, hiding behind some garbage cans for four or five hours, until it got dark. I sat the whole time, chanting and wondering what was going on and what I could do next. For a couple of hours, I heard them scouring the neighborhood and I even saw a police cruiser go by, wondering if they were looking for me. After dark, I went downtown and went to a Chinese restaurant, where I called the senior devotee at the university. He already knew I had gotten away because the deprogrammers had called him and asked for me, which of course was a dumb thing to do. He immediately called San Diego, and as Krishna would have it, the San Diego people knew there was a devotee named Prabhupada Das in Tucson. He came and picked me up, took me to his place, and drove me on to San Diego, which was four hundred miles away.

We drove straight overnight to reach the temple. He didn't want to put me on a bus or anything, because he figured they might be watching the bus terminals and the airports. I stayed in San Diego all day Sunday and then I went to Los Angeles. I could just see how the devotees cooperate with each other. Everybody started arranging this and arranging that and being so nice and everything. In a short time, I was back at the university and then hid out at Gita Nagari, the farm in Pennsylvania.

My parents called various Krishna temples almost every day, but the devotees would not say I was there. However, one day my mother called the temple in Maryland and a young devotee, who didn't know I was hiding, said my mother was calling. And as I talked to my mother on the phone, she simply said, "I just want you to understand why we had done this." I said to her, "I understood from the minute that it happened why you had done this." She said, "You do?" And I said, "Yeah. You were misled by these con-men, you know. Their business," I said, "is that they deal with fear. That's all it is. They deal with fear. They played on your fears; they played on your family affection."

I think the thing that really upset my parents was when I told them, "You didn't have to do this. I was walking out the door anyway." Since that time I always have my bags half packed. I have left the temple several times, only to return. I've always been in perfect agreement with the philosophy of the Hare Krishna temples; it's just the Sankirtan thing that I have difficulty with. That's the one thing I've ever disagreed with in ISKCON. It's the way some things are done, not even that they're done, it's just the way they're done. You know, it's just the deceit.[6]

I've been back home a couple of times since my deprogramming, but I can't trust my parents any longer. Things are really strained when I go home, and I am aware that my parents understand me even less well than they thought they did.

Deprogramming as Reconversion

Deprogramming only makes sense as a radical solution if one accepts the notion that cult members have been "brainwashed" or programmed through "mind control." Flo Conway and Jim Siegelman state clearly the necessary and dependent relationship between brainwashing and deprogramming as they extol the work of the original deprogrammer, Ted Patrick:

> In all the world, there is nothing quite so impenetrable as a human mind snapped shut with bliss. No call to reason, no emotional appeal can get through its armor of self-proclaimed joy. . . . A man named Ted Patrick has developed the only remedy currently available . . . an antidote he named "deprogramming," a remarkably simple and—when properly used—nearly foolproof process for helping cult members regain their freedom of thought.[7]

Marvin Galper, a West Coast clinical psychologist, agrees when he asserts that "brainwashing is to implant definite attitudes and beliefs into the person," while deprogramming is "to help the person regain the ability to make his own free choices, . . . to think for himself again."[8]

While the techniques of contemporary deprogramming may be more refined, the attempt to dissuade persons forcibly to abandon their chosen faith is as old as religion itself. Hostilities toward new religions have ranged from the parental furor that led to altered practices of initiation for Buddhist youths in the fifth century B.C. to the death of Jain adherents at the hands of Hindu kings in the second century A.D. in South India. Attempts to force renunciation of a new faith include the persecution of Christians at the hands of angry mobs and the emperor Nero's persecutions as well as the Islamic jihads, or "holy wars," of forced conversions. However, the closest thing to contemporary deprogrammings occurred in the thirteenth century when both Thomas Aquinas and Francis of Assisi were abducted by family members in order to discourage their new ascetic lives.

In the case of Thomas Aquinas, his brothers, who were noblemen from Naples, kidnapped him and imprisoned him in Monte Cassino because he had become a Dominican monk. One brother is reported to have sent a prostitute to visit him and encourage him to break his vow of celibacy. Francis of Assisi was abducted by his own father, who thought his son had gone insane. The bishop of Assisi rescued Francis from his imprisonment and assisted him in returning to his Franciscan way of life.[9] In both cases, it was the newness and strangeness of the mendicant way of life that concerned the families of the converts. Likewise, both men were viewed as having gone too far when they adopted a totalistic way of life (i.e., full-time religious commitment undergirded by theological justification) that was foreign to those less committed.

In our day, a variety of practices are lumped together under the rubric "deprogramming." Bromley and Shupe make a distinction between "coercive deprogramming," which refers to any practice that entails forcible removal of the cult member from the cult, and "reevaluation," which consists of voluntary consultation between a cult member and a counselor outside the cult.[10] Each of these two main types of deprogramming includes a considerable diversity of practices, depending upon the background, style, and viewpoints of the specific deprogrammer.

For example, Willa Appel notes that Ted Patrick, Galen Kelly, and John Clark approach deprogramming very differently from each other.[11] Patrick uses a "snapping" technique that is meant to be quick and appears to be as radical as the brainwashing it attempts to eradicate. Kelly chooses a three-stage approach that takes two weeks or more to apply and focuses upon education and reindoctrination. According to Appel, Clark's method is the mildest of the three and resembles a modified psychoanalytic approach.

While it is important to distinguish among the various types of deprogramming occurring today, all forms involve a significant degree of belief confrontation and all attempt, in a heavily value laden way, to change the beliefs of cult members. Like Conway and Siegelman, those who believe adamantly in the ubiquitousness of some form of mind control in cult conversions also trust in coercive deprogramming as the only way to extricate youths from the cults.[12]

The noted lawyer and president of the New York Civil Liberties Union, Jeremiah Gutman, describes the steps and the pattern of a typical deprogramming.[13] First, the deprogrammers "case the victim" as they determine the routine of the cult convert and arrange for the kidnapping. Second, the deprogrammers enact a "rescue"—usually with the family's assistance—that legally can only be understood as a kidnapping. Third, a "chase" usually ensues, with the victim physically restrained and whisked off in a van or a car. Fourth, the cult member is taken to a motel or a borrowed house (to avoid obvious detection) for the actual "deprogramming" to be conducted. This stage usually involves physical restraint, sleep deprivation, stripping of all vestiges of cult dress and artifacts, and intense interrogation. Sometimes food deprivation, physical abuse, and threats of harm are included in the intractable cases. Fifth, a period of "rehabilitation" and/or milder forms of psychological counseling follows the successful breaking of the will of the cult convert. Often this stage occurs in pleasant surroundings in the company of an ex-member of the same cult.

Gutman says that the period of "floating" that deprogrammers say occurs after the initial break and before the rehabilitation is complete is really a "pseudoscientific" rationalization by deprogrammers to allow for the cases where a youth returns to his or her cult. The fees charged by deprogrammers depend to a great degree on the ability of the family to pay and have resulted in homes being mortgaged, life savings being depleted, and pensions turned over to deprogrammers.

Ted Patrick was the first person to develop the coercive deprogramming technique which is described in some detail in *Let Our Children Go!*[14] Born in Chattanooga, Tennessee, Theodore (Ted) Roosevelt Patrick was raised in a poor, black family. Patrick had a speech impediment which led his mother to try all kinds of faith healers, fortune-tellers, and religious quacks who came through town. Patrick says proudly of his educational past, "I am a tenth-grade dropout with a Ph.D. in common sense." Patrick was appointed a community relations representative for the State of California by Governor Reagan's administration, and it was while in that position that Ted performed his first deprogramming.

Patrick's first contact with the cults was through an irate parent who came to report her son missing after a July 4, 1971, Mission Beach party. Patrick discovered the young man in the Children of God (COG) group and nearly joined the group himself according to his account. After conducting several deprogrammings of members of COG, Patrick resigned his job with the state and declared "all out war against the cults."[15] While there are good reasons for Patrick to have considered COG a dangerous cult—it has now moved with its founder, David Berg, to Europe—his war is with all cults. He says, "You name 'em. Hare Krishna, The Divine Light Mission, Guru Maharaj Ji, . . . The Children of God. Not a brown penny's worth of difference between any of 'em."[16]

Patrick's deprogramming tactics include all the ones outlined by Gutman. In the early 1970s, Patrick would assist in the kidnappings himself, until his first brush with a possible lengthy prison term altered that practice. Patrick has used strong-armed tactics to kidnap and detain cult members and brags that he has deprogrammed more than twenty-six hundred cult members in the last decade.[17] He talks tough and describes deprogrammings in which he has had to get rough with resistant cult members. He often uses bodyguards and trained dogs to control and to confine his subjects. He has used bright lights and a video camera in some of his deprogrammings and usually tries to wear down his victims by depriving them of sleep. He has used threats of physical harm and psychological badgering as common elements in his aggressive style of deprogramming.

Patrick says that the hallmark of his deprogramming technique is his uncanny way of finding the chink in the armor of faith the disciple of a cult tries to defend.[18] Patrick often asserts that he can do a deprogramming in thirty minutes or an hour, but in any case in a day. One of the main weapons in his arsenal is the Christian Bible. In describing Patrick's deprogramming of a Krishna devotee named Tom Koppelman (not his real name), Conway and Siegelman say, "Surprisingly, to deprogram this ascetic follower of Krishna, a Hindu God, Patrick used the same tool he might use on a Moonie or a Jesus Freak: the Bible."[19] Koppelman was impressed with Patrick's knowledge of the Bible and said, "He started pulling out verse after verse from the Bible that really cut down the Krishna movement. . . . 1 Timothy 4 . . . blew the groundwork out of the whole vegetarian business."[20]

To his critics who say that his methods are just like the brainwashing he is combating, Patrick demurs: "It's nothing of the kind. Essentially it's just talk. I talk to the victim, for as long as I have to."[21] Patrick argues that the effects of brainwashing are that the cult victim can no longer think for himself or herself. Therefore, he concludes, "the cult completely destroys the mind. . . . When you deprogram people, you force them to think."[22] Among the devotees who were interviewed and who had been unsuccessfully deprogrammed by Patrick there was near-unanimous agreement that he was a man who tried to engender fear. He would spit on Prabhupada's picture and then tear it up dramatically. He also physically threatened and tried to humiliate each devotee. But there was also agreement that he was easily duped by the devotee who was well-grounded in his or her faith.

The real danger of the Ted Patrick type of conviction that brainwashing is a widespread practice is that *anyone* in *any situation* is a potential victim. Two members of the Tucson Freedom of Thought Foundation deprogrammed an Old Catholic priest because his Episcopalian parents objected to his faith choice.[23] Patrick has tried to deprogram two Greek Orthodox women ages twenty-one and twenty-three "because the parents were upset that their daughters had resisted the traditional Greek custom of living at home until the parents found them 'suitable' husbands."[24] In a similar vein,

Patrick was hired by a mother to deprogram her thirty-one-year-old daughter because she was under the mental control of her fiancé (who was not a member of any cult).[25] Patrick has also tried to deprogram a young woman who joined an unpopular political party![26] Finally, as we have seen, Ted Patrick was a central figure in the Stephanie Reithmiller case where his associates kidnapped, sexually affronted, and tried to deprogram Stephanie in order to free her from the mind control of her reputedly lesbian roommate.

Deprogrammers are self-appointed and seldom have any credentials, education, or experience that warrant their claims to expertise. Most deprogrammers are parents or friends of someone who has been in the cults or ex-members of the cults themselves. Some are lawyers whose professional contacts and clients have opened the door to deprogramming as a central part of their business. Few have any professional training related to their newly found careers. Certainly Ted Patrick has no special education or training that warrants respect for his overly simplistic analysis of brainwashing as "instant hypnosis." Likewise, Neil Maxwell is a San Francisco pharmacist who has reportedly deprogrammed more than fifty cult members, likening deprogramming to a "surgical process."[27]

Such are the people who are the self-appointed "new vigilantes" who place themselves above the law where the cults are concerned.[28] Bromley and Shupe assess the matter succinctly: "Deprogrammers are self-serving, illegal, and fundamentally immoral."[29] As we will observe later in this chapter, few persons in the clinical psychological professions have ever been involved as deprogrammers, although some, like John Clark and Margaret Singer, have been central to the anticult movement.

If it is true that "deprogramming is not brainwashing any more than indoctrination into a new religion is," then why or how does deprogramming work?[30] To this question several answers have been given. First, critics of deprogramming recognize that all forms of deprogramming involve rational dialogue as a key element in their techniques.[31] In spite of the claims that cult members can't think, even Ted Patrick's heavy-handed and radical process is based upon rational dialogue and the conveying of information. Bromley and Shupe agree that the deprogrammers rely to a great extent upon "reason, logic, and ideas. . . . Thus the very logic of deprogramming and why it should work is hopelessly inconsistent, contradictory, and illogical."[32] One obvious answer to the question then is that deprogramming is essentially aggressive or coercive persuasion.

However, Melton and Moore argue that deprogramming "is far from . . . talk [alone]. It involves a complex, pressured massage of the person's total inner life."[33] They go on to describe seven basic pressures that are rooted in the deprogramming process.[34] First, there is the feeling of hopelessness that comes from the forced imprisonment. Second, cult members experience a loss of privacy as they are escorted everywhere twenty-four hours a day—even to the bathroom. Third, most deprogrammers wear down their victims by marathon talk sessions that leave little or no time for sleep. Fourth, cult members experience personal abuse during the deprogramming in the form of verbal harangues and physical threats. Fifth, deprogrammers purposely desecrate and debunk what the cult member deems to be holy or sacred, from forcing cult members to eat forbidden food to encouraging sexual relations for celibate devotees. Sixth, parental pressure is used throughout most deprogrammings as an attack on the emotions and family loyalties of the cult member. Finally, the rational dialogue that is central to all deprogrammings usually takes the form of an intense interrogation that utilizes "badgering, leading questions, and theological and biblical dialectics."

According to Melton and Moore, the above practices "cause physical and emotional fatigue and create a strong sense of humiliation and guilt."[35] This direct attack on the whole system of emotional, physical, and psychological defenses of the individual results in a collapse of conviction in the cult member.[36] Because a deprogrammer like Ted Patrick does use the Bible or Lifton's book or some other basis for a standard of judgment of the cult's beliefs, he teaches the cultist not *how* to think but *what* to think. In most deprogrammings, therefore, the deprogrammed ex-cult member has simply "exchanged one totalistic commitment for another."[37]

Bromley and Shupe take a slightly different and equally profitable tack. From their point of view, a deprogramming is a "power confrontation" between the parents and the cult over who should control the cult member. Deprogrammers and their critics alike recognize that the cult member's family is a key to understanding cult membership. On the one hand, some see cults breaking up the American family, while on the other hand critics have seen the rise in cult membership as a sign that the American family was already in trouble. What Bromley and Shupe point out is that there is an implicit or explicit rejection of one's family values when a child joins a cult and trades the relationships and goals of his or her parents for those of the cult. Bromley and Shupe conclude, "This is a basic conflict between generations of parental hopes and plans versus youth self-determination. It is this conflict that the deprogramming is meant to resolve."[38]

The power confrontation that occurs in a deprogramming is stacked against the cult member. The coercive deprogramming allows the cult member little room for negotiation. The parents are brought in usually weeping and saying they love their son or daughter who is in the cult. A central ploy of Ted Patrick and other deprogrammers is to encourage the cult member to feel guilty for rejecting his or her parents. As Melton and Moore's family system analysis points out, the joining of a cult may sometimes consciously or unconsciously be an assertion of independence by the child from rigid family control.[39] Deprogramming can then often essentially be an attempt by parents to reassert their authority over their children. Certainly, this element was present in Laksmana's deprogramming. His father knew what was right for his son and, after failing to convince him, was willing to impose his will.

Bromley and Shupe also give a number of other contributing reasons for the success of deprogrammings: (1) The recent convert may be shocked by unsavory evidence that is presented from newspapers, ex-members, or other sources; (2) perhaps the cult member already had doubts that the deprogramming encouraged (this was the case for Laksmana even when he wanted to oppose his deprogrammers); (3) some devotees or disciples simply get burned out from the hectic schedule of cult fund-raising or other such activities; and finally, (4) perhaps there were already strong feelings of guilt over the turmoil the cult caused for the family that were easily tapped by this focus of most deprogrammings.[40] Whatever the contributing factors, however, successful deprogrammings almost always contain a cathartic breakdown on the part of the cult member as he or she tearfully embraces his or her parents once again.[41] A familiar scene at deprogrammings is the parental reclaiming of authority in physical and psychological terms. From this author's point of view, a reconversion process has occurred. A cult member's former identity has been reclaimed.

If deprogramming can be understood, at least in part, as a way of resolving family conflicts, then apostate stories by deprogrammed youths clearly attempt to exonerate both the parents and the child from guilt. After a deprogramming, a natural tendency is not to want to blame oneself for misplaced idealism or to blame one's parents for accomplishing the rescue. Consequently, brainwashing becomes a convenient scapegoat that absolves the cult member of the act of joining, and reunion with the family puts pressure on the child to reinforce the parents for what they did and blame the cult for the necessity of such a strong action as deprogramming.[42] As we saw at the beginning of the chapter, apostate atrocity stories are intended to outrage the general public and cast blame on the cults. What we now can see is that another primary function of such stories is to absolve families and the ex-member from any responsibility for their actions.[43]

A counterbalance to the logic of the deprogrammers and to the horrific stories of the deprogrammed apostates is the silent testimony of those who have left the cults voluntarily and have chosen not to rant against their former groups. As we saw from Eileen Barker's study of the Unification Church, only a very small percentage (12 percent) of converts are gained from a Moonie weekend and longer training sessions, and of those who do join, a great many leave during the first year of their own volition. Likewise we saw that approximately seventy-five hundred of the nine thousand Krishna devotees initiated by Prabhupada have left ISKCON, and nearly all have left voluntarily. Why, if the cults are so evil and their practices so dangerous, do not most of these apostates speak out?

In his participant observation study of Mormon defections, Armand Mauss discovered three basic types: intellectual defections, social defections, and emotional defections.[44] *Intellectual* defections occur when the basic tenets of one's faith no longer seem plausible. Implausibility may arise when competing beliefs (e.g., agnosticism or the eating of meat) come to appear better explanations for lived experiences. Implausibility may also arise when the gap between ideal religious behavior and real behavior in a group becomes too great. *Social* defection occurs when a member's social bonds weaken. This weakening can occur if one's friend leaves the group or if deep disagreements or conflicts disrupt the relationship. Finally, *emotional* defections are comprised of deep-seated emotional reactions to the religious groups, such as the rebellion of adolescents to their parents' religion. Likewise, claims of hypocrisy or politicization of the religious institution constitute emotional grounds for defection. What should be obvious is that these categories are not mutually exclusive but overlapping spheres of influence that lead to cult defections.

In his study of Divine Light Mission disciples ("premies"), James Downton, Jr. found all three of Mauss's categories of defectors.[45] Downton did find several premies whose reasons for disaffiliation were complex and spanned at least two of Mauss's types. In fact, Downton discovered an interrelationship of all three basic reasons to defect and offers a scenario of "leave-taking." Among the premies, departure was often incremental.[46] First, social bonds with other members were gradually broken. Simultaneously, new relationships with people outside the group were forged. Contact with outsiders also usually meant hearing criticism of the Divine Light Mission which deepened the premie's own intellectual doubts and criticisms. Such disenchantment made being around other premies less satisfying, which weakened further the social bonds that helped maintain commitment.

As reported earlier, a longtime Krishna woman devotee related in her 1981 interview that she was becoming more and more disenchanted with the role and status of women in ISKCON. Her disgruntlement stemmed, in great part, from her realization that in the early days of the movement she had more opportunities to assume leadership roles. In the early days of the movement, she had served as a *pujari,* or ritual priest, and had also given morning classes on the scriptures. While women are still permitted to become *pujaris,* they are no longer permitted to officiate at the primary ritual occasion of the day, the morning deity worship *(mangala-aratrika).* Furthermore, while it was rare even in the early days of ISKCON for women to address the whole temple as the leader of the morning class, it is now not permitted at all. Thus, this devotee's disaffection was both *intellectual* (she disagreed with the current interpretations of Krishna theology that put women in a more subordinate position than had Prabhupada) and *emotional* (she felt offended that her spiritual worth had been lowered, while less worthy men could assume her previous positions). I was not surprised to learn that this devotee had voluntarily left ISKCON less than a year after her interview (though she has now returned to ISKCON).

Laksmana's basic disgruntlement was with the discrepancy between Krishna theology and his temple's practices. As one who sought models of perfection (remember his dismay over the Edgar Cayce Institute's materialism based upon a spiritualist theology), Laksmana could not tolerate in ISKCON the same lax morality he sometimes practiced himself. When he was asked to give false stories about himself and the paintings he was supposed to peddle, seeds of discontent sprouted in him. According to his own account, he "already had doubts," and these intellectual questions were simply magnified by the emotional distress he felt from his street selling. If one were able to look deeper into Laksmana's reasons for leaving ISKCON, it would not be surprising if one found a lack of social bonding with other devotees and with his guru. What Laksmana's story reveals clearly is that his deprogramming was counterproductive to its intended goal, since it caused him to question his doubts and decision to leave ISKCON.

While systematic studies of voluntary defectors are just beginning to appear, the results are predictable, given the above alternative explanations for the effectiveness of coercive deprogrammings and their connection to apostate atrocity stories. For example, Stuart Wright recently investigated forty-five voluntary defectors from the Moonies, the Krishnas, and the Children of God and found among voluntary defectors attitudes very different from those among deprogrammed ex-members.[47] One question that was asked of these defectors was, "When you think about having been a member, how do you feel?" To the five choices of response that Wright gave them, the defectors responded: Indifferent 0%; Angry 7%; Duped/Brainwashed 9%; Wiser for the experience 67%; Variety of other responses 18%.[48]

Unlike deprogrammed apostates who are forcibly and rapidly removed from the cult, voluntary defectors "often experience a disengagement sequence that will last for months."[49] Comparing cult defection to marital divorce, Wright rehearses the literature on divorce that indicates that the more sudden and unexpected the marital breakup, the more acrimonious the emotional reaction. Since voluntary defection "involves a whole sequence of cognitive and emotional maneuvers," the willing deserter gradually assumes a different perspective on his or her involvement with the cult without usual recourse to the brainwashing interpretation (of which all the respondents were quite aware). Essentially, the voluntary defector's revised perspective on her or his cult rested somewhere between that of the hyperbolic anticult description and the continuing idealism of most of the committed followers.[50]

One of the most readable accounts of a voluntary defection from a cult is that of Chris Elkins in his book *Heavenly Deception*. As a young Moonie who was deeply committed to the Rev. Moon and the Unification Church, Chris appeared to his family as just another brainwashed robot for Moon. At the very time that his family was arranging his deprogramming, Chris was going through a period of doubting his faith and the practices of the Unification Church. Escaping before he could be deprogrammed, Chris later left the Unification Church on his own. His very reasoned account (seen through the eyes of his new evangelical Christian faith) ends with the dual assertions, "I don't believe that Moonies are brainwashed," therefore, "Parents, don't consider deprogramming as a solution to your problem."[51]

What all the above examples and this author's research show is that, far from being unthinking and unfeeling robots as critics claim, Krishna devotees are converted to a great extent by the group's theology. While there are also social and emotional components to any conversion process (though in various mixtures), the dominant force is usually the convert's rational (or rationalized) quest for meaning that is satisfied by the Krishna story. Therefore those who choose to leave must rationalize their rejection of the religious worldview and life-style they previously thought made sense. Consequently, both the joining process and the exiting process are primarily willful and thoughtful, unless violent extraction through deprogramming is used. Just as we saw how commitment to ISKCON involved a total personal commitment (intellectual assent supported by the ritual cycle and the complete life-style), so too defections have intellectual, social, and emotional components.

If there is anything to add to the foregoing analyses, it would be that deprogramming must be seen finally as an attack on the belief systems of Krishna devotees that will be as varied and fragile as the various stages of faith that Fowler describes. From this point of view, the success of deprogrammings will depend to a great extent on the maturity of the Krishna (or other) faith that is being challenged. In the story of Laksmana we find a young man who was a thoughtful experimenter. Consequently, Laksmana was at-

tracted to ISKCON by its unity of idea and act in devotion to Krishna. Therefore, even when he had doubts and was frustrated with the selling practices
of his temple, Laksmana was more than a match for his captors, who believed
there was a magic button they could press to "snap" him out of his cult
"disease."

If conversion to ISKCON means that young persons freely choose to adopt
the Krishna story as their own, then deprogramming can only be viewed as
an attempt to impose an alternate worldview on an unwilling or bewildered
subject. Clearly in the case of Ted Patrick, this is exactly what deprogramming is—the substitution of a more normative biblical worldview for that of
the cult. In criticizing the Ted Patrick type of deprogramming, Galen Kelly,
another deprogrammer, tells this story: One time a deprogrammer
"snapped" a young woman out of her "cult mind" and then proudly announced to her parents, "You'll be glad to know your daughter's a Christian
again." "But," said the dazed parents, "she used to be Jewish."[52]

In one of the most unusual interviews conducted for this study, the author
heard the remarkable story of a young woman who was deprogrammed, left
ISKCON and served as a counselor to other deprogrammed devotees, and
then decided to return to ISKCON. The young woman, who will be called
Radha, was raised in the home of a Congregational minister. A nonconform-
ist throughout her youth, Radha rebelled in the late 1960s and early 1970s
through the drugs and free living common to her hippie friends.

With a B.A. in social work and a new live-in boyfriend to talk with, Radha
began passionately to explore the Asian scriptures she hoped would hold
answers to her unresolved religious questions. Convinced by Prabhupada's
interpretation of the *Bhagavad Gita,* Radha and her boyfriend moved to the
Gita Nagari farm without ever having met a Krishna devotee.

The first stay at the farm lasted only ten days, after which time Radha and
her boyfriend went to Philadelphia to get married. Shortly afterward, they
both joined the Philadelphia Krishna temple and remained there until Radha
was kidnapped and deprogrammed approximately eighteen months later. In
a letter that Radha wrote just after her deprogramming in 1976 she said, "My
father said that he just wanted me to talk to some people. . . . However, you
don't get out of the deprogramming until you agree that all cults are bad and
that you don't want to go back." Radha's deprogramming took place in her
grandfather's cabin in the Pocono Mountains under the guidance of a well-
known rabbi deprogrammer.

Radha remembers the deprogrammers attacking all the cults and then
putting Hare Krishna beliefs in that context. Radha explains her deprogramming this way:

Anyone put in such a situation where all the bad points of his belief were
brought out and emphasized and put down over and over and over and over
again would certainly begin to doubt his belief. Why? Because we all know deep
inside that we are not perfect and can be wrong and we don't want to be
cheated. For two days I was told that I was brainwashed and was under mind
control and that I needed to get my freedom back. . . . They screamed at me
again and again, "You're not going back to that cult!" On the one hand, I just
wanted to get out of this deprogramming. On the other hand, I really wanted
to go back to the movement. . . . After being in such a fix, I just broke down

and cried. After that I was very susceptible to what they were saying, and consciously and subconsciously I began to accept what they were saying.[53]

Unknown to Radha, her husband also had been kidnapped and deprogrammed at the same time. Dismayed at the disappearance of his wife, Radha's husband agreed to come back to his hometown to meet with his father, knowing he was going to be deprogrammed, as his wife was. He was willing to risk even his Krishna faith to be with Radha. However, his deprogrammers—the same ones who had deprogrammed Radha—were easily fooled into believing he had snapped back. He then was sent to be rehabilitated, as had Radha.

Meanwhile Radha was living back home with her family and had fallen into many of her old habits, including smoking marijuana. She was asked to host a young woman who had just been deprogrammed out of the Krishnas, and this woman moved into her house for a period of time. After several episodes of talking with ex-devotees, Radha began to rethink what had happened to her. She was left on her own most of each day and she began to remember the positive things that had drawn her to ISKCON, especially the teachings on the need to liberate the soul and on the personal nature of God. Even though she was not chanting or keeping up any daily devotional activity, she said, "I still wanted to come back. I knew it was my own free will and that it wasn't mind control."

The problem was that she was convinced that her parents would just come and get her again and so she planned her escape legally. She went to a lawyer and had him write a paper denouncing the statement she was forced to sign at the end of her deprogramming. Radha was back with her husband now and they both lived with her parents. They would arise at 5:00 or 5:30 A.M. just to talk out their faith and to be sure they wanted to return to ISKCON for the right reasons and not as a protest against their families. Radha and her husband were convinced that the discipline of ISKCON is what they both wanted and needed. They then plotted their final return.

A second letter was drafted by Radha's attorney and delivered to her parents. It said that Radha would press criminal charges if her parents tried to kidnap and deprogram her again. Then Radha wrote a personal letter to her parents in which she said, "Sorry I had to be so heavy, but I just wanted you to understand, I mean it. Just leave me alone and let me live my own life." Radha and her husband went back to ISKCON and chose to live on the Gita Nagari farm, where they now reside with their young son and daughter.

Deprogrammings are a "traumatic attack" on the total person, as Melton and Moore suggest, and in many cases represent the "power confrontation" between parents and their children that Bromley and Shupe describe. In one sense, then, deprogrammings are forceful and coercive attempts by a group of persons to impose their will upon an individual. In another sense, deprogrammings are attempts at "reconversion" in that deprogrammers use appeals to reason to offer an alternative worldview—one that is more socially acceptable.

Deprogramming is the most destructive of the legacies of the great American cult scare and can, as we have seen in both Laksmana's and Radha's cases, actually intensify the conflict between parents and their children in ISKCON and other cults. In their psychological testing of ten cultists affected by deprogramming, J. Thomas Ungerleider and David K. Wellisch concluded that persons in the cults who actually experienced or were threatened with deprogramming had greater feelings of hostility toward their parents than those who had voluntarily left the cults.[54] Supporting the earlier conclusions of this chapter, Ungerleider and Wellisch suggest that the hostility of this group of threatened cult members likely predates their cult affiliation.

Deprogramming may be the most violent and repressive legacy of cult prejudice and fear. However, it is joined by other hostile practices and unfortunate consequences that are not as readily discernible to the public's eye.

The Anticult Movement and the Media

The anticult movement in America took on formal institutional shape in 1972 with the FREECOG (Free the Children of God) association. With Ted Patrick's assistance, families in the San Diego area banded together to get their children out of the Children of God. Since that beginning, the anticult movement has taken national (e.g., Citizens Freedom Foundation) as well as local (Tucson Freedom of Thought Foundation) forms. Opponents from the mainline or evangelical religious communities have supported such groups as the Spiritual Counterfeits Project in Berkeley or worked through campus ministry programs on many of America's college campuses. While this is not the place to rehearse the history and motives of the anticult movements in America, Anson Shupe and David Bromley have provided a comprehensive overview in their book *The New Vigilantes.*

One example of an anticult association that represents the legacy of cult fear and prejudice is the American Family Foundation, headquartered in Weston, Massachusetts. The stated purpose of the organization is to combat mind control and the destructive cults: "The American Family Foundation is a non-profit tax-exempt organization established in response to the problems caused . . . by persons and groups which employ mind-control technologies and irresponsible forms of behavior modification."[55] According to an interview with Robert Schwartz, a full-time staff person in the Weston office, the American Family Foundation grew out of the wedding of two different forces. On the one hand, K. H. Barney, a project director at the Raytheon Corporation, had two children in the Unification Church and paid to have them deprogrammed. Barney wanted an avenue to warn the public about the dangers of the "destructive cults" and through his initial financial support, the American Family Foundation (AFF) was founded in 1978. On the other hand, the Center for Destructive Cultism, founded by the psychiatrist Dr. John Clark, joined forces with the AFF in 1980 to provide some legitimacy to the research and work of the association and to pool the resources of these two anticult groups to fight the cults.

In the interview with Robert Schwartz, the AFF was presented as a research and educational association, a clearinghouse for information on the cults. There was a paid staff of only three to four persons in the Weston office, although the literature of the organization listed more than a dozen regional and local officers who volunteer their time to the AFF. The picture that

Schwartz painted of the AFF was one of balanced information gathering and dissemination. In comparison to other anticult groups Schwartz said, "I think you probably are going to find a little more even-temper around here."[56] Schwartz named a list of foundations that had chosen to support the AFF which ranged from private to religious financial trusts.

Schwartz had been a professor of African history at the University of Florida and the University of Virginia but "was unable to find continuing, permanent work." He knew Dr. Clark socially and was looking for an opportunity to do social-scientific research at a time when the AFF needed such a staff member. Hence Schwartz joined AFF to provide strength in the research area but has been given responsibility for the development of the fledgling organization. One could not help feeling initially comforted by the credentials and attitude conveyed by this AFF representative.

However, while the AFF promotes itself as a cut above the other anticult organizations, its literature, leadership, and activities contradict any claims to balance or neutrality. One full-page solicitation advertisement of the AFF begins with the announcement, "Cult activity didn't die at Jonestown" and ends with a plea for funds by pleading "Prevent another Jonestown." Half of the page of this advertisement is covered with a scene of the dead victims spread on the streets of Jonestown. The intervening text says in part, "Cult activity is still alive in this country. Maybe in your own neighborhood. They're stealing your children and possessing their minds. We, the American Family Foundation, are fighting back, but we need your help."

The Advisor, which is published by the AFF, has essentially the same anticult presuppositions and skewed analyses. Likewise, the published bulletins and monographs of the AFF decry the balanced work of Bromley and Shupe while lauding that, for instance, of Conway and Siegelman. Far from a critical and balanced attempt to discriminate between the dangerous and the benign or beneficial cults, the AFF lumps them all together as "destructive."

The names of the persons on the AFF's Board of Directors and Advisory Board read like a "who's who" of anticult spokespersons. These boards include psychiatrist Dr. John Clark, sociologist Edward Levine, writer Willa Appel, deprogrammer George Swope, minister Rev. John Blackwell, and Rabbi James Rudin. Through workshops, publications, and public lectures, the leadership of the AFF promotes the very cult fear that we have seen lead to destructive consequences for individuals and families. Nonetheless, the AFF promotes itself as a basic information resource for parents of cult converts.

Although not a deprogramming agency, the AFF seemingly attempts to engender fear and mistrust through its literature on the cults while making the same exaggerated and inaccurate generalizations common to most anticult groups. And while not as directly engaged in the violence that deprogramming represents, the AFF is a good example of anticult institutions that can frighten parents of cult converts into taking drastic actions such as deprogramming. Consequently, anticult groups such as the AFF are a part of the legacy of the brainwashing/mind control fear and suspicion that are indiscriminately linked with all cults.

As was said earlier, "cults" range along a continuum from dangerous and/or illegal groups (e.g., People's Temple and Synanon) to groups that are essentially new religions in America (e.g., Mormons and Hare Krishnas). For groups like the AFF (and the nationally active Citizens Freedom Foundation) not to make such distinctions is to create for parents of cult members an illusion that *all* parents of *all* cult members are failing in their familial responsibilities if they do not oppose their child's group and attempt to extract their child—one way or another. Thus parents of Scientology and Krishna converts are falsely led to believe that these two groups are essentially the same in their recruiting techniques, life-style, and general orientation when they are lumped together as two of the major "destructive cults."

The sometimes unwitting and often straightforward accomplices of anticult institutions are the print media and the film media. From the striking headlines that often exaggerate the content of the story that follows to the uncritical acceptance and publication of atrocity stories, the print media continue to provide additional fuel to the fires of cult fear. For example, the way the national press handled the deprogramming story of Herb Tucker in the fall of 1980 turned that ex-devotee into a virtual media phenomenon overnight. In a sensationalist essay, "Eat, Sleep, Drink Krishna," Roger Verdon of the *Kansas Hutchinson News* uncritically accepts the brainwashing stereotype and uses it to tell Tucker's story.[57] After less than a year in ISKCON, Tucker was deprogrammed in less than six hours by a deprogrammer who used Conway and Siegelman's concept of "snapping" to convice Tucker that he had been duped. Tucker was convinced that his entry into ISKCON was not something for which he was responsible. The article closes with a report of a victory letter sent by the deprogrammers to the Hare Krishnas which simply said, "We got another one." The envelope also contained Herb Tucker's ponytail.

Over the next three months after the *Kansas Hutchinson News'* article, Herb Tucker was interviewed by the *National Examiner* in an article entitled "It's Great to Be Free Again, Says Rescued Krishna Cultist"[58] and appeared on NBC's *To Tell the Truth*. Tucker spoke to ministerial groups about the dangers of the cults and spoke on several radio talk shows. Herb Tucker had been a Krishna devotee for less than six months, and yet through the creation of the media, the public had come to accept Herb Tucker as an expert witness on all of ISKCON and the cults. For our consideration, it is important to understand what an influential role the media play in cases like Tucker's which spread cult fear.

The danger of continually reporting only one side of the cult story is that reporters and editors too begin to accept and to generalize from the logic and language of the anticult community. For example, in reporting the tragic beating and shooting of a policeman in Memphis, Tennessee, one Ohio newspaper announced in bold headlines, "8 Die in Memphis Cop-Cult Battle."[59] The first paragraph of the story says, "Police firing tear gas stormed the home of a religious zealot early today." Later on in the story the reader learns that the killer was named Lindberg Sanders, a black man who was ' described as a religious zealot with a history of mental illness" who thought police were "anti-Christ."

A neighboring Ohio newspaper announced the same shooting with the headline, "Eight Slain in Memphis Shootout."[60] Calling the seven black men a "religious sect," this article stressed the connection of the mental illness of the leader with his aberrant Christian teachings. The basic difference in the reporting of this tragic story for the readers of these two competing newspapers was that one drew upon images and stereotypes of the anticult movement to depict this tragic story, while the other newspaper used categories that were more neutral and less inflammatory.

In recent years, many major newspapers have tried to balance their reporting of the cults and especially of ISKCON. We saw earlier that the *Cleveland Plain Dealer* and the *Los Angeles Times* both did lengthy Sunday feature stories on the Hare Krishnas that were balanced and nonjudgmental. Likewise, several television programs have done a documentary on the Palace of Gold in New Vrindaban. In 1984 the opening of the Detroit Krishna center supported by grandchildren of Henry Ford and Walter Reuther was a gala media event that resulted in positive front-page coverage in *USA Today*. Still, the balance is tipped in favor of those who await a new Jonestown to report and who turn a racially and psychologically nuanced police shooting event into a "cop-cult shootout."

The film media have likewise capitalized on the dramatic atrocity stories as frightful accounts of one cult victim after another are presented to the viewing public. Nearly every cult film is modeled after a thinly veiled combination of images and misconceptions associated with Jonestown and the Moonies. Some examples include *Ticket to Heaven, Moonchild,* and *Blinded by the Light*. In each case, the cult victim is brainwashed by the cult and only saved by some violent intervention, such as a deprogramming. As those who organized anticult conferences know, such films reinforce and accentuate the cult brainwashing stereotype. Therefore, the film media have also been agents, knowingly and unknowingly, in the great American cult scare.

Psychiatry and the Law

Nearly a decade ago, a *Boston Sunday Globe* reporter, Mary Thornton, observed, "American psychiatry appears to be moving toward a head-on collision with the US Constitution over a fundamental question: Are members of unusual religious groups exercising their right to religious freedom or are they victims of brainwashing and mind control?"[61] In this prophetic essay, Thornton rightly stated the cult riddle still not solved a decade later on the psychiatrist's couch or at the judge's bench.

Courts of law try to be rational and logical in their interpretation of evidence and to accept the precedents of history as a guide to wise and fair judgments. Psychiatry and clinical psychology, however, comprise an imprecise science in which subjectivity and ideological biases abound. As one reflective court observer puts it, "Law tends to be absolutist, psychiatry relativist; law tends to see the world in terms of black and white, psychiatry in graduations."[62] Many Americans probably agreed with this assessment of the relationship of psychiatry and the law as they expressed confusion over the psychiatric testimony that reduced the culpability of John Hinckley in an insanity plea in the assassination attempt on President Reagan's life.[63] Just as confusing was the court's ruling that Patricia Hearst was not brainwashed by the Symbionese Liberation Army and thus had to stand trial for the acts she committed as the SLA rebel "Tanya."

The brainwashing legacy with its attendant emotions of fear and suspicion has nowhere had a more deleterious influence than in the psychiatric and legal arenas. Court trials involving the cults become as much a question of whether or not the defendants can dispel the mind control image as they do an adjudication of the specific charges of the case. One good example of this phenomenon is the case of Robin George mentioned earlier.[64] The case pitted Robin George and her mother, Marcia, against several ISKCON corporations. The trial was a lengthy one, and thousands of pages of testimony resulted. However, the essence of the trial was a brainwashing/mind control charge upon which all the other charges (false imprisonment, infliction of emotional distress, wrongful death, and libel) rested. And it was a clinical psychologist, Margaret Thaler Singer, who set down the parameters of what mind control meant in this context.

Shying away from the term "brainwashing," Singer instead talked about "behavior change technology" and "thought reform."[65] Singer confessed in cross-examination that she had seen Robin George only two times previously for a total of approximately four and a half hours and only in the presence of her mother and brother (i.e., never alone). Furthermore, Singer admitted that Robin's mother and brother both contributed answers to the questions she asked Robin, making Singer's data, methodology, and conclusions more than a little questionable. Singer further admitted that, while she had access to tests done by other psychologists years earlier, she had administered no psychological tests to Robin George herself. Finally, Robin George was fifteen when she ran away from home in 1975 to join the Krishnas, and Singer interviewed Robin six years later when Robin was twenty-one. Nonetheless, on this questionable data base, Singer built her mind control edifice.

Singer claimed that the thought control the Krishnas utilized to entrap the young Robin George was a "systematic manipulation of psychological and social influences"—what most scholars would call "socialization" and what is common to many institutions from the army to Alcoholics Anonymous. During her lengthy testimony, Singer developed two quite different scenarios of thought reform, one based on fear and the other on deception. Though the recruiting techniques of ISKCON and the Moonies are strikingly different, Singer's testimony in the George case was echoed nearly verbatim in a subsequent *Barbara Dole* v. *Unification Church* hearing.[66]

In the Dole affidavit, Singer summarizes her theory of brainwashing this way:

> I have found the Plaintiff, Barbara Dole, was rendered incapable of exercising her own will and judgment as a result of the deceptions and manipulations performed by the UNIFICATION CHURCH members. . . . Plaintiff, Barbara Dole, was subject to such social and psychological manipulations by the UNIFICATION CHURCH members that her own volition, judgment, and free will were subverted.[67]

Singer says that "flattery is part of the systematic manipulation" and that "love bombing is a technique used by recruiters to make a potential recruit feel unconditionally loved and special."[68] It is with such obviously subjective analysis that Singer built her case for brainwashing in the Dole case as well.

Some mental health professionals and researchers have warned psychologists against using mental health categories as a social weapon.[69] The use of the value-laden and imprecise categories of psychiatric analysis in the courtroom often leads to conflicting testimony that can mislead or confuse a lay jury or audience.[70] Lee Coleman warns, "I have tried to demonstrate that whenever psychiatry is given state power, no one is well served. It is simply too easy for psychiatric authority to become a vehicle of social policy more than a system of individual help."[71]

John Clark has been one psychiatrist who has been willing to use his authority as a mental health authority to denounce the cults. In his wide travels Clark has altered his analysis again and again to meet the criticisms of his opponents and to try to find a way to convince mental health professionals that brainwashing/mind control should be a pathological category for a psychological illness. Originally Clark tried categories such as "borderline schizophrenia" and analogies such as "temporal lobe epilepsy" to describe the cult victim's psychological syndrome.[72] Calling questions of civil liberty irrelevant when talking about cult victims, Clark has served as an apologist for those who declare war on the cults.[73]

Clark achieved some notoriety in 1976 for his testimony in the Ed Shapiro/New York Krishnas case. At a conservatorship hearing in which Shapiro's father wanted to have his son admitted to a mental institution to be deprogrammed, Clark testified that since Ed Shapiro was under the influence of "mind control," standard psychological tests might not reveal his mental illness.[74] When Clark was pressed by the judge to state the basis for his medical judgment, Clark admitted that an October 12 interview with Ed Shapiro had lasted fifteen minutes, but that he then watched and observed Shapiro for an hour and a half after the young man refused to talk to Clark anymore. On this basis, Clark signed an affidavit on September 29, 1976, stating that he recommended that Shapiro be admitted to the McLean Hospital (where Clark was a staff member) for psychological stress tests that would determine whether this Krishna devotee was under "mind control."

The brainwashing legacy has reached deep into home and family. Perhaps no pain is as great as that of parents who feel their son or daughter has been "lost to the cults," unless it is the grief of parents who have gambled and lost in a deprogramming attempt. Laksmana's parents will likely never enjoy their son's full trust again. Just as tragically, Laksmana really feels he has no home to which he can return if he were to leave ISKCON permanently. Both parents and children can be the victims of the anticult rhetoric of fear and suspicion that lead to deprogrammings that fail. Ironically, in terms of personal freedom and maturation, there may not be any victors in successful deprogrammings either.

9

Through a Dark Looking Glass

We began this study by observing that the critics of the cults uniformly make two assumptions: first, that all cults are the same; and second, that all cults are dangerous or destructive. We have listened to the pervasive charges of many anticult spokespersons and have outlined the main features of the anticult argument. However, we have also seen the extent to which the stereotypic picture painted of the cults clearly does not fit like a template upon the realities of the Hare Krishna movement, a group always included in any list of "destructive cults." It should be quite clear by now that the Hare Krishnas are different from groups with which they are usually lumped, such as the Moonies, the Scientologists, or the People's Temple of Jim Jones. Furthermore, ISKCON's twenty-year history in America has amply demonstrated that it is not a single group with a single mind-set that is likely to become violent.

One obvious question arises. If the anticult stereotypes are so exaggerated or inaccurate with respect to ISKCON, how well do they fit *any* of the major cults they are designed to attack? The work of David Bromley and Anson Shupe as well as that of Eileen Barker on the Moonies suggests that at least the Unification Church joins ISKCON as a cult that is far more benign than cult stereotypes would suggest. To be sure, there are significant differences between the Krishnas and the Moonies that do not allow an easy grouping of these two movements on such issues as their recruiting processes or the perception of their founders (Prabhupada and the Rev. Moon). Still, neither movement poses the danger to society that the reading public has been led to believe.

Not only is ISKCON as a religious institution not a comfortable match—except very superficially—with the pejorative images associated with all cults, it is even wrong to assume that ISKCON is a single organism itself. It is an international organization whose various cultural locations have played a major role in determining local institutional forms and practices. For example, ISKCON began as a missionary movement in North America (the United States and Canada) and was headquartered in Los Angeles for much of the first decade of its existence. The primary economic base for most American temples is some form of street selling (books, paintings, etc.). At the present time, ISKCON in America has ceased to grow numerically (dropouts each year approximate the number of new converts), has fallen on hard times economically, and has encountered significant social and legal opposition.

In contrast, ISKCON in India now thrives institutionally, with increasing numbers of Indian Krishna devotees claiming ISKCON's temples as their own. Consequently, very little street selling occurs in India because the essential economic foundation for ISKCON communities in India is their extensive life membership program which has attracted considerable lay Indian monetary support. Hence, ISKCON's fate in America will not necessarily be the same as that of its Indian temples and communities. The same is true of comparisons of Australian or Italian Krishna centers with American ones. In short, ISKCON is a very diverse international missionary organization.

Even within America, another obvious element of ISKCON's complexity is the autonomous nature of its various farms and temples and the distinctiveness this factor has bred. Los Angeles is famous for its large "fringe" community, for its loose adherence to the prescribed religious discipline, and for stressing book distribution above all other means of economic sustenance. New Vrindaban, on the other hand, is a close-knit, though large, community and has as its central focus the building of an appealing architectural and religious sight-seeing attraction to introduce outsiders to ISKCON. Already, nearly a half million visitors have come to see what the Krishnas are building in this sleepy part of West Virginia. With its Palace of Gold and developing temple-pilgrimage complex, New Vrindaban relies upon tourist trade and the support of Indians in America, not on book distribution, for much of its income. Because of ISKCON's federation type of institutional organization, each zone and each temple has a degree of autonomy that has led to heterogeneity, not to conformity. When one adds to this picture the impact and authority of the various new gurus over certain temples and zones, the complexity of Krishna communities in America is further increased.

What both the above characteristics—geographic and institutional diversity—point to is the variety of ideologies, communities, and expressions of mission among ISKCON communities that often gets overlooked in critiques that assume there is a single entity called ISKCON. To be sure, the common adherence to certain beliefs and practices described in this book does support such a generalization. Likewise, the influence of the Governing Body Commission has had a stabilizing and cohesive effect. Yet it is important to recognize that whenever a newsworthy event is reported regarding one ISKCON community, it must be weighed against the location, type, and history of each ISKCON community before any generalizations are made.

Since the information presented within these pages is open for anyone to discover, is it not reasonable to ask why it is that the anticult groups have persisted in using unitary images and negative stereotypes when describing such groups as ISKCON? One obvious answer is that the information that the anticult antagonists and groups like the American Family Foundation collect is skewed and selective. Deprogrammed ex-members, angry parents, and antagonistic psychiatric professionals do not constitute a solid basis for acquiring a balanced truth. While the experience of ex-members should be considered when one is trying to understand the nature and dynamics of a group like ISKCON, such testimony should be considered the least reliable source —not the primary source—for an accurate description. Furthermore, those forcibly removed, deprogrammed ex-members who serve as the informants for most anticult presentations, represent only a minority of even this group. As we have seen, the books by Conway and Siegelman and the Rudins suffer from this distorted information base.

Nonetheless, a skewed sampling group is not a sufficient reason to explain why anticult spokespersons have persisted with their stereotypes and attacks in the face of mounting contradictory evidence from solid scholarly studies of which they are aware. In conversations between this author and a variety of anticultists one impression was consistent: most cult antagonists mistrust, if not fear, that which is religiously "foreign" or different from liberal American Christian/Jewish cultural values. Repeatedly, critics of the cults chastised them for not having a social or religious ethic that focused upon the corporate good. For instance, in one conversation with Ed Levine, a sociology professor from Chicago and a member of the American Family Foundation board, he insisted again and again that the Krishnas did nothing for the public good, nor taught their disciples "to love their neighbor as themselves." Levine repeatedly asserted that the Ten Commandments were the least common denominator that should be used to judge the cults.[1] What should be obvious in such a critique is that a new and foreign faith like ISKCON that stresses individual salvation is being judged as different and unacceptable according to normative American cultural/religious values. It was precisely to eradicate religious persecution based upon such normative judgments that the First Amendment to our Constitution was written.

Finally, it is not simply skewed data and normative assessments of the Krishnas and the cults that shine through the anticult literature as motivations for continuing the cult scare in America. It is also the case that cult antagonists are at their root opponents of deep-felt religions of any kind. For example, during a lengthy interview, John Clark made it quite clear that he had difficulty accepting not only the cult convert's mind-set but also that of the monk or nun in the Catholic monastery.[2] Just as Freud before them, the anticult psychologists and antagonists appear to be suspicious of *any* person or group who takes her or his religion too seriously.

Conway and Siegelman in their book *Snapping* finally assert categorically.

> It seems clear to us that, confronted by the demands of a complex, ever-changing, and often overwhelming mass society, an individual cannot elect mindless happiness over everything and everyone else in his or her life. That kind of happiness is information disease.[3]

It appears inconceivable to Conway and Siegelman that anyone could *choose* to devote his or her life completely to a religious faith.

Consequently—and anticipating their subsequent book—Conway and Siegelman broaden their attack on the cults in *Snapping* to include evangelical Christians. They simply state, "The Evangelical movement shares many characteristics with religious cults and mass therapies."[4] What begins in *Snapping* as an attack upon the new cults in America culminates in their most recent book, *Holy Terror,* as a full-fledged attack upon evangelical Christianity. In

Holy Terror, Conway and Siegelman assert that the evangelical (fundamentalist) Christian movement seeks to impose new forms of "political and social control" on all Americans through a program of "deception and distortion."[5]

Conway and Siegelman state openly their fear of persons who are fully committed to their religious faith:

> We cannot live as machines surrendered to Christ and computers. Nor can the United States long endure as a fundamentalist nation. But neither can we survive as two nations—one fundamentalist, one secular. If the leaders of the fundamentalist right really cared about this country . . . they would see the inevitable end of what they wish for America. They would also realize that totalism is not triumph. . . . But they can continue to divide us as Americans. They can play upon our panic in the face of complexity.[6]

The irony of the conclusions of Conway and Siegelman is that their book *Holy Terror* openly attempts to create fear in the face of the complexity of the fundamentalist religious right in America.

In the hostile charges of Conway and Siegelman we observe clearly what is an undercurrent in many, if not most, anticultists' critiques of the cults, that is, a real fear of *any* full commitment to a religious life. Therefore, perhaps a third reason for the strength of *anticult* sentiments and critiques is that they are in the end *antireligious* statements as well. Gordon Melton and Robert Moore put the matter this way: "The new bigotry turns both the ideology and the new scientific perspectives of the Enlightenment into the effective tools of ancient scapegoating."[7]

Liberal Christian and Jewish institutions require very little from their adherents in terms of commitment of time, money, or life orientation. Consequently, most mainline American churches may seem to be beyond the pale of anticult activity. Nonetheless, it would seem reasonable to ask: If anticult images or stereotypes are permitted to set the agenda and parameters for psychiatric and legal debates on religion, are not all religious institutions fair game for the secular liberal critique?[8] It is clear that anticult groups such as the American Family Foundation think that besides the cults, there is a threat from groups masquerading as churches. Furthermore, it is the anticultists that believe it is they who should decide who will be lumped together as dangerous opponents of freedom.

Perhaps the most frightening examples of the anticult movement's attempts to undermine civil and religious freedoms in America under the guise of anticult legislation are the spate of conservatorship and cult-study bills that were introduced in the early 1980s. A landmark bill that served as a precedent for many in other states was that introduced in 1980 and 1981 by Howard Lasher, an assemblyman from New York State. Lasher's bill was an amendment to the mental hygiene law and began with this description of the persons who were deemed incapable of conducting their own affairs:

> The person has undergone a sudden and dramatic personality change which is identifiable by the following characteristics:
> 1. Abrupt and drastic alteration of basic values and lifestyle, as contrasted with gradual change such as that which might result from maturation or education;
> 2. Lack of appropriate emotional response;

3. Regression to child-like behavior;
4. Physical changes [including "weight changes," "wooden, mask-like expression," and "dilated pupils"];
5. Reduction of decisional capacity . . . ;
6. Psychopathological changes . . . [including "dissociation, obsessional ruminations, delusional thinking"].[9]

When a person could be shown to exhibit *some* of the above characteristics, he or she had "to show cause" why the court should not grant the petitioners (assumed to be the parents or guardians) a forty-five-day conservatorship over their child. The defendant was not to be permitted a jury trial and hearsay evidence was to be allowed. If the defendant was found incapable according to the above criteria, he or she was to be put through "a court approved program [i.e., deprogramming] which shall be designed to enable the person to make informed and independent judgments."[10]

Some legislators argued that certainly Jesus and his disciples would have been found mentally ill according to the characteristics named in Lasher's bill. Others argued that the list of characteristics described nearly verbatim any modern "born again" Christian. Still others pleaded that such a bill opened the door to widespread religious oppression, and that it could be applied to a person's dramatic shift in political or social orientation too. Nonetheless, the Lasher bill passed by a wide margin in the New York Assembly in 1980 and by a comfortable margin in 1981. Only vetoes by Governor Carey two years in a row prevented Lasher's bill from becoming law.

The Lasher bill has been but one notable instance when anticult leaders in the legislative and psychiatric communities in the United States have joined forces to attack the "cults" and, in the process, have attacked the very heart of the First Amendment's guarantee to freedom of religion. If the stories of the Krishna devotees presented in this volume have taught us anything, it is that some persons do attempt to surrender some of the control over their lives for what they perceive to be the positive spiritual effect of a "second birth." Likewise, most religions of the world require a process of socialization that hopes to bring about the dramatic change in values and life orientation that the Lasher bill identifies as mentally incapacitating. Consequently, the antireligious bias that undergirds the Lasher bill and many of the anticult interpretations of groups like the Krishnas is the dark, antireligious prism through which many antagonists look at the cult data they have selectively collected and pejoratively assessed.

The Attraction of the Dark Lord

It is not only the anticultists whose vision is clouded by selective remembering and biased interpretation. The devotees of Krishna who were interviewed obviously remembered their life histories selectively and interpreted favorably most controversial events or actions associated with ISKCON. We should not be surprised when the most consistent prism through which devotees view the world is that of their Krishna faith.

Therefore devotees repeatedly explain fortuitous or tragic events in their lives with the phrase, "It is Krishna's arrangement." As we saw in chapter

5, the ⸗ogency and completeness of the worldview provided by Krishna theology is one major reason for its attractiveness to new converts. So too the new life of faith that encompasses both private worship and public ministry is a drawing card for those young people who want to live out their faith in all that they say and do.

However, there are additional reasons why some converts are attracted to the emotional devotionalism of ISKCON that appear to be connected to the convert's previous life history. While the number of new converts to ISKCON from Jewish backgrounds has dropped to 15 percent or lower in recent years, the number ranged above 20 percent for the first decade of ISKCON's history in America. Likewise, the proportion of youths from Catholic backgrounds ran above 30 percent in a survey this author did of six temples several years ago. Why are Jewish and Catholic youths in particular attracted to ISKCON? Interviews with devotees from these traditional backgrounds have provided some help in unraveling this mystery.

One common attraction of Jewish and Catholic youths to ISKCON is ISKCON's stress on its ancient Indian scriptural tradition that is mediated through a formal and complex ritual cycle. However, while both Jewish and Catholic traditions extol the value of history and tradition, the theological orientation of these traditions is dramatically different. On the one hand, most devotees raised in a Jewish context saw their decision to join ISKCON as a *break* with their ethnic/religious family tradition that practiced no devotion to a personal God. On the other hand, most devotees raised in Catholic homes felt that becoming a Krishna devotee was a *continuation* or deepening of their Catholic faith. One young woman said bluntly, "I am a better Catholic now." As we saw earlier, Mahema went to the Catholic church to get Jesus' permission prior to her joining ISKCON.

When pressed, however, both young women admitted they had ceased to attend Catholic mass and both felt that while the Krishna theology included their previous faith, their new faith also superseded their old one. Nonetheless, there is a similarity in the Krishna and the Catholic traditions in their stress on formal rituals, the abundant use of iconography, their hierarchical institutional/authority structure, their strong emphasis on the private prayer life, and their ideals of the monastic life of full-time religious service and personal piety.

The insistence by many devotees of Jewish descent that it was the "personalistic theism" of ISKCON that attracted them is perhaps an important clue to Krishna's overall appeal. Many devotees remarked that they were attracted to ISKCON because they could know who God was, what he looked like, what name(s) to call him, and how to achieve a close personal relationship with him. Those from Reform Jewish homes often said that their home life was nonreligious and that even their rabbis were uninterested in serious questions about personal religiosity. None of the interviewees from Jewish backgrounds came from an Orthodox religious background, where a stress on personal piety is more likely. Most converts from Jewish homes would have agreed with one ex-Jewish devotee who said, "When I joined ISKCON, I found God was a person for the first time."

While there are likely many variables that account for the relatively high percentage of devotees from Catholic and Jewish backgrounds, what the above summary sketch suggests is that a major factor in all conversions to ISKCON is the unabashed personal devotionalism of the Krishna faith and practice. Not only do the Krishna faith (chapter 5) and practice (chapter 6) make sense and fully encompass all of life, the playful Krishna is appealing as a friend, a lover, and a personal God.

Not to recognize the serendipitous quality of Krishna devotion is to miss the attraction of Krishna's many *lilas*, or playful "pastimes." As much as anything else, it is the sense that God is real and as available as any friend on earth that animates the faith of devotees regardless of background.

In spite of the commonalities of the attraction of Krishna to potential converts to ISKCON, the stories contained in this volume point to *many paths* into ISKCON, not one. Govinda's quest was that of a religious seeker who was slow to commit himself and who sought spiritual satisfaction above all else. Mahema's search revealed a strong interest in social relationships and a life of service to those whom she considered soul brothers and sisters. Lakshmi sought isolation and protection from a world that had abused her and found in ISKCON a supportive community in which she need not fear sexual imposition. Sita joined ISKCON in a fit of psychological desperation only to discover that the Krishna teachings about love of God did answer her long-standing questions. Finally, Laksmana thought philosophical speculation about the afterlife and human potential as taught by Edgar Cayce was the path to fulfillment, but joined ISKCON instead because he saw in the Krishna life a blending of faith and practice he still seeks to perfect.

From the dozens of devotee interviews collected over four years one central impression remains: there are many types of religious seekers who came to Krishna by many paths—some circuitous and some direct. No single explanation can do justice to the shifting nuances of the conversion processes of Krishna devotees. Clearly the brainwashing interpretation is not of any help at all, since it finally is a *predictive* categorization, as we have seen above, not a *descriptive* account at all. However, if there is one common thread in Krishna conversions, it is the explicit or implicit search by devotees for a meaningful context into which they can put their living and their dying. In this respect, ISKCON is like all religions that provide not simply answers to life's questions but a framework within which the devotee can live.

The Future of ISKCON

While it would be foolish to attempt to predict the exact nature of ISKCON's future in America, there are some important factors internal and external to ISKCON that will affect its viability as a religion in America in the years ahead. First of all, ISKCON has weathered the stormy turmoil caused by Prabhupada's death. While the charisma of Prabhupada was not fully transferred, it was institutionalized in the eleven successors (now expanded) whom he appointed and in the GBC, which was instituted as a guardian of Krishna faith and practice. However, the tension between the individualistic and potentially authoritarian office of the guru and the GBC as the collective overseer of ISKCON's welfare will not disappear. In ISKCON there is always opportunity for a headstrong leader to break off to start his own movement as Dheera Krishna (the Los Angeles temple president) did and as Bhaktipad has essentially done. Nonetheless, the conservative force of the GBC and the new flexibility in appointing gurus give ISKCON a better chance than its Indian predecessor to make a confederation of gurus and senior disciples work.

A second serious challenge that ISKCON faces is finding a stable and dependable economic base for its many programs and activities. Certainly, the Indian community in America has provided increasing financial support for many city temples and special projects such as the Palace of Gold in New Vrindaban. However, the book ministry of ISKCON is very expensive and is being met with more informed resistance than it was ten years ago. It still remains to be seen if ISKCON can develop a large enough lay community to underwrite the work of its temples and farms. Devotees in ISKCON sometimes underestimate the negative impact their questionable economic practices have on neutral or even sympathetic outsiders. While it is true that corruption can be found in all sectors of American business and industry, devotees' willful flaunting of local and state laws in their selling practices continues to give ISKCON's opponents a strong lever on public opinion.

A third complex challenge that ISKCON faces is how it will educate its children and what role it will give to young women who are raised entirely within the Krishnas' educational institutions. As the *gurukula* school system evolves, it will have to decide just how much secular education and skills it will permit its children to learn. Furthermore, only time will tell if ISKCON can raise young women who will live out the idealized religious and social roles assigned to them when many senior women devotees have education more like that of their male counterparts.

A fourth factor in ISKCON's ultimate success is its adoption as a legitimate child by the Indian community in America and India. With the completion of the Juhu Beach (Bombay) temple and Prabhupada's Samadhi (burial memorial) in Vrindavan, and its active building program in Mayapur, ISKCON now has a strong identity in India that has both psychological and economic advantages for American Krishna communities. On the one hand, devotees can look to India as their spiritual homeland, an orientation that can provide some solace now that the full-time membership of the American movement has stabilized at about twenty-five hundred to three thousand adults. On the other hand, Indians in India and America form a critical economic base for many ISKCON temples. Furthermore, ISKCON provides for Indians in America a home away from home. In sum, ISKCON may always be a marginal religious movement in America, but it clearly has India as its spiritual home and the Indian community in America as its first line of economic and social defense.

Perhaps the most ominous challenge to ISKCON's future in America is the anticult movement's success in arousing suspicion and fear of the cults in the general public as well as in the more narrowly circumscribed legal and psychiatric communities. The anticultists' attempts to depict the Hare Krishna movement as a dark and demonic cult that seduces the minds of unsuspecting youth has been successful to the extent to which images of Jonestown are successfully transferred.

However, more mainline churches in America are beginning to realize that much of the anticultists' critique is thinly disguised opposition to deep-felt religious piety of any kind. Therefore, to a great extent, all persons who value their religious freedom have a stake in how well a new and marginal missionary movement like ISKCON is treated. As Lord Acton reminds us:

> The most certain test by which we judge whether a country is really free is the amount of security enjoyed by minorities. Liberty, by this definition, is the essential condition and guardian of religion.[11]

The Hare Krishna movement in America reflects the same limitations and foibles as any religious institution. Devotees are human beings who, like most religious disciples, have higher aspirations for themselves than they often can achieve in practice. Devotees often fall short of that which they know to be right and good and yet seek a level of religious commitment that is uncommon in most religious institutions in America. (Compare Paul's words in Romans 7.) Nonetheless, the stylized anticult images of Krishna devotees as slaves of a dark and demonic Lord are inappropriate caricatures if one is truly interested in understanding why thousands of American youths have sought religious satisfaction in the Indian tradition of the dark Lord Krishna.

Notes

Chapter 1: The Great American Cult Scare

1. Jack Sparks, *The Mind Benders: A Look at Current Cults*, p. 115.
2. Lita Schwartz, "The Cult Phenomenon," in *Cults and the Family*, ed. Florence Kaslow and Marvin B. Sussman.
3. J. Gordon Melton and Robert L. Moore, *The Cult Experience: Responding to the New Religious Pluralism*, p. 15.
4. Ibid., pp. 18–28.
5. For an insight into the nature of the descriptive debate regarding cults, see Jacob Needleman and George Baker, eds., *Understanding the New Religions*, pp. 1–47; Melton and Moore, *The Cult Experience*, ch. 1; Thomas Robbins and Dick Anthony, *In Gods We Trust: New Patterns of Religious Pluralism in America*, pp. 9–86; Robert S. Ellwood, Jr., *Alternative Altars: Unconventional and Eastern Spirituality in America*, pp. 1–64; and Robert Wuthnow, *The Consciousness Reformation*. In addition, two books which appeared as this book was going to press and which call attention to sociological (Rochford) and psychological (Poling and Kenney) dimensions of ISKCON are E. Burke Rochford, *Hare Krishna in America* and Tommy H. Poling and J. Frank Kenney, *The Hare Krishna Character Type: A Study of the Sensate Personality*.
6. Flo Conway and Jim Siegelman, *Snapping: America's Epidemic of Sudden Personality Change*, p. 15.
7. Ibid., pp. 58, 62.
8. Quoted in Robert McCory's "Prisoners of Sects: Parents Fight Back Against the Cults."
9. Margaret T. Singer, "Coming out of the Cults."
10. For example, Conway and Siegelman, *Snapping*, p. 81; Ted Patrick and Tom Dulack, *Let Our Children Go!* p. v and passim.
11. Patrick and Dulack, *Let Our Children Go!* p. 50.
12. Quoted in Dick Brenneman, "SM Trial Ends Like a Family Reunion."
13. John Clark, Jr. "Cults," pp. 279–281.
14. A popular book that explored well the variety of emotions and reactions to the horror of Jonestown and reported his impressions from the tapes

made in Jonestown is James Reston, Jr., *Our Father Who Art in Hell.* A book that explores from a variety of academic perspectives the implications of the violence perpetrated by Jim Jones is Ken Levi, ed., *Violence and Religious Commitment: Implications of Jim Jones' People's Temple Movement.*

15. A. James and Marcia R. Rudin, *Prison or Paradise? The New Religious Cults,* p. 8.

16. Ibid., pp. 28–29.

17. Patrick and Dulack, *Let Our Children Go!* p. 11.

18. Two wire stories entitled "Mom of Dead Boy Goes on Trial" and "Fatal Spanking Left Bruises from Tot's Back to Thigh."

19. A. James and Marcia R. Rudin, *Prison or Paradise?* p. 52.

20. Patrick and Dulack, *Let Our Children Go!* p. 171.

21. Melton and Moore, *The Cult Experience,* pp. 99, 103.

Chapter 2: Godmen and Gurus

1. When a person is initiated into the International Society for Krishna Consciousness he or she is given a spiritual name in the Sanskrit language (e.g., Govinda Dasa). I have used such authentic Sanskrit names for the persons whose life stories are told at the beginnings of chapters but have disguised the devotees' identity by using Sanskrit pseudonyms, since often their pre-Krishna life contains sensitive or embarrassing events and episodes. I would also remind the reader that ISKCON is the acronym the Hare Krishnas use for their society and will be used to refer to their institution and movement throughout this book.

2. Andrew J. Pavlos, *The Cult Experience,* p. 13.

3. Lowell D. Streiker, *The Cults Are Coming!* p. 13.

4. Ronald Enroth, *The Lure of the Cults,* pp. 55–56.

5. "Cult Investigator Gives the PTA the Anti-Krishna Word."

6. Ibid.

7. Enroth, *The Lure of the Cults,* p. 61. See also Dusty Sklar, *Gods and Beasts: The Nazis and the Occult,* pp. 169–170.

8. For a fuller understanding of the important distinction being made between "man-god" and "god-man," see Marvin Henry Harper, *Gurus, Swamis, and Avataras: Spiritual Masters and Their American Disciples,* pp. 70–71; see also Peter Brent, *Godmen of India.*

9. Quoted in Satsvarupa dasa Goswami, *Planting the Seed: New York City 1965–1966,* p. 179.

10. "The Qualifications of the Spiritual Master," p. 4.

11. "The Self Outside the Boundaries of Time," p. 5.

12. Brent, *Godmen of India,* p. 13.

13. For a good description of the spiritual guide in Christian history, see Kenneth Leech, *Soul Friend: The Practice of Christian Spirituality,* pp. 34–89.

14. Ibid., pp. 88–89.

15. Sheldon B. Kopp, *Guru: Metaphors from a Psychotherapist,* pp. 4–5.

16. Satsvarupa dasa Goswami has written in six volumes the complete biography of the Hare Krishnas' founding guru, Prabhupada, which has been published by the Bhaktivedanta Book Trust under the series title *Śrīla Prabhupāda-līlāmṛta.* Each volume also has its own name. Volume 1 is enti-

tled *A Lifetime in Preparation: India, 1896–1965* and should be consulted for the life of Prabhupada prior to his coming to America. The main story line and, unless otherwise noted, all quotes from Prabhupada come from *A Lifetime in Preparation.*

17. Goswami, *A Lifetime in Preparation,* p. 141.

18. Quoted in Goswami, *A Lifetime in Preparation,* p. 240.

19. For the full text of this prayer/poem, see Goswami, *Planting the Seed,* pp. 277–279.

20. Ibid., pp. 281–284.

21. "My Impressions of Srila Prabhupada: A Historical and Personal View by J. Stillson Judah," pp. 29–33.

22. "He Was the Perfect Example: An Interview with George Harrison," p. 9.

23. Max Weber, *The Theory of Social and Economic Organization,* p. 341; see also pp. 341–358.

24. Max Weber, *The Sociology of Religion,* p. 46.

25. For a look at the political and personal dimensions of charisma as viewed by a psychoanalyst, see Irvine Schiffer, *Charisma: A Psychoanalytic Look at Mass Society.*

26. Weber, *The Theory of Social and Economic Organization,* p. 358; see also pp. 358–369.

27. David G. Bromley and Anson D. Shupe, Jr., *Strange Gods: The Great American Cult Scare,* p. 155.

Chapter 3: The Transmission of Charisma

1. While the other stories of devotees' lives told in this book are related in some detail and in the first person, Satsvarupa, the guru whose life is summarized in a third person account here, asked that I not present full details of the story he told me. I have only summarized his pre-Krishna life and have reported directly his views regarding the place of the new gurus in ISKCON.

2. A. James and Marcia R. Rudin, *Prison or Paradise? The New Religious Cults,* pp. 48–54.

3. Carroll Stoner and Jo Anne Parke, *All God's Children: The Cult Experience —Salvation or Slavery?* pp. 112–113.

4. "Srila Prabhupada Departs."

5. Ibid., p. 36.

6. "His Final Instructions."

7. Max Weber, *The Theory of Social and Economic Organization,* p. 364.

8. Interview in the Los Angeles temple, June 1980.

9. A lengthy personal letter from Panchadrivida Swami to his godbrothers in ISKCON dated December 8, 1983.

10. *Brijabasi Spirit* magazine, 1983, p. 1. This magazine is an occasional publication from the New Vrindaban community which describes the work and extols the guru of that community.

11. Max Weber, *The Sociology of Religion,* p. 39.

12. Satsvarupa dasa Goswami, "Initiation Means to Become Submissive," p. 10. The point of this quote is that it is important to the guru/disciple

relationship for the disciple to trust his or her spiritual master and not question the instructions that are given. Still, when a guru acts or asks his disciples to act in ways that clearly contradict scriptures or tradition, his disciples have the obligation to question, and if necessary to abandon, him.

13. Satsvarupa dasa Goswami, "After Initiation the Disciple Must Accept the Spiritual Master as Absolute," p. 9.

14. Satsvarupa dasa Goswami, *In Every Town and Village,* p. 104.

15. Interview, July 6, 1981.

16. Ibid.

17. "Trouble in Krishnaland," p. 32.

18. *Sacramento Bee,* June 23, 1980.

19. Transcribed interview with Sridara Maharaja which took place in India on October 21, 1980.

20. "Excerpts from Srila Prabhupada's Will Regarding Land and Buildings," a letter dated June 1977, p. 1.

21. "ISKCON News Release," Miami, Florida, July 9, 1983.

Chapter 4: Surrender and Authority Among the Krishnas

1. For Eric Hoffer's conclusions regarding submission to cult or group authorities, see his *The True Believer,* pp. 103–109.

2. Lowell D. Streiker, *The Cults Are Coming!* pp. 91–95, 110–118.

3. Ibid., p. 114.

4. Ibid., pp. 112–113.

5. A. James and Marcia R. Rudin, *Prison or Paradise? The New Religious Cults,* p. 111.

6. "Investigating the Effects of Some Religious Cults on the Health and Welfare of Their Converts," testimony given to the Vermont Senate, 1976. All quotations from John Clark in this chapter come from this unpublished testimony.

7. Francine Jeanne Daner, *The American Children of Krsna: A Study of the Hare Krishna Movement,* pp. 9–14, 72–77.

8. Ibid., p. 10.

9. Ibid., p. 19.

10. Ibid., p. 20.

11. Ibid., pp. 74–77.

12. Ibid., p. 75.

13. Kenneth Cragg, *The House of Islam,* p. 133, esp. n. 1.

14. *The Koran Interpreted,* p. 75. Suras are "chapters" or "books" of the Quran.

15. Cragg, *The House of Islam,* p. 7.

16. Fazlur Rahman, *Islam,* p. 34.

17. Tor Andræ, *Mohammed: The Man and His Faith,* p. 68.

18. See "Cautions Which Must Be Kept in Mind by All Who Would Become Truly Religious and Attain Perfection," p. 16.

19. Thomas Merton, *The Monastic Journey,* pp. 113–114.

20. David G. Bromley and Anson D. Shupe, Jr., *Strange Gods: The Great American Cult Scare,* p. 130.

21. Fred Rothbaum, John R. Weiss, and Samuel S. Snyder, "Changing the

World and Changing the Self: A Two-Process Model of Perceived Control,"
pp. 5–37.

22. Ibid., p. 7.

23. Ibid., p. 8.

24. Ibid., p. 11.

25. Ibid., p. 20.

26. Erich Fromm, *Escape from Freedom*, p. 155.

27. Rothbaum and others, "Changing the World and Changing the Self,"
p. 24.

28. Michael W. Ross, "Clinical Profiles of Hare Krishna Devotees," pp.
416–420.

29. Rothbaum and others, "Changing the World and Changing the Self,"
p. 24.

30. Ibid., p. 27.

31. Carroll Stoner and Jo Anne Parke, *All God's Children: The Cult Experience—Salvation or Slavery?* p. 4.

Chapter 5: Why Worship a Blue God?

1. The name Krishna *(Krsna)* literally means "black" or "dark blue" as
found in the dark thundercloud. While traditionally Krishna and his various
manifestations are depicted with black skins (reflecting perhaps the indige-
nous, tribal origins of this deity), artistic representations from medieval times
to the present have often substituted the artistically preferred robin's-egg or
sky-blue color for Krishna's skin.

2. This story was told to me October 10, 1983, by Kalaknatha dasa, a
Krishna devotee who in his devotional role has served as an editor for
ISKCON but who in his secular vocation is a self-employed businessman. The
story he related to me has been altered stylistically only in a few places for
clarity of expression. This is a story that *all* Indian and American Krishna
devotees consider as Krishna's (i.e., God's) *lila,* or "play," usually translated
as "Krishna's pastimes."

3. In the *Bhagavad Gita,* Vishnu declares, "Though unborn, eternal, and
though creator of all beings, I enter the world and assume a material nature
by my own mysterious power *(maya).* For whenever a languishing of righteousness and a rising up of unrighteousness on earth appears, I send myself
forth. For the protection of the good, and for the destruction of evil doers,
to make a firm footing for the right, I come into being from age to age"
(IV.6–8).

4. For a comparative description of this erotic mystic tradition, see Edward
C. Dimock, Jr., *The Place of the Hidden Moon: Erotic Mysticism in the Vaisnava-sahajiyā Cult of Bengal.*

5. For an excellent portrayal of the interconnectedness of the butter-thief
stories, sculptures, paintings, poems, and literary interpretations, see John
Stratton Hawley, *Krishna, the Butter Thief.* For a more general interpretation
of the role and significance of Krishna in Indian mythology, see David R
Kinsley, *The Sword and the Flute: Kālī and Krsna, Dark Visions of the Terrible
and the Sublime in Hindu Mythology,* pp. 9–82, 151–160.

6. For an introduction to the dramas that depict the Krishna *lila,* see John

Stratton Hawley, *At Play with Krishna: Pilgrimage Dramas from Brindavan*, and Norvin Hein, *The Miracle Plays of Mathura*.

7. An accessible and brief discussion of ISKCON's "Roots in India" can be found in Francine Jeanne Daner, *The American Children of Krsna: A Study of the Hare Krishna Movement*, pp. 23–32. For an insider's view, see Subhananda dasa Brahmacari, "Is the Krishna Consciousness Movement 'Hindu'?" pp. 1–29.

8. *The Krsna Consciousness Handbook: For the Year 484, Caitanya Era (March 24, 1970–March 12, 1971)*, pp. 108–109.

9. Carroll Stoner and Jo Anne Parke, *All God's Children: The Cult Experience —Salvation or Slavery?* p. 190.

10. "This Material World Is Zero," p. 24.

11. A. C. Bhaktivedanta Swami Prabhupada, *The Bhagavad Gita as It Is*, pp. 32–33.

12. Ibid., p. 34.

13. Besides Kinsley, *The Sword and the Flute*, for a brief discussion of the three primary Krishna traditions in Indian mythology, see Thomas J. Hopkins, *The Hindu Religious Tradition*, pp. 89–95.

14. For an instance of a Krishna devotee who views ISKCON as a nonsectarian tradition and superior to his previous Christian faith, see Kirtananda Swami, "The Things Christ Had to Keep Secret," pp. 10–13. For a recent defense of the notion that ISKCON's theology is inherent in and superior to all other religious traditions, see Ravindra Svarupa Dasa, "How I Was Saved from Being 'Saved,' " pp. 21–23.

15. Andrew J. Pavlos, *The Cult Experience*, p. 16.

16. Daner, *The American Children of Krsna*, p. 76.

17. "This Material World Is Zero," p. 24.

18. Ibid.

19. "Toward a Religious Criterion of Religion," in *Understanding the New Religions*, ed. Jacob Needleman and George Baker, pp. 131–132.

20. Anthony F. C. Wallace, "Revitalization Movements," in *Reader in Comparative Religion: An Anthropological Approach*, pp. 421–429; Michael Novak, *Ascent of the Mountain, Flight of the Dove*, pp. 28–41; Peter L. Berger, *The Sacred Canopy*, pp. 3–28; Clifford Geertz, "Religion as a Cultural System," in *Anthropological Approaches to the Study of Religion*, pp. 1–46.

21. William James, *The Varieties of Religious Experience*, pp. 114–160.

22. Geertz, "Religion as a Cultural System," p. 4.

23. Ibid., p. 13.

24. Ibid., p. 5.

25. Ibid., p. 8.

26. These accusations were made by the prosecuting attorney of the *Robin and Marcia George* v. *International Society of Krishna Consciousness* trial in the cross-examination of this author near the end of the trial during the third week of May 1983.

27. Geertz, "Religion as a Cultural System," pp. 24–34.

28. Ibid., p. 14.

29. Terry Godlove, in "In What Sense Are Religions Conceptual Frameworks?" pp. 289–305, points out that it is not the unique nature or the broad application of the concepts of religion that give them their credence, but

rather their ability to provide timely and plausible interpretations for common, if problematic, events such as death and suffering.

30. Peter Berger says that the religious worldview ("nomos") must provide interpretations for the "marginal" situations of life (*The Sacred Canopy*, p. 43).

31. Geertz, "Religion as a Cultural System," p. 19.

32. Eileen Barker's studies of Moonies in England confirms the notion that specific theological content is important in determining who joins the Unification Church. For a summary of her findings, see "Who'd Be a Moonie? A Comparative Study of Those Who Join the Unification Church," pp. 59–96. The fact that most Moonie converts were concerned about "doing good" *in the world* precludes their interest in such "otherworldly" groups as the Krishnas—and vice versa. The sketchy statistical evidence available about the lack of such crossover conversions supports this conclusion.

33. A. James and Marcia R. Rudin, *Prison or Paradise? The New Religious Cults*, pp. 20–23.

34. Robert Jay Lifton, *Thought Reform and the Psychology of Totalism: A Study of "Brainwashing" in China*, p. 419.

35. Ibid.

36. Daner, *The American Children of Krsna*, pp. 12–14.

37. Ibid., p. 77.

38. For example, see Novak, *Ascent of the Mountain*, pp. 154–156.

39. Eric Hoffer, *The True Believer*, p. 77.

40. Milton Rokeach, *The Open and Closed Mind*, p. 6.

41. Ibid., pp. 43–45.

42. Ibid., pp. 58–63.

43. Ibid., p. 57.

44. Ibid., p. 67.

45. Ibid., p. 404.

46. Since its inception, ISKCON has been under nearly constant attack by its opponents. Consequently, it usually has chosen to deny *any* guilt. The effect has, of course, been to cast suspicion on ISKCON's public announcements, not to alleviate the public's fears.

47. T. W. Adorno and others, *The Authoritarian Personality*, p. 52.

48. David Loye, *The Leadership Passion: A Psychology of Ideology*, pp. 153–155.

49. J. Gordon Melton and Robert L. Moore, *The Cult Experience: Responding to the New Religious Pluralism*, pp. 98–99.

50. See J. Stillson Judah, *Hare Krishna and the Counterculture*, pp. 187–197; see also Larry D. Shinn, *Two Sacred Worlds: Experience and Structure in the World's Religions*, pp. 85–120.

Chapter 6: New Identities: Secure in the Arms of Krishna

1. Ted Patrick and Tom Dulack, *Let Our Children Go!* p. 171.

2. The Krishnas quote Jiva Goswami as saying, "Diksa is the process by which one can awaken his transcendental knowledge and vanquish all reactions [karman] caused by sinful activity" (A. C. Bhaktivedanta Swami Prabhupada, *The Spiritual Master and the Disciple*, p. 363).

3. Ibid.

4. For examples of anticult deprecation of chanting, see Andrew J. Pavlos, *The Cult Experience*, pp. 51–52; Patrick and Dulack, *Let Our Children Go!* pp. 171ff.; Flo Conway and Jim Siegelman, *Snapping: America's Epidemic of Sudden Personality Change*, pp. 137ff.

5. A. C. Bhaktivedanta Swami Prabhupada, *Śrī Nāmāmṛta: The Nectar of the Holy Name*, p. 3.

6. For an excellent description of the physiology and psychology of meditation practices, see Claudio Naranjo and Robert E. Ornstein, *On the Psychology of Meditation*.

7. *Śrimad Bhāgavatam* 7.6.24, translation and commentary by A. C. Bhaktivedanta Swami Prabhupada (Los Angeles: Bhaktivedanta Book Trust), vol. 2, pt. 1, p. 149.

8. See "The Ordination Service," in *Buddhism: In Translation*, ed. Henry Clarke Warren, pp. 395–401. Two outsiders to ISKCON who explain the Krishna's vows in social, ethical, and psychological terms are J. Stillson Judah, *Hare Krishna and the Counterculture*, pp. 124–137, and Francine Jeanne Daner, *The American Children of Krsna: A Study of the Hare Krishna Movement*, pp. 13–14, 60–61.

9. For a summary description of the first American initiation, see Srila Satsvarupa dasa Goswami, "The First Initiation," *Back to Godhead* 15, no. 11 (1980), pp. 5–7, 20.

10. Ibid., p. 6.

11. Standard prayers and songs used in Krishna temples in India and throughout the world are collected in *Songs of the Vaiṣṇava Ācāryas*, trans. A. C. Bhaktivedanta Swami Prabhupada.

12. While not widely circulated among devotees, there is a full and precise description of basic ISKCON rituals in *The Process of Deity Worship (Arcana-Paddhati)*, trans. Jayasacinanda dasa Adhikari and ed. Jayatirtha dasa Adlukari. This book is one example of the Indianization process that continues to go on in ISKCON.

13. Prabhupada used to call the neck beads "Krishna's dog collar" because they symbolize the same faithful submission to Krishna that a dog gives to its master.

14. Clifford Geertz, "Religion as a Cultural System," in *Anthropological Approaches to the Study of Religion*, p. 28.

15. Building upon the work of Arnold van Gennep, Victor Turner focuses upon the transition or "liminal" stage of ritual in his book *The Ritual Process: Structure and Anti-Structure*, esp. pp. 94–130.

16. J. Gordon Melton and Robert L. Moore in their book *The Cult Experience: Responding to the New Religious Pluralism* expand Victor Turner's analysis of ritual liminality to include the whole transition period of cult members (see pp. 47–60). For a fuller understanding of the potential effect of initiation and other rituals in ISKCON, see Larry D. Shinn, *Two Sacred Worlds: Experience and Structure in the World's Religions*, pp. 85–98.

17. Ravindra Svarupa Dasa, "Encounter with the Lord of the Universe, p. 9.

18. Ibid.

19. Ibid., p. 14.

20. Jayadvaita Swami, "The Transcendence Comes Into View," p. 7.

21. Ibid., p. 8.

22. *Śrī Caitanya-Caritāmṛta*, Madhya 20.344, as quoted in *Śrī Nāmāmṛta: The Nectar of the Holy Name*, Subhananda dasa, p. 4. For an extensive compilation of scriptural injunctions on chanting in the Indian Krishna and ISKCON traditions, see *Śrī Nāmāmṛta*. For an introduction to the connections in Indian devotional religion between deity worship and chanting, see the essays "Bhakti Hinduism," "mantra," and "puja" in *Abingdon Dictionary of Living Religions*, ed. Keith Crim. Also see relevant sections of Thomas J. Hopkins' *The Hindu Religious Tradition*.

23. For example, see Carroll Stoner and Jo Anne Parke, *All God's Children: The Cult Experience—Salvation or Slavery?* p. 48, and Patrick and Dulack, *Let Our Children Go!* p. 165.

24. *Śrī-Caitanya-Caritāmṛta*, Madhya 16.64, translation and commentary by A. C. Bhaktivedanta Swami Prabhupada, Madhya-lila: vol. 6, p. 188.

25. *Śrīmad Bhāgavatam* 7.6.24, vol. 2, pt. 1, p. 149.

26. *Śrīmad Bhāgavatam* 2.3.17, vol. 2, pt. 1, p. 149.

27. Interview with Kirtananda Swami in New Vrindaban in January 1981.

28. Interview with Ramesvara Swami in Los Angeles, June 1980. (It should be noted that this guru softened this point of view subsequently and now raises money in his zone through a variety of means.)

29. See, for example, A. C. Bhaktivedanta Swami Prabhupada, *Preaching Is the Essence*, pp. 93–95.

30. ISKCON devotees have been arrested or charged with such solicitation scams as posing as Vietnam veterans (*Albany* [New York] *Times Union*, May 27, 1982, and *Beloit* [Wisconsin] *News*, September 25, 1981), selling art reproductions fraudulently (*Bangor* [Maine] *Daily News*, December of 1981), and supposedly collecting money for the hungry children of America or India (Syracuse, New York, November 26, 1980). David G. Bromley and Anson D. Shupe, Jr., offer a balanced view of the competing claims of anticultists and the rationalized defenses of ISKCON and other cults in their chapter called "Fund-Raising and the New Religions: Charities or Rip-offs?" in *Strange Gods: The Great American Cult Scare*, pp. 157–176.

31. Patrick and Dulack, *Let Our Children Go!* p. 46.

32. Pavlos, *The Cult Experience*, p. 133.

33. "Beyond Sexism, Beyond Tokenism," *Back to Godhead* 14, no. 9 (1979), p. 10.

34. A genuine conflict of cultures and ideological perspectives arises when a traditional Indian religious teacher, a man, defends his tradition's theological justifications for the social subordination of women in the face of current American women's critiques of Western patriarchal theistic religions such as ISKCON. For example, see the various essays edited by Carol Christ and Judith Plaskow in *Womanspirit Rising: A Feminist Reader in Religion* (New York: Harper & Row, 1977).

35. "Status and Duties of Women," in *The Laws of Manu* IX.2, 3, as translated and edited by Sarvepalli Radhakrishna and Charles A. Moore in *A Sourcebook in Indian Philosophy*, p. 190.

36. "Beyond Sexism, Beyond Tokenism," p. 10.

37 Sitarani dasi, 'What's the Role of Women in Kṛṣṇa Consciousness?''

p. 12. See also Visakha Devi Dasi, "Women in Krsna Consciousness: Questions and Answers," pp. 6–7. For an opinion by a woman reporter who lived with some Krishna women in Boston and New York, see Faye Levine, *The Strange World of the Hare Krishnas,* pp. 145–150.

38. Sitarani, "What's the Role of Women in Krsna Consciousness?" p. 12.

39. "Krishna School Seems Another World," *Denver Post,* September 6, 1974, p. 3HH.

40. Stoner and Parke, *All God's Children,* p. 86.

41. See the descriptive account of Krishna's schools and child-rearing practices by Daner, *The American Children of Krsna,* pp. 68–71.

42. The clinical studies of ISKCON children done by Lawrence Lilliston (see "Children in ISKCON: A Clinical View," a paper presented at a conference in New Vrindaban, July 22–26, 1985) show that Krishna children test in the normal range on psychological tests for children and perform above their age group academically.

43. "His Final Instructions," p. 25.

44. Amodha Dasa, "At School with Krsna's Canadian Kids," p. 12. Another devotee essay is Ravindra Svarupa Dasa, "A Teacher for Krsna's Children," pp. 21–27.

45. Daner, *The American Children of Krsna,* p. 75.

46. Ibid., p. 60.

47. For a summary of the radical feminists' critiques of patriarchal religions and an analysis of some underlying assumptions of these critiques, see Larry D. Shinn, "The Goddess: Theological Sign or Religious Symbol?" pp. 178–195.

48. Ravindra Svarupa, "A Teacher for Krsna's Children," p. 21.

Chapter 7: Pathways to Krishna

1. "Krishna Case May Be First of Brainwashing."

2. Murray Schumach, "Judge Dismisses Charges in Hare Krishna 'Brainwashing' Case," p. B3.

3. "Krishna Disciple's Sanity Challenged."

4. Timothy Carlson, "Landmark Case Awards Cult Victim $32.5 Million: Jury Says Krishnas Brainwashed Teen."

5. Ibid.

6. Dave Golowenski, "Tribe's Cold Shoulder Worries Super Joe."

7. Mike Pulfer, "Lawyer for Goss Doubts Leis Will Seek Retrial," p. B2.

8. Robert J. Lifton, *Thought Reform and the Psychology of Totalism: A Study of "Brainwashing" in China.*

9. The deprogrammer Ted Patrick with his "instant hypnosis" arguments, the psychologist Margaret Singer with her theory of the "manipulation of the psychological and social environment," and psychologist John Clark's "syndrome of sudden change" all mention Lifton's work. Yet all these critics tend to go their own ways with very generalized and elusive definitions of the brainwashing process and state of mind.

10. See the work of Flo Conway and Jim Siegelman *(Snapping: America's Epidemic of Sudden Personality Change)* and Willa Appel *(Cults in America).*

11. All the stages that follow are paraphrased from Lifton, *Thought Reform and the Psychology of Totalism,* pp. 65–85.

12. Ibid., p. 66.

13. Ibid., p. 84.

14. Ibid., p. 85.

15. The ideas of John G. Clark and Margaret T. Singer will be presented more fully in the next chapter.

16. Conway and Siegelman, *Snapping: America's Epidemic of Sudden Personality Change.*

17. Ibid., pp. 102–103.

18. Ibid., p. 58.

19. Ibid., p. 114.

20. Ibid., p. 73.

21. Ibid., p. 109.

22. Ibid., pp. 118–121.

23. Ibid., p. 123.

24. Ibid., p. 126; see also pp. 127, 128.

25. Ibid., p. 133.

26. Ibid., p. 137.

27. Ibid., p. 225.

28. Ibid., p. 226.

29. For example, Ted Patrick and Tom Dulack, *Let Our Children Go!;* Carroll Stoner and Jo Anne Parke, *All God's Children: The Cult Experience— Salvation or Slavery?;* and A. James Rudin and Marcia R. Rudin, *Prison or Paradise? The New Religious Cults.*

30. John Lofland, " 'Becoming a World Savior' Revisited," in *Conversion Careers: In and Out of the New Religions,* ed. James T. Richardson, pp. 10–23.

31. Ibid., pp. 20 and 11.

32. Ibid., p. 22.

33. J. A. C. Brown, *Techniques of Persuasion: From Propaganda to Brainwashing,* p. 226.

34. Ibid., p. 290.

35. Ibid., p. 291.

36. "Who'd Be a Moonie?" in *The Social Impact of New Religious Movements,* ed. Bryan Wilson (New York: Rose of Sharon Press, 1981), p. 64.

37. Michael W. Ross, "Clinical Profiles of Hare Krishna Devotees," pp. 417–418.

38. Ibid., p. 419.

39. See the court testimony of Allan Gerson related to the Shapiro trial (October 21, 1976) which predates and confirms Ross's later findings.

40. Marc Galanter and others, "The 'Moonies': A Psychological Study of Conversion and Membership in a Contemporary Religious Sect," p. 168.

41. Sigmund Freud, "A Religious Experience," in *The Standard Edition of the Complete Psychological Works of Sigmund Freud,* ed. and trans. James Strachey (London: Hogarth Press, 1961), pp. 169–172.

42. Sigmund Freud, *The Future of an Illusion,* trans. W. D. Robson-Scott, pp. 86–87.

43. Leon Salzman, "The Psychology of Religious and Ideological Conver-

sion," pp. 177–187, and Carl Christensen, "Religious Conversion," pp. 207–216.

44. Erik H. Erikson, *Young Man Luther,* pp. 265–266.

45. Francine Jeanne Daner, *The American Children of Krsna: A Study of the Hare Krishna Movement,* pp. 14 and 12.

46. J. Gordon Melton and Robert L. Moore, *The Cult Experience: Responding to the New Religious Pluralism,* pp. 65–69.

47. Erik H. Erikson, *Identity: Youth and Crisis,* pp. 49–50, 165ff.

48. Rodney Stark and William Bainbridge, "Networks of Faith: Interpersonal Bonds and Recruitment to Cults and Sects," pp. 1376–1395.

49. Ibid., p. 1377.

50. Ibid., p. 1379.

51. Larry D. Shinn, "Conflicting Networks: Guru and Friend in ISKCON," in *Genesis, Exodus, and Numbers.*

52. See David G. Bromley and Anson D. Shupe, Jr., *"Moonies" in America: Cult, Church and Crusade; Strange Gods: The Great American Cult Scare;* and Anson D. Shupe, Jr., and David G. Bromley, *The New Vigilantes: Deprogrammers, Anti-Cultists, and the New Religions.*

53. David Bromley and Anson Shupe, "Just a Few Years Seem Like a Lifetime: A Role Theory Approach to Participation in Religious Movements," in *Research in Social Movements: Conflict and Change,* ed. Louis Kriesberg, pp. 162, and 159–185.

54. See *The Republic of Plato,* trans. Allan Bloom, pp. 193–220.

55. William James, *The Varieties of Religious Experience,* p. 160.

56. James W. Fowler, *Stages of Faith: The Psychology of Human Development and the Quest for Meaning,* pp. 119–211.

57. Ibid., p. 200.

58. See Larry D. Shinn, "The Many Faces of Krishna," in *Alternatives to American Mainline Churches,* pp. 122–125.

59. For a good example of how a psychologist can appreciate religious conversion as a psychological/spiritual process, see Herbert Fingarette, *The Self in Transformation* (New York: Harper & Row, Harper Torchbooks, 1965). For a representative sociological analysis of conversion—in this case to a utopian faith—see Rosabeth Moss Kanter, *Commitment and Community: Communes and Utopias in Sociological Perspective.* Particularly useful to the understanding of cult conversions as a sometimes sudden and othertimes gradual transition process is Melton and Moore's *The Cult Experience,* pp. 46–60. What is missing from the above studies of conversion as a *process of transformation* is the theological and/or religious emphasis on the *rational content* of this gradual shifting of faith standpoints. This emphasis on the content of faith is the thrust of Fowler's *Stages of Faith.* So too most devotees' stories of their conversion to ISKCON reveal a definite and sometimes determinative reliance on the "philosophy" of Krishna. However else one may view conversion to ISKCON, it is clear that it is an intellectual process of rational and emotional transformation.

60. Thomas Robbins and Dick Anthony, "New Religions, Families, and 'Brainwashing,'" in their book *In Gods We Trust: New Patterns of Religious Pluralism in America,* pp. 268–269.

61. Lifton, *Thought Reform and the Psychology of Totalism,* p. 4.

Chapter 8: Deprogramming: Fear and Its Legacies

1. For brief histories of previous "new" religions in America and the persecution they experienced, see David G. Bromley and Anson D. Shupe, Jr., *Strange Gods: The Great American Cult Scare,* pp. 6–20, and J. Gordon Melton and Robert L. Moore, *The Cult Experience: Responding to the New Religious Pluralism,* pp. 18–28.
2. Bromley and Shupe, *Strange Gods,* p. 16.
3. Ibid.
4. Susan Murphy is one ex-devotee who, at one point, sided with her mother in trying to get her sister (Eileen) out of ISKCON by using the print media to rail against ISKCON's abuse and denigration of women. See "Sisters on Opposite Sides of Religious Cult Hassle" and "Girl Sues Hare Cult for $2.5M." Genny Ayer's brief account of her eighteen months in ISKCON included charges of prostitution and shoplifting as likely Krishna practices even though they are not condoned at present; see "Life Inside a Hare Krishna Sect," *Fairfield Republic,* July 17, 1977.
5. Ted Patrick and Tom Dulack, *Let Our Children Go!* p. 180.
6. Laksmana explains in another part of the interview that he agreed with Sankirtan as *book distribution* but couldn't accept the "selling" of secular goods as a part of his Krishna faith.
7. Flo Conway and Jim Siegelman, *Snapping: America's Epidemic of Sudden Personality Change,* pp. 62f.
8. Rudy Aversa, "Psychologist Deals with Cultic 'Brainwash.' "
9. Frank Flynn, "Deprogramming in the Middle Ages," p. 5.
10. Bromley and Shupe, *Strange Gods,* pp. 194–196.
11. Willa Appel, *Cults in America: Programmed for Paradise,* pp. 138–160.
12. Ibid., p. 145. Consequently, in this essay I will use "deprogramming" to refer to the coercive type.
13. Jeremiah Gutman, "Deprogramming: Step by Step," pp. 1–4.
14. Patrick and Dulack, *Let Our Children Go!* passim.
15. Ibid., p. 74.
16. Ibid., p. 11.
17. Camilla Warriel, "Patrick Criticizes Reithmiller Fiasco."
18. Conway and Siegelman, *Snapping,* p. 66.
19. Ibid., p. 71.
20. Ibid.
21. Patrick and Dulack, *Let Our Children Go!* p. 69.
22. Conway and Siegelman, *Snapping,* pp. 64–65.
23. William Willoughby, " 'Old Catholic' Sues Parents, Deprogrammers."
24. Bromley and Shupe, *Strange Gods,* p. 184.
25. Ibid.
26. Nat Hentoff, "The New Body Snatchers."
27. Robert W. Dellinger, "Cults and Kids," p. 12.
28. Anson D. Shupe, Jr., and David G. Bromley, *The New Vigilantes: Deprogrammers, Anti-Cultists, and the New Religions,* pp. 124–144.
29. Bromley and Shupe, *Strange Gods,* p. 204.
30. Ibid., p. 197.

31. Melton and Moore, *The Cult Experience*, p. 74.
32. Bromley and Shupe, *Strange Gods*, p. 185.
33. Melton and Moore, *The Cult Experience*, p. 75.
34. Ibid., pp. 75–80.
35. Ibid., p. 79.
36. Ibid., p. 83.
37. Ibid.
38. Bromley and Shupe, *Strange Gods*, p. 190.
39. Melton and Moore, *The Cult Experience*, p. 68.
40. Bromley and Shupe, *Strange Gods*, p. 196.
41. Ibid., p. 197.
42. Ibid., p. 198.
43. Ibid., p. 201.
44. Armand L. Mauss, "Dimensions of Religious Defection," *Review of Religious Research*, vol. 10, no. 3 (Spring 1969).
45. James V. Downton, Jr., *Sacred Journeys: The Conversion of Young Americans to Divine Light Mission*, pp. 211–220.
46. Ibid., p. 218.
47. Stuart A. Wright, "Post-Involvement Attitudes of Voluntary Defectors from Controversial New Religious Movements," pp. 172–182.
48. Ibid., p. 175.
49. Ibid.
50. Ibid., p. 181.
51. Chris Elkins, *Heavenly Deception*, p. 140.
52. Appel, *Cults in America*, p. 148.
53. Part of the text of the letter that Radha wrote to her parents when she reentered ISKCON.
54. J. Thomas Ungerleider and David K. Wellisch, "Cultism, Thought Control and Deprogramming: Observations on a Phenomenon," pp. 10–15. See also Ungerleider and Wellisch, "Coercive Persuasion, Religious Cults, and Deprogramming," pp. 279–282.
55. Frontispiece in *Proposal for Support* (Weston, Mass.: American Family Foundation, 1982).
56. All comments from Robert Schwartz quoted here come from an interview with him in the Weston office of the American Family Foundation, August 5, 1982.
57. *Kansas Hutchinson News*, October 12, 1980.
58. *National Examiner*, December 23, 1980.
59. *(Elyria) Chronicle-Telegram*, January 13, 1983, front page lead story.
60. *Lorain Journal*, January 13, 1983, lead story.
61. Mary Thornton, "The Hare Krishna Puzzle."
62. Jonas B. Robitscher, *Pursuit of Agreement: Psychiatry and the Law*, p. 13.
63. For an excellent assessment of the various roles that psychiatry plays in the courtroom (from the insanity defense to diminished capacity arguments), see Lee Coleman, *The Reign of Error: Psychiatry, Authority and Law*.
64. This author served as an expert witness for the defense in the Robin George trial. A reading of several hundred pages of testimony plus eight hours on the witness stand over three days constitutes the background for this example.

65. Testimony of Margaret Singer, May 2, 1983.

66. A sworn affidavit by Margaret Thaler Singer dated February 28, 1984.

67. Ibid., p. 2.

68. Ibid., p. 4.

69. Steven Chorover, "Mental Health as a Social Weapon," in *New Religions and Mental Health: Understanding the Issues,* pp. 14–20.

70. David L. Bazelon, "Psychiatrists and the Adversary Process," in *Biomedical Ethics and the Law,* ed. J. M. Humber and R. F. Almeder (New York: Plenum Publishing Corp., 1979), pp. 185–193.

71. Coleman, *The Reign of Error,* p. 242.

72. See Jim Hodge, "Local Youth Lost to Hare Krishnas," *Lafayette Advertiser,* June 19, 1977.

73. Blaine Harden, "Cultists Victims of Brainwashing?"; John G. Clark, Jr., "The Manipulation of Madness," a paper presented to the New Jersey Psychological Association, November 7, 1977.

74. Clark testified at the "Petition of Guardianship of Edward David Shapiro," November 3, 1976, and all quotations on this case come from that hearing's transcripts.

Chapter 9: Through a Dark Looking Glass

1. Interview with Ed Levine in Cleveland, Ohio, July 6, 1981.

2. Interview with John G. Clark, Jr., at his Weston home on July 16, 1981.

3. Flo Conway and Jim Siegelman, *Snapping: America's Epidemic of Sudden Personality Change,* p. 225.

4. Ibid., p. 44.

5. Flo Conway and Jim Siegelman, *Holy Terror: The Fundamentalist War on American Freedoms in Religion, Politics, and Our Private Lives,* pp. 3, 4, and passim.

6. Ibid., p. 347.

7. J. Gordon Melton and Robert L. Moore, *The Cult Experience: Responding to the New Religious Pluralism,* p. 95.

8. For an excellent survey of the legal issues and the primary positions taken by lawyers on both sides of the cult issue, see Thomas Robbins, "Cults, Brainwashing and Deprogramming: The View from the Law Journals," *Religious Studies Review* (forthcoming). Besides the psychological studies cited in chapters 7 and 8, see also James S. Gordon, M.D., "The Cult Phenomenon and the Psychotherapeutic Response," *Journal of the American Academy of Psychoanalysis* 11, no. 4 (1983), pp. 603–615.

9. Amendment to the mental hygiene law, sponsored by Howard Lasher, bill number 1-44-30-901, March 10, 1981, p. 3.

10. Ibid., p. 11.

11. As quoted in Sharon Worthing, "Courts, 'Cults,' Conservators: A Constitutional Challenge," *Christianity and Crisis,* March 16, 1981, p. 59.

Bibliography

Adlukari, Jayatirtha dasa, ed. *The Process of Deity Worship (Arcana-Paddhati).* Translated by Jayasacinanda dasa Adhikari. Los Angeles: Bhaktivedanta Book Trust (hereafter cited as BBT), 1978.

Adorno, T. W., and others. *The Authoritarian Personality.* New York: Harper & Row, 1950.

Allport, Gordon W. *The Nature of Prejudice.* (Unabridged.) London: Addison-Wesley Publishing Co., 1979.

Andræ, Tor. *Mohammed: The Man and His Faith.* New York: Harper & Row, Harper Torchbook, 1960.

Appel, Willa. *Cults in America: Programmed for Paradise.* New York: Holt, Rinehart & Winston, 1983.

Atkins, Susan. *Child of Satan, Child of God.* Plainfield, N.J.: Logos International, 1977.

Aversa, Rudy. "Experts' Beliefs Differ on 'Cults' Brainwashing." *Los Angeles Herald Examiner,* n.d.

———. "Psychologist Deals with Cultic 'Brainwash.' " *Los Angeles Herald Examiner,* September 11, 1976.

Bagwell, Robert. "The Abrupt Religious Conversion." *Journal of Religion and Health* 8, no. 2 (1969).

Barker, Eileen. "Who'd Be a Moonie? A Comparative Study of Those Who Join the Unification Church." In *The Social Impact of New Religious Movements,* edited by Bryan Wilson. New York: Rose of Sharon Press, 1981.

———, ed. *New Religious Movements: A Perspective for Understanding Society.* New York: Edwin Mellen Press, 1982.

Batson, C. Daniel, and W. Larry Ventis. *The Religious Experience: A Social-Psychological Perspective.* New York: Oxford University Press, 1982.

Bedell, George C., Leo Sandon, Jr., and Charles T. Wellborn. *Religion in America.* New York: Macmillan Co., 1982.

Berger, Peter L. *The Sacred Canopy: Elements of a Sociological Theory of Religion.* Garden City, N.Y.: Doubleday & Co., Anchor Books, 1967.

Berger, Peter, Brigitte Berger, and Hansfried Kellner. *The Homeless Mind: Modernization and Consciousness.* New York: Random House, Vintage Books, 1973.

Bianco, Joseph R. "The Deprogrammers Part II: Who Are They?" *Northwest Magazine.* Oregon Publishing Co., 1977.

Bloom, Allan, trans. *The Republic of Plato.* New York: Basic Books, 1968.

Brahmacari, Subhananda dasa. "Is the Krishna Consciousness Movement 'Hindu'?" Paper presented at the Fifth Annual Conference of the Australian Association for the Study of Religion, May 11–15, 1980, at Australian National University, Canberra.

Brenneman, Dick. "SM Trial Ends Like a Family Reunion." *Santa Monica Evening Outlook,* July 21, 1980.

Brent, Peter. *Godmen of India.* New York: Quadrangle Books, 1972.

Brijabasi Spirit. (Magazine.) New Vrindaban, W. Va.: Palace Press, 1983.

Bromley, David G., and Anson D. Shupe, Jr. *"Moonies" in America: Cult, Church and Crusade.* Beverly Hills, Calif.: Sage Publications, 1979.

———. *Strange Gods: The Great American Cult Scare.* Boston: Beacon Press, 1981.

Brown, J. A. C. *Techniques of Persuasion: From Propaganda to Brainwashing.* New York: Penguin Books, 1963.

Bryant, M. Darrol, and Herbert W. Richardson, eds. *A Time for Consideration. A Scholarly Appraisal of the Unification Church.* New York: Edwin Mellen Press, 1978.

Carlson, Timothy. "Landmark Case Awards Cult Victim $32.5 Million: Jury Says Krishnas Brainwashed Teen." *Los Angeles Herald Examiner,* June 18, 1983.

Caulfield, Sean. *The Experience of Praying.* New York: Paulist Press, 1980.

"Cautions Which Must Be Kept in Mind by All Who Would Become Truly Religious and Attain Perfection." In *Councils of Light and Love.* New York: Paulist Press, 1978.

Ch'en, Kenneth. *Buddhism in China: A Historical Survey.* Princeton: Princeton University Press, 1964.

Chorover, Steven. "Mental Health as a Social Weapon." In *New Religions and Mental Health: Understanding the Issues,* edited by Herbert Richardson. New York: Edwin Mellen Press, 1980.

Christensen, Carl. "Religious Conversion." *Archives of General Psychiatry* 9, no. 3 (September 1963).

Cinnamon, Kenneth, and Dave Farson. *Cults and Cons: The Exploitation of the Emotiona Growth Consumer.* Chicago: Nelson-Hall, 1979.

Clark, John G., Jr. "Cults." *Journal of the American Medical Association,* July 20, 1979

———. "The Manipulation of Madness." A paper presented to the New Jersey Psychological Association, November 7, 1977.

"Clinical Profiles of Hare Krishna Devotees." *American Journal of Psychiatry* 140, no. 4 (April 1983).

Coan, Richard W. *Hero, Artist, Sage, or Saint? A Survey of Views on What Is Variously Called Mental Health, Normality, Maturity, Self-Actualization, and Human Fulfillment* New York: Columbia University Press, 1977.

Coleman, Lee. *Psychiatry the Faithbreaker.* Sacramento: Printing Dynamics, 1982.

———. *The Reign of Error: Psychiatry, Authority and Law.* Boston: Beacon Press, 1984

Conn, Walter E., ed. *Conversion: Perspectives on Personal and Social Transformation.* New York: Alba House, 1978.

Conway, Flo, and Jim Siegelman. *Holy Terror: The Fundamentalist War on American Freedoms in Religion, Politics, and Our Private Lives.* New York: Doubleday & Co. 1982.

———. *Snapping: America's Epidemic of Sudden Personality Change.* Philadelphia: J B Lippincott Co., 1978.

Cox, Harvey. *The Feast of Fools: A Theological Essay on Festivity and Fantasy.* Cambridge: Harvard University Press, 1969.

———. *Turning East: Why Americans Look to the Orient for Spirituality—and What That Search Can Mean to the West.* New York: Simon & Schuster, 1977.

Cragg, Kenneth. *The House of Islam.* Belmont, Calif.: Wadsworth Publishing Co., 1975.

Crim, Keith, and others, eds. *Abingdon Dictionary of Living Religions.* Nashville: Abingdon Press, 1981.

"Cult Investigator Gives the PTA the Anti-Krishna Word." *Glendale News-Press,* March 15, 1977.

Daner, Francine Jeanne. *The American Children of Krsna: A Study of the Hare Krishna Movement.* New York: Holt, Rinehart & Winston, 1976.

Dasa, Amodha. "At School with Krsna's Canadian Kids." *Back to Godhead* 17, no. 10 (1982).

Dasa, Ravindra Svarupa. "Celibacy: Exquisite Torture, or a 'Yes to God'?" *Back to Godhead* 15, no. 1–2 (1980).

———. "Encounter with the Lord of the Universe." *Back to Godhead* 15, no. 6 (1980).

———. "How I Was Saved from Being 'Saved.' " *Back to Godhead* 15, no. 5 (1980).

———. "A Teacher for Krsna's Children." *Back to Godhead* 17, no. 1 (1982).

dasi, Sitarani. "What's the Role of Women in Krsna Consciousness?" *Back to Godhead* 17, no. 12 (1982).

Dasi, Visakha Devi. "Women in Krsna Consciousness: Questions and Answers." *Back to Godhead* 16, no. 3–4 (1981).

Deikman, Arthur J. *The Observing Self: Mysticism and Psychotherapy.* Boston: Beacon Press, 1982.

Dellinger, Robert W. *Cults and Kids.* Boys Town, Neb.: Boys Town Center, n.d.

Dimock, Edward C., Jr. *The Place of the Hidden Moon: Erotic Mysticism in the Vaisnava-sahajiyā Cult of Bengal.* Chicago: University of Chicago Press, 1966.

Double-Cross. Crusader Comicbook series. Chino, Calif.: Chick Publications, 1981.

Downton, James V., Jr. *Sacred Journeys: The Conversion of Young Americans to Divine Light Mission.* New York: Columbia University Press, 1979.

Eck, Diana L. *Darsan: Seeing the Divine Image in India.* Chambersburg, Pa.: Anima Books, 1981.

Edgerton, Franklin, trans. *The Bhagavad Gita.* Cambridge: Harvard University Press, 1972.

Edwards, Christopher. *Crazy for God: The Nightmare of Cult Life.* Englewood Cliffs, N.J.: Prentice-Hall, 1979.

"8 Die in Memphis Cop-Cult Battle." *Elyria Chronicle-Telegram,* January 13, 1983.

"Eight Slain in Memphis Shootout." *Lorain Journal,* January 23, 1983.

Elkins, Chris. *Heavenly Deception.* Wheaton, Ill.: Tyndale House, 1980.

———, *What Do You Say to a Moonie?* Wheaton, Ill.: Tyndale House, 1981.

Ellison, Craig W., ed. *Your Better Self: Christianity, Psychology and Self-Esteem.* San Francisco: Harper & Row, 1983.

Ellwood, Robert S., Jr. *Alternative Altars: Unconventional and Eastern Spirituality in America.* Chicago: University of Chicago Press, 1979.

———. *Religious and Spiritual Groups in Modern America.* Englewood Cliffs, N.J.: Prentice-Hall, 1973.

Enroth, Ronald. *The Lure of the Cults.* Chappaqua, N.Y.: Christian Herald Books, 1979.

Erikson, Erik H. *Identity: Youth and Crisis.* New York: W. W. Norton & Co., 1968.

———. *Young Man Luther.* Garden City, N.Y.: Doubleday & Co., Anchor Books, 1964.

Evans, Christopher. *Cults of Unreason.* New York: Dell Publishing Co., 1973.

Evenson, Janet. "Reprimand Urged for Salem Attorney." *Oregon Statesman,* May 15, 1980.

'Fatal Spanking Left Bruises from Tot's Back to Thigh." *Elyria Chronicle-Telegram,* July 13, 1983.

Fichter, Joseph H., ed. *Alternatives to American Mainline Churches.* New York: Rose of Sharon Press, 1983.

Flynn, Frank. "Deprogramming in the Middle Ages." *New Era* 1, no. 1 (March/April 1981).

Fowler, James W. *Stages of Faith: The Psychology of Human Development and the Quest for Meaning.* San Francisco: Harper & Row, 1981.

Frankl, Viktor E. *Man's Search for Meaning.* New York: Pocket Books, 1963.

———. *The Unconscious God: Psychotherapy and Theology.* New York: Simon & Schuster, 1975.

———. *The Unheard Cry for Meaning: Psychotherapy and Humanism.* New York: Simon & Schuster, 1978.

Freud, Sigmund. *The Future of an Illusion.* Translated by W. D. Robson-Scott. Revised and edited by James Strachey. Garden City, N.Y.: Doubleday & Co., Anchor Books, 1961.

Fromm, Erich. *Escape from Freedom.* New York: Avon Books, 1969.

Fuller, Andrew Reid. *Psychology and Religion: Eight Points of View.* Washington: University Press of America, 1977.

Galanter, Marc. "Charismatic Religious Sects and Psychiatry: An Overview." *American Journal of Psychiatry* 139, no. 12 (December 1982).

——— and others. "The 'Moonies': A Psychological Study of Conversion and Membership in a Contemporary Religious Sect." *American Journal of Psychiatry* 136, no. 2 (February 1979).

Geertz, Clifford. "Religion as a Cultural System." In *Anthropological Approaches to the Study of Religion: The Social Anthropology of Complex Societies,* edited by Michael P. Banton. London: Tavistock Publications, 1966.

Gelberg, Steven J., ed. *Hare Krishna, Hare Krishna: Five Distinguished Scholars on the Krishna Movement in the West.* New York: Grove Press, 1983.

Ghurye, G. S. *Indian Sadhus.* Bombay: Popular Prakashan, 1964.

Gibbs, Jack P., ed. *Social Control: Views from the Social Sciences.* Beverly Hills, Calif.: Sage Publications, 1982.

"Girl Sues Hare Cult for 2.5M." *Boston Herald American,* April 20, 1977.

Glock, Charles Y., ed. *Religion in Sociological Perspective: Essays in the Empirical Study of Religion.* Belmont, Calif.: Wadsworth Publishing Co., 1973.

Glock, Charles Y., and Robert N. Bellah, eds. *The New Religious Consciousness.* Berkeley and Los Angeles: University of California Press, 1976.

Glock, Charles Y., with Robert Wuthnow, Jane Allyn Piliavin, and Metta Spencer. *Adolescent Prejudice.* New York: Harper & Row, 1975.

Godlove, Terry. "In What Sense Are Religions Conceptual Frameworks?" *Journal of the American Academy of Religion* 52, no. 2 (June 1984).

Goff, Kenneth. *The Soviet Art of Brainwashing: A Synthesis of the Russian Textbook on Psychopolitics.* Torrance, Calif.: Noontide Press.

Goffman, Erving. *Asylums: Essays on the Social Situation of Mental Patients and Other Inmates.* Garden City, N.Y.: Doubleday & Co., Anchor Books, 1961.

Golowenski, Dave. "Tribe's Cold Shoulder Worries Super Joe." *Lorain Journal,* October 29, 1981.

Gonda, J. *Aspects of Early Visnuism.* Delhi: Motilal Banarsidass, 1969.

Goswami, Bhakti Raksaka Srila Sridhara Deva. *The Search for Sri Krsna: Reality the Beautiful.* San Jose, Calif.: Guardian of Devotion Press, 1983.

Goswami, Satsvarupa dasa. "After Initiation the Disciple Must Accept the Spiritual Master as Absolute." *Sadhu-bhusanam,* 1981.

———. *In Every Town and Village.* Vol. 4 of *Śrīla Prabhupāda-līlāmṛta.* Los Angeles: BBT, 1982.

———. "Initiation Means to Become Submissive." *Sadhu-bhusanam,* January–February 1982.

———. *A Lifetime in Preparation: India, 1896–1965.* Vol. 1 of *Śrīla Prabhupāda-līlāmṛta.* Los Angeles: BBT, 1980.

———. *Only He Could Lead Them: San Francisco/India, 1967.* Vol. 3 of *Śrīla Prabhupāda-līlāmṛta.* Los Angeles: BBT, 1981.

————. *Planting the Seed: New York City, 1965–1966.* Vol. 2, of *Śrīla Prabhupāda līlāmṛta.* Los Angeles: BBT, 1980.

————. *Readings in Vedic Literature: The Tradition Speaks for Itself.* New York: BBT, 1977.

Gould, Roger L. *Transformations: Growth and Change in Adult Life.* New York: Simon & Schuster, 1978.

Gunther, Bernard. *Neo-Tantra: Bhagwan Shree Rajneesh on Sex, Love, Prayer and Transcendence.* San Francisco: Harper & Row, 1980.

Gutman, Jeremiah. "Deprogramming: Step by Step." *New Era* 2, no. 1 (March/April 1982).

Harden, Blaine. "Cultists Victims of Brainwashing?" *Trenton Times,* November 9, 1977.

Harper, Marvin Henry. *Gurus, Swamis, and Avataras: Spiritual Masters and Their American Disciples.* Philadelphia: Westminster Press, 1972.

Hawley, John Stratton. *At Play with Krishna: Pilgrimage Dramas from Brindavan.* Translated and introduced; in association with Shrivatsa Goswami. Princeton: Princeton University Press, 1981.

————. *Krishna, the Butter Thief.* Princeton: Princeton University Press, 1983.

Hein, Norvin. *The Miracle Plays of Mathura.* New Haven: Yale University Press, 1972.

Hentoff, Nat. "The New Body Snatchers." *Playboy* 25, no. 2 (February 1978).

"He Was the Perfect Example: An Interview with George Harrison." *Back to Godhead* 18, no. 2–3 (1983).

"His Final Instructions." *Back to Godhead* 13, no. 1–2 (1978).

Hoffer, Eric. *The True Believer.* New York: Mentor Books, 1951.

Hoge, Jim. "Local Youth Lost to Hare Krishnas." *Lafayette Advisor,* June 19, 1977.

Hook, Sidney, ed. *Psychoanalysis, Scientific Method, and Philosophy.* New York: New York University Press, 1959.

Hopkins, Thomas J. *The Hindu Religious Tradition.* Encino, Calif.: Dickenson Publishing Co., 1971.

Horowitz, Irving Louis, ed. *Science, Sin, and Scholarship: The Politics of Rev. Moon and the Unification Church.* Cambridge: Massachusetts Institute of Technology Press, 1978.

Hubbard, L. Ron. *Dianetics: The Modern Science of Mental Health.* Los Angeles: Bridge Publications, 1978.

Hunter, James Davison. *American Evangelicalism: Conservative Religion and the Quandary of Modernity.* New Brunswick, N.J.: Rutgers University Press, 1983.

Hyde, Margaret O. *Brainwashing and Other Forms of Mind Control.* New York: McGraw-Hill Book Co., 1977.

James, William. *The Varieties of Religious Experience.* New York: Collier Books, 1961.

Judah, J. Stillson. *Hare Krishna and the Counterculture.* New York: John Wiley & Sons, 1974.

Kakar, Sudhir. *Shamans, Mystics and Doctors: A Psychological Inquiry Into India and Its Healing Traditions.* Boston: Beacon Press, 1982.

Kalupahama, David J. *Buddhist Philosophy: A Historical Analysis.* Honolulu: University Press of Hawaii, 1976.

Kanter, Rosabeth Moss. *Commitment and Community: Communes and Utopias in Sociological Perspective.* Cambridge: Harvard University Press, 1972.

Kemperman, Steve. *Lord of the Second Advent: A Rare Look Inside the Terrifying World of the Moonies.* Ventura, Calif.: Regal Books, 1981.

Kim, Young Oon. *Faiths of the Far East.* Vol. 3 of *World Religions.* New York: Golden Gate Publishing Co., 1976.

————. *India's Religious Quest.* Vol. 2 of *World Religions.* New York: Golden Gate Publishing Co., 1976.

————. *Living Religions of the Middle East.* Vol. 1 of *World Religions.* New York: Golden Gate Publishing Co., 1976.

————. *Unification Theology and Christian Thought.* Revised. New York: Golden Gate Publishing Co., 1975.

Kinsley, David R. *The Divine Player: A Study of Krsna Lila.* Delhi: Motilal Banarsidass, 1979.

————. *The Sword and the Flute: Kālī and Krsna, Dark Visions of the Terrible and the Sublime in Hindu Mythology.* Berkeley and Los Angeles: University of California Press, 1975.

Koller, John M. *The Indian Way.* New York: Macmillan Co., 1982.

Kopp, Sheldon B. *Guru: Metaphors from a Psychotherapist.* Palo Alto, Calif.: Science and Behavior Books, 1971.

————. *If You Meet the Buddha on the Road, Kill Him! The Pilgrimage of Psychotherapy Patients.* New York: Bantam Books, 1972.

The Koran Interpreted. Translated by Arthur J. Arberry. New York: Macmillan Co., 1955.

Kriesberg, Louis, ed. *Research in Social Movements: Conflict and Change.* Greenwich: JAI Press, 1979.

"Krishna Case May Be First of Brainwashing." *New York Times,* October 14, 1976.

"Krishna Disciple's Sanity Challenged." Denver Colorado, Associated Press story. April 14, 1979.

The Krsna Consciousness Handbook: For the Year 484, Caitanya Era (March 24, 1970– March 12, 1971). Los Angeles: ISKCON Press, 1970.

Kumarappa, Bharatan. *The Hindu Conception of the Deity as Culminating in Ramanuja.* London: Luzac and Co., 1934.

Lasch, Christopher. *The Culture of Narcissism: American Life in the Age of Diminishing Expectation.* New York: Warner Books, 1979.

————. *Haven in a Heartless World: The Family Besieged.* New York: Basic Books, 1979.

LeCron, Leslie M. *The Complete Guide to Hypnosis.* New York: Harper & Row, 1971.

Lee, Philip, with Robert E. Ornstein; David Galin; Arthur Deikman; and Charles Tart. *Symposium on Consciousness: Presented at the Annual Meeting of the American Association for the Advancement of Science Feb. 1974.* New York: Penguin Books, 1974.

Leech, Kenneth. *Soul Friend: The Practice of Christian Spirituality.* San Francisco: Harper & Row, 1980.

Lele, Jayant, ed. *Tradition and Modernity in Bhakti Movements.* International Studies in Sociology and Social Anthropology, vol. 31. Leiden: E. J. Brill, 1981.

Levi, Ken, ed. *Violence and Religious Commitment: Implications of Jim Jones's People's Temple Movement.* University Park: Pennsylvania State University Press, 1982.

Levine, Faye. *The Strange World of the Hare Krishnas.* Greenwich, Conn.: Fawcett Publications, 1974.

Levinson, Henry Samuel. *The Religious Investigations of William James.* Chapel Hill: University of North Carolina Press, 1981.

Lewis, I. M. *Ecstatic Religion: An Anthropological Study of Spirit Possession and Shamanism.* New York: Penguin Books, 1971.

Lifton, Robert Jay. *The Broken Connection.* New York: Simon & Schuster, 1979.

————. *Thought Reform and the Psychology of Totalism: A Study of "Brainwashing" in China.* New York: W. W. Norton & Co., 1969.

Lofland, John. *Doomsday Cult: A Study of Proselytization and Maintenance of Faith.* New York: Irvington Publishers, 1981.

Loye, David. *The Leadership Passion: A Psychology of Ideology.* Washington: Jossey-Bass, 1977.

McCory, Robert. "Prisoners of Sects: Parents Fight Back Against the Cults." *Reader: Chicago's Free Weekly,* June 17, 1983.

Main, John. *Word Into Silence.* New York: Paulist Press, 1981.

Malony, H. Newton, ed. *Current Perspectives in the Psychology of Religion.* Grand Rapids: Wm. B. Eerdmans Publishing Co., 1977.

May, Gerald G. *Care of Mind, Care of Spirit: Psychiatric Dimensions of Spiritual Direction.* San Francisco: Harper & Row, 1982.

Mead, Sidney E. *The Old Religion in the Brave New World: Reflections on the Relation Between Christendom and the Republic.* Berkeley and Los Angeles: University of California Press, 1977.

Meadow, Mary Jo, and Richard D. Kohoe. *Psychology of Religion: Religion in Individual Lives.* New York: Harper & Row, 1984.

Melton, J. Gordon, and Robert L. Moore. *The Cult Experience: Responding to the New Religious Pluralism.* New York: Pilgrim Press, 1982.

Merton, Thomas. *The Monastic Journey.* New York: Doubleday & Co., 1978.

"Mom of Dead Boy Goes on Trial." *Elyria Chronicle-Telegram,* July 13, 1983.

Moore Robert L. *John Wesley and Authority: A Psychological Perspective.* Missoula, Mont.: Scholars Press, 1979.

Mukherjee, Dilip Kumar. *Chaitanya.* New Delhi: National Book Trust, India, 1970.

Murray, Andrew. *Absolute Surrender.* Springdale, Pa.: Whitaker House, 1981.

"My Impressions of Srila Prabhupada: A Historical and Personal View by J. Stillson Judah." *Back to Godhead* 14, no. 8 (1979).

Naranjo, Claudio, and Robert E. Ornstein. *On the Psychology of Meditation.* New York: Viking Press, 1971.

Needleman, Jacob. *The New Religions.* New York: E. P. Dutton & Co., 1970.

Needleman, Jacob, and George Baker, eds. *Understanding the New Religions.* New York: Seabury Press, 1978.

Needleman, Jacob, and Dennis Lewis, eds. *On the Way to Self Knowledge.* New York: Alfred A. Knopf, 1976.

Nelson, Rob, and Robin Smith, eds. *The Mind Benders.* Toronto: McGraw-Hill Ryerson, 1969.

Novak, Michael. *Ascent of the Mountain, Flight of the Dove: An Invitation to Religious Studies.* New York: Harper & Row, 1971.

Oaks, Dallin H., ed. *The Wall Between Church and State.* Chicago: University of Chicago Press, Phoenix Books, 1963.

"On Christ, Christians and Krsna." *Back to Godhead* 12, no. 12 (1977), p. 16.

Ornstein, Robert E. *The Mind Field: A Personal Essay.* London: Octagon Press, 1983.

————, ed. *The Nature of Human Consciousness: A Book of Readings.* San Francisco: W. H. Freeman & Co., 1973.

Otto, Rudolf. *India's Religion of Grace and Christianity Compared and Contrasted.* Translated by Frank Hugh Foster. New York: Macmillan Press, 1930.

Paloutzian, Raymond F. *Invitation to the Psychology of Religion.* Glenview, Ill.: Scott, Foresman & Co., 1983.

Patrick, Ted, and Tom Dulack. *Let Our Children Go!* New York: Ballantine Books, 1976.

Pavlos, Andrew J. *The Cult Experience.* New York: Greenwood Press, 1982.

Pelletier, Kenneth R. *Holistic Medicine: From Stress to Optimal Health.* A Delta/Seymour Lawrence Edition. New York: Dell Publishing Co., 1979.

————. *Toward a Science of Consciousness.* New York: Delta Books, 1978.

Penfield, Wilder, and others. *The Mystery of the Mind: A Critical Study of Consciousness and the Human Brain.* Princeton: Princeton University Press, 1975.

Poling, Tommy H., and J. Frank Kenney. *The Hare Krishna Character Type: A Study of the Sensate Personality.* Lewiston, N.Y.: Edwin Mellen Press, 1986

Prabhupada, A. C. Bhaktivedanta Swami. *The Bhagavad Gita as It Is.* New York: Collier Books, 1968.

————. *The Bhagavad Gita as It Is.* (Abridged Edition.) Los Angeles: BBT, 1972.

————. *Chant and Be Happy: The Story of the Hare Krishna Mantra.* Los Angeles: BBT, 1982.

————. *Coming Back: The Science of Reincarnation.* Los Angeles: BBT, 1982.

————. *Consciousness: The Missing Link.* Los Angeles: BBT, 1980.

————. *Easy Journey to Other Planets.* Los Angeles: BBT, 1972.

————. *Krishna Consciousness: The Topmost Yoga System.* Los Angeles: ISKCON Books, 1970.

————. *The Nectar of Devotion: The Complete Science of Bhakti Yoga.* Los Angeles: BBT, 1970.

————. *The Nectar of Instruction.* Los Angeles: BBT, 1975.

————. *Perfect Questions Perfect Answers.* Los Angeles: BBT, 1977.

————. *Preaching Is the Essence.* Los Angeles: BBT, 1977.

————. *Raja-Vidya: The King of Knowledge.* Los Angeles: BBT, 1973.

————. *The Science of Self-Realization.* Los Angeles: BBT, 1980.

————. *The Spiritual Master and the Disciple.* Edited by Subhananda dasa Brahmacari. Los Angeles: BBT, 1978.

————. *Sri Isopanisad: The Knowledge That Brings One Nearer to the Supreme Personality of Godhead, Krsna.* Los Angeles: BBT, 1974.

————. *Śrī Nāmānṛta: The Nectar of the Holy Name.* Edited by Subhananda dasa. Los Angeles: BBT, 1982.

————. *Teaching and Study Guide to Bhagavad Gita as It Is.* Los Angeles: BBT, 1977.

————. trans. *Songs of the Vaiṣṇava Ācāryas.* Los Angeles: BBT, 1979.

Prebish, Charles S. *American Buddhism.* North Scituate, Mass.: Duxbury Press, 1979.

Proposal for Support. Weston, Mass.: American Family Foundation, 1982.

Pulfer, Mike. "Lawyer for Goss Doubts Leis Will Seek Retrial." *Cincinnati Inquirer,* April 25, 1982.

Purdom, Charles B. *The God-Man: The Life, Journeys and Work of Meher Baba.* London: George Allen & Unwin, 1964.

"The Qualifications of the Spiritual Master." *Back to Godhead* 13, no. 1–2 (1978), p. 4.

Radhakrishna, Sarvepalli, and Charles A. Moore, eds. *A Sourcebook in Indian Philosophy.* Princeton: Princeton University Press, 1967.

Rahman, Fazlur. *Islam.* Garden City, N.Y.: Doubleday & Co., Anchor Books, 1968.

Rajneesh, Bhagwan Shree. *The Book of the Secrets.* Edited by Ma Ananda Prem and Swami Ananda Teerth. New York: Harper & Row, Harper Colophon Books, 1974.

Ramanujan, A. K., trans. *Hymns for the Drowning: Poems for Visnu by Nammalvar.* Princeton: Princeton University Press, 1981.

Reich, Charles A. *The Greening of America.* New York: Bantam Books, 1971.

Reston, James, Jr. *Our Father Who Art in Hell.* New York: Times Books, 1981.

Richardson, James T., ed. *Conversion Careers: In and Out of the New Religions.* Beverly Hills, Calif.: Sage Publications, 1977.

Ricoeur, Paul. *Interpretation Theory: Discourse and the Surplus of Meaning.* Fort Worth: Texas Christian University Press, 1976.

Robbins, Thomas, and Dick Anthony. "Cults, Brainwashing and Counter-Subversion." *Annals, AAPSS,* 446, November 1979.

————. *In Gods We Trust: New Patterns of Religious Pluralism in America.* New Brunswick, N.J.: Transaction Books, 1981.

Robitscher, Jonas B. *Pursuit of Agreement: Psychiatry and the Law.* Philadelphia: J. B. Lippincott Co., 1966.

Rochford, E. Burke. *Hare Krishna in America.* New Brunswick, N.J.: Rutgers University Press, 1985.

Rokeach, Milton. *Beliefs, Attitudes and Values.* San Francisco: Jossey-Bass, 1972.

————. *The Open and Closed Mind: Investigation Into the Nature of Belief Systems and Personality Systems.* New York: Basic Books, 1960.

————. *The Three Christs of Ypsilanti: A Psychological Study.* New York: Alfred A. Knopf, 1964.

Ross, Michael W. "Clinical Profiles of Hare Krishna Devotees." *American Journal of Psychiatry* 140, no. 4 (April 1983).

Roth, Guenther, and Wolfgang Schluchter. *Max Weber's Vision of History: Ethics and Methods.* Berkeley and Los Angeles: University of California Press, 1979.

Rothbaum, Fred, John R. Weiss, and Samuel S. Snyder. "Changing the World and Changing the Self: A Two-Process Model of Perceived Control." *Journal of Personality and Social Psychology* 42, no. 1 (1982).

Rudin, A. James, and Marcia R. Rudin. *Prison or Paradise? The New Religious Cults.* Philadelphia: Fortress Press, 1980.

Salzman, Leon. "The Psychology of Religious and Ideological Conversion." *Psychiatry* 16, no. 2 (May 1953).

Sargant, William W. *Battle for the Mind: A Physiology of Conversion and Brain-washing.* New York: Doubleday & Co., 1957.

————. *The Mind Possessed: A Physiology of Possession, Mysticism and Faith Healing.* Philadelphia: J. B. Lippincott Co., 1974.

Schiffer, Irvine. *Charisma: A Psychoanalytic Look at Mass Society.* Toronto: University of Toronto Press, 1973.

Schumach, Murray. "Judge Dismisses Charges in Hare Krishna 'Brainwashing' Case." *New York Times,* March 18, 1977.

Schwartz, Lita. "The Cult Phenomenon." In *Cults and the Family,* edited by Florence Kaslow and Marvin B. Sussman. New York: Haworth Press, 1982.

"The Self Outside the Boundaries of Time." *Back to Godhead* 14, no. 11 (1979), p. 5.

Shinn, Larry D. "Conflicting Networks: Guru and Friend in ISKCON." In *Genesis, Exodus, and Numbers,* edited by Rodney Stark. New York: Paragon House Publishers, 1986.

————. "The Goddess: Theological Sign or Religious Symbol?" *NVMEN: International Review for the History of Religions* 31, no. 2 (December 1984).

————. "The Many Faces of Krishna." In *Alternatives to American Mainline Churches,* edited by Joseph H. Fichter. New York: Rose of Sharon Press, 1983.

————. *Two Sacred Worlds: Experience and Structure in the World's Religions.* Nashville: Abingdon Press, 1977.

Shupe, Anson D., Jr., and David G. Bromley. *The New Vigilantes: Deprogrammers, Anti-Cultists, and the New Religions.* Beverly Hills, Calif.: Sage Publications, 1980.

Sims, Robert. *The Art of Intelligent Living.* Gunnison, Conn.: Ananta-Unlimited, 1979.

Singer, Margaret T. "Coming out of the Cults." *Psychology Today* 12, no. 8 (1979).

Singer, Milton, ed. *Krishna: Myths, Rites, and Attitudes.* Chicago: University of Chicago Press, 1966.

Singh, Khushwant. *Gurus, Godmen and Good People.* New Delhi: Orient Longman, 1975.

"Sisters on Opposite Sides of Religious Cult Hassle." *Waterbury Republican,* January 27, 1977.

Sklar, Dusty. *Gods and Beasts: The Nazis and the Occult.* New York: Thomas Y. Crowell Co., 1977.

Slater, Philip. *The Pursuit of Loneliness: American Culture at the Breaking Point.* Boston: Beacon Press, 1970.

Smart, Ninian. *The Religious Experience of Mankind.* 3d ed. New York: Charles Scribner's Sons, 1984.

Smith, Timothy L. *Revivalism and Social Reform: American Protestantism on the Eve of the Civil War.* Baltimore: Johns Hopkins University Press, 1980.

Sontag, Frederick. *Sun Myung Moon and the Unification Church.* Nashville: Abingdon Press, 1977.

Sparks, Jack. *The Mind Benders: A Look at Current Cults.* Nashville: Thomas Nelson Publishers, 1979.

Spear, Percival. *A History of India; Vol. II.* Baltimore: Penguin Books, 1970.

Śrī Caitanya-Caritāmṛta, Antya 3.139 and Madhya 16.64. Translated by A. C. Bhaktivedanta Swami Prabhupada. Los Angeles: BBT, 1975.

"Srila Prabhupada Departs." *Back to Godhead* 13, no. 1–2 (1978).

Stark, Rodney, and William Bainbridge. "Networks of Faith: Interpersonal Bonds and Recruitment to Cults and Sects." *American Journal of Sociology* 85 (1980).

Steiger, Brad. *Gods of Aquarius: UFOs and the Transformation of Man.* New York: Harcourt Brace Jovanovich, 1976.

Stoner, Carroll, and Jo Anne Parke. *All God's Children: The Cult Experience—Salvation or Slavery?* Radnor, Pa.: Chilton Book Co., 1977.

Strachey, James, trans, and ed. *The Standard Edition of the Complete Psychological Works of Sigmund Freud.* London: Hogarth Press, 1961.

Streiker, Lowell D. *The Cults Are Coming!* Nashville: Abingdon Press, 1978.

Swami, Jayadvaita. "The Transcendence Comes Into View." *Back to Godhead* 14, no. 8 (1979).

Swami, Kirtanananda. "The Things Christ Had to Keep Secret." *Back to Godhead* 12, no. 12 (1977).

"This Material World Is Zero." *Back to Godhead* 14, no. 6 (1979), p. 24.

Thornton, Mary. "The Hare Krishna Puzzle." *Boston Sunday Globe,* January 23, 1977.

Tiemann, William Harold, and John C. Bush. *The Right to Silence: Privileged Clergy Communication and the Law.* Nashville: Abingdon Press, 1983.

Tipton, Steven M. *Getting Saved from the Sixties: Moral Meaning in Conversion and Cultural Change.* Berkeley and Los Angeles: University of California Press, 1982.

Tisdale, John R., ed. *Growing Edges in the Psychology of Religion.* Chicago: Nelson-Hall, 1980.

Toffler, Alvin. *Future Shock.* New York: Bantam Books, 1970.

"Trouble in Krishnaland." *Courier-Journal Magazine: L.A. Times,* March 27, 1981.

Turner, Victor W. *The Ritual Process: Structure and Anti-Structure.* Chicago: Aldine Publishing Co., 1969.

Underwood, Barbara, and Betty Underwood. *Hostage to Heaven: Four Years in the Unification Church, by an Ex-Moonie and the Mother Who Fought to Free Her.* New York: Clarkson N. Potter, 1979.

Ungerleider, J. Thomas, and David K. Wellisch. "Coercive Persuasion, Religious Cults, and Deprogramming." *American Journal of Psychiatry* 136, no. 3 (March 1979).

———. "Cultism, Thought Control and Deprogramming: Observations on a Phenomenon." *Psychiatric Opinion* 16, no. 1 (January 1979).

Verdier, Paul A. *Brainwashing and the Cults: An Exposé on Capturing the Human Mind.* North Hollywood, Calif.: Wilshire Book Co., 1977.

Wallace, Anthony F. C. "Revitalization Movements." In *Reader in Comparative Religion: An Anthropological Approach,* edited by William A. Lessa and Evon Z. Vogt. 4th ed. New York: Harper & Row, 1979.

Wallis, Jim. *The Call to Conversion: Recovering the Gospel for These Times.* San Francisco: Harper & Row, 1981.

Wallis, Roy. *The Road to Total Freedom: A Sociological Analysis of Scientology.* New York: Columbia University Press, 1977.

Warren, Henry Clarke, ed. *Buddhism: In Translation.* New York: Atheneum Publishers, 1968.

Warriel, Camilla. "Patrick Criticizes Reithmiller Fiasco." *Cincinnati Inquirer,* April 25, 1982.

Weber, Max. *The Sociology of Religion.* Translated by Ephraim Fischoff. Boston: Beacon Press, 1963.

————. *The Theory of Social and Economic Organization.* Translated by A. M. Henderson and Talcott Parsons. Glencoe, Ill.: Free Press, 1947.

White, John, ed. *Frontiers of Consciousness.* New York: Avon Books, 1974.

Willoughby, William. " 'Old Catholic' Sues Parents, Deprogrammers." *Washington Star,* April 21, 1977.

Wilson, Bryan. *Religion in Sociological Perspective.* London: Oxford University Press, 1982.

Wilson, Frances, ed. *The Love of Krishna: The Kṛṣṇakarṇāmṛta of Līlāśuka Bilvamaṅgala.* Philadelphia: University of Pennsylvania Press, 1975.

Winquist, Charles E. *Homecoming: Interpretation, Transformation and Individuation.* American Academy of Religion: Studies in Religion, no. 18. Missoula, Mont.: Scholars Press, 1978.

Wood, Allen Tate. *Moonstruck: A Memoir of My Life in a Cult.* New York: William Morrow & Co., 1979.

Wrenn, Gilbert C., and Shirley Schwarzrock. *The Mind Benders.* Circle Pines, Minn.: American Guidance Service, 1971.

Wright, Stuart A. "Post-Involvement Attitudes of Voluntary Defectors from Controversial New Religious Movements." *Journal of the Scientific Study of Religion* 23, no. 2 (June 1984).

Wuthnow, Robert. *The Consciousness Reformation.* Berkeley and Los Angeles: University of California Press, 1976.

Yanoff, Morris. *Where Is Joey? Lost Among the Hare Krishnas.* Athens, Ohio: Swallow Press, 1981.

Zablocki, Benjamin. *The Joyful Community.* Baltimore: Penguin Books, 1971.